Introduction to Video Game Design and Development

Joseph Saulter   American InterContinental University

 **McGraw-Hill Irwin**

INTRODUCTION TO VIDEO GAME DESIGN AND DEVELOPMENT

Published by McGraw-Hill/Irwin, a business unit of The McGraw-Hill Companies, Inc., 1221 Avenue of the Americas, New York, NY, 10020. Copyright © 2007 by The McGraw-Hill Companies, Inc. All rights reserved. No part of this publication may be reproduced or distributed in any form or by any means, or stored in a database or retrieval system, without the prior written consent of The McGraw-Hill Companies, Inc., including, but not limited to, in any network or other electronic storage or transmission, or broadcast for distance learning.

Some ancillaries, including electronic and print components, may not be available to customers outside the United States.

This book is printed on acid-free paper.

1 2 3 4 5 6 7 8 9 0 CCI/CCI 0 9 8 7 6

ISBN-13: 978-0-07-340300-7
ISBN-10: 0-07-340300-8

Editorial director	John E. Biernat
Publisher	Linda Schreiber
Senior sponsoring editor	Doug Hughes
Editorial coordinator	Peter Vanaria
Marketing manager	Keari Bedford
Producer, Media technology	Janna Martin
Project manager	Bruce Gin
Lead production supervisor	Michael R. McCormick
Coordinator freelance design	Artemio Ortiz Jr.
Photo research coordinator	Lori Kramer
Senior media project manager	Susan Lombardi
Cover illustration	Bill Blakesley
Typeface	10.25/15 Bethold Baskerville Book
Compositor	International Typesetting and Composition
Printer	Courier Kendallville

Library of Congress Cataloging-in-Publication Data

Saulter, Joseph.
    Introduction to video game design and development / Joseph Saulter. —1st ed.
        p. cm.

Dedication

This book is dedicated to my father and brother, Lloyd Saulter and Raymond Saulter; your spirit continues to motivate me every day. To my mother Ethel Saulter, the first call of my day and the best call of my day. To my loving wife Charlene Saulter: You complete my life and my family, your support and encouragement inspire me to be the best I possibly can. To my pastor, mentors, and friends, whose dedication to perfection and creative collaboration is worth more than financial rewards. Finally this book is dedicated to all my students, who over the past 15 plus years have challenged, molded, and inspired me.

This book is dedicated to world peace and diversity.

Joseph Saulter earned his master from State University of New York, Empire State College. He is currently the chairman of the Game Design and Development Department at American InterContinental University in Atlanta and CEO of Entertainment Arts Research, one of the first African American 3D Video Game Development Companies in the United States. Entertainment Arts Research is currently working on three major new game titles, including Kaotic Foolz, an urban stealth third-person game, and the Seventh Day, a highly anticipated Christian-based gospel 3D video game unlike anything currently available. Joseph is the chairman of the International Game Developers Association (IGDA) Diversity Advisory Board; cofounder of the Urban Video Game Academy; and a member of the American Society of Composers, Authors, and Publishers (ASCAP), American Federation of Musicians (AFM) Local 802, New York State School Music Association (NYSSMA), and the Professional Composers of America. He has served as a technology professor and musical director for the entertainment industry from Broadway to the outermost bush areas of Africa. His Broadway credits are *Hair* and *Jesus Christ Superstar,* and he also wrote the drum book for Doug Hennings's Broadway hit *The Magic Show*. Joseph has received numerous awards and certifications in the music and entertainment industry, one of which is the Drama Desk Award for his role in the Broadway musical *I Love My Wife* staring the Smothers brothers. For you old school fans, Joseph Saulter was the coauthor of the legendary *Twilight 22* album with the smash hit "Electric Kingdom." He presented for the Tavis Smiley and Microsoft collaboration, Blacks in Technology National Tour. He is also a professional jazz drummer for over 30 years and author of a new series of game design and development textbooks published by McGraw-Hill.

Brief Table of Contents

TABLE OF CONTENTS

CHAPTER 4

Game Components: Part Two   110

CHAPTER 5

Serious Games   134

CHAPTER 6

The Game Development Team   154

CHAPTER 7

Game Development Process Part One: Concept and Preproduction   186

About the Book

In recent years, video and computer games have become an incredibly popular form of mainstream entertainment. Some of the more popular game titles have had sales rivaling or in excess of big-budget Hollywood movies. In 2005 the game industry recorded nearly $14 billion in U.S. sales alone, up 10 percent from the previous year. By comparison, the MPAA ("Motion Picture Association of America") recorded ticket sales of approximately $9.5 billion that same year. Why are these games so popular? Who makes them, and how are they developed? What makes a great game?

This book explores the various elements and principles of video and computer game design and technology. Chapter 1 examines what a game is, why people play games, and what sort of people play video and computer games. Chapter 2 present a compelling overview of the history of game development, from the first computer games through the current crop of computer and next generation consoles. Chapter 3 gives us a look at the components used to create games, and Chapter 4 continues this examination. Chapter 5 introduces the reader to serious games, a game arena where new developers are making a difference in education as well as simulations. Chapter 6 takes a look at the people who typically make up a game development team and describes their backgrounds, responsibilities, and tools. Chapter 7 explores the game development process from game conception to preproduction. Chapter 8 continues to probe the development process by looking at the production phase to postrelease and selling game products. Finally, Chapter 9 discusses some important aspects of the business of developing games and wraps up with a look at popular current trends and their impact on the future of the industry.

The book is accompanied by a series of lab sessions that present various hands-on activities designed to illustrate some of the more important concepts discussed in the chapters. Students will have an opportunity to play some classic games and discuss their impact on future titles. Students will also get to play a number of modern games and discuss various critical design elements and how they affect gameplay. Most important, students will take part in a number of exercises that involve creating original game concepts and designs.

Acknowledgments

The author would like to thank contributing author Dr. Thelma Looms. Without your dedication to perfection and collaboration this book would not have been possible.

Thanks also to all of the following people for your contribution to my life as well as this book. I appreciate the opportunity to work with such dedicated professionals:

Frank Able, Ernest Adams, Asante Addae, Adrienne Anderson, Valetta Anderson, Joseph Aranyosi, Mario Armstrong, Geoffrey Aronson, Dr. Alfred Basta, Gordon Bellamy, Big Boss, Becky Blakenship, Bill Blakesley, Walter Bland, Todd Borghesani, Nichole Bradford, Jon Crispin, Don Daglow, Ola and Joe Gardner, Kevin Gillis, Jennifer Goldfinch, Douglas Green, Clifford Hawkins, Ethelia Hines, Jaymes Hines, Maribeth Hines, Dr. David Holness, David Honig, Ross Horrocks, Doug Hughes, Jon James, Dr. Leslie Jarvis, Pamela Jolly, Chris Klaus, Debra Langford, Peter Leahy, Dr. Gene Loflin, Dr. Thelma Looms, Marcus Matthews, Leslie McCoy, Greg Meier, Will Mendez, Joe Morton, Cheryl Albert Reed, Steve Steinman, Lex Suvanto, Steve Sherman, Robert Tassinari, Dr. Diane Weber, Jo Ann Wilson, John Walker, Doug Wood, and Dr. Melissa Williams.

I would also like to extend thanks to all of the individuals who took the time to review my text. Your insight and input were essential in the final shaping of the text;

Mark Baldwin
President
Baldwin Consulting
Golden, Colorado

Richard Blunt
Associate Professor of Game and Simulation Studies
DeVry University
Arlington, Virginia

Drew Davidson
Director—Game Art & Design, Interactive Media Design
Art Institute of Pittsburgh, Art Institute Online
Pittsburgh, Pennsylvania

Michelle Hansen
Division Chair, Computer Information Systems
and Programming
Davenport University
Kalamazoo, Michigan

Chris McGhee
Academic Director
Art Institute of Phoenix
Phoenix, Arizona

Kevin O'Gorman
Chair, Game Design & Development
American InterContinental University–Dunwoody
Atlanta, Georgia

(I would also like to thank Kevin for his extensive contributions to Chapter 5)

Phillip Tavel
Curriculum Manager for Game and Simulation Programming
DeVry University
Seattle, Washington

Terrasa E. Ulm
Professor of Game Design
Becker College
Worcester, Massachusetts

Tim Warchocki
Department Chair—Game Design and Development
International Academy of Design and Technology
Orlando, Florida

Using the Book: Students

Chapter Openers

Each chapter of *Introduction to Video Game Design and Development* begins with a short introduction which previews the chapter's topics and their role in the game development process.

Learning objectives serve as the chapter sections and appear in the chapter opener and in each corresponding section, noted by a separate icon. These learning objectives serve as progress markers and help the students read with purpose.

Dynamic Graphics

The majority of the images included in the text, including our cover image, are created and provided by **Bill Blakesley,** one of the top 3D animators in the business.

Bill is a master degreed medical illustrator with over 10 years of experience in 3D medical visualization. He is employed as a medical animator at Shaw Science Partners and serves as an assistant adjunct faculty member at the Medical College of Georgia. Bill also sits on the advisory board and conducts an introduction to 3D animation at American InterContinental University. In the gaming industry, Bill consults with Entertainment Arts Research in the development of several future projects. He can be contacted at bblakesley@mindspring.com.

Introduction to Video Game Design and Development is also pleased to include a number of images from the **Into the Pixel** art exhibition for our chapter opening and end-of-chapter images.

Into the Pixel is a juried exhibition of the art of the video game, curated by experts from world-renowned art museums, cutting-edge galleries, and interactive industry veterans.

Into the Pixel is videogame artists' one annual opportunity to receive recognition for their creative achievements by peers in both the digital and fine art worlds.

Video games are an influential aspect of pop-culture and entertainment whose impact goes beyond the digital arts to influence perspectives in art, cinematography, literature, and even fashion. And behind every game character and dynamic environment are artists whose talents birthed the image seen in the 3D world.

The charts, tables, and figures in the text have a fresh, vibrant look in order to present important information in an easily understandable manner.

CHAPTER 1

Overview of Games, Gameplay, and the Game Experience

As a prelude to any discussion of game design, it is important to establish a fundamental orientation. This chapter defines the concept of a game, explores the behavioral, cultural, and societal motivations behind the playing of games, and identifies what makes a game enjoyable and satisfying.

After completing this chapter, you will be able to:

* Identify the characteristics common to all games.
* Identify the traditional game categories.
* Describe the social and cultural motivations behind game playing.
* Identify the types of people who play computer and video games.
* Classify various player archetypes and their reasons for playing games.
* Summarize the elements of a satisfying and enjoyable gaming experience.
* Describe common mistakes made by game designers that lead to player dissatisfaction.

TABLE 1.1   Summary of player archetypes.

Player Archetypes	Characteristics	Example Games
The Berserker	Solves problems through combat and/or destruction.	Doom, Duke Nukem, Quake, Unreal
The Detective	Enjoys finding clever ways to solve puzzles and problems.	Myst, Thief: The Dark Project, Grim Fandango, Syberia
The Power-Leveler	Enjoys character abilities.	Everquest, Morrowind or Ultima
The Strategist	Enjoys tactical decision-making.	Civilization, Starcraft, Command & Conquer, Warcraft, Age of Empires
The Socializer	Views games as a social experience.	The Sims Online, There, Second Life
The Thespian	Enjoys role-playing.	Everquest, Neverwinter Nights, Star Wars Galaxies
The Griefer	Makes other players miserable.	Ultima Online, Everquest, Counterstrike, Unreal, Battlefield 1942

Pro Tips

This boxed feature, indicated by a star icon in each chapter, provides insight into the video gaming industry by current top professionals. Each successful individual offers advice and perspective to new students or further develops certain essential topics introduced in the chapter.

Bill Blakesley

Pro Tips 6.1

SoftImage Master Class Developer

So you've decided to get into the game market. It is a lot of fun and it is always a lot of work. I will do my best to pass along things I have learned from my experience that you may find helpful.

The most important thing to strive for in a creative environment is to be a team player. You may be the next Einstein of 3D modeling, but if your colleagues cannot stand you it's going to be a long road. As artists, we are all trying hard to get better and better. Do not let self-achievement get in the way of the product goal.

If you are in an environment where roles are well defined, focus on an area that you enjoy and are proficient in. Again, your contribution to the team is important. It is a good idea to learn other areas of content creation because it makes you more marketable. Just make sure that if you are a texture artist on the project you strive to be the best texture artist on the planet.

Game Cheats

This marginal feature, indicated by an exclamation point icon, provides additional useful information on the subjects of certain chapters.

165

involved in the game through a communicator gives the player a power unlike any other entertainment vehicle.

A good game writer, under the best of circumstances, will work with the lead designer from the beginning. The writer will develop a detailed "bible" for the game containing the history of the game's world and the backstory that sets the plot in motion, as well as background information about the major characters. Incorporating this information into the game's design document is at the lead ... riter is also responsible for creating all of the NPC ... riters also write, edit, and polish any on-screen text or ... ntained in the game's manual.

... rief and to the point, yet it must convey character and ... nature of games frequently sees the player repeating ... mes. Long verbose dialogue that may sound good at ... iatingly dull with repetition. Game writers must write ... e. Dialogue that reads well is not always dialogue that ... ear requires a distinct talent.

Game Cheats 6.1

Interactivity in game design along with new technology will allow the storyteller to immerse the player while the developers figure out how to bring emotion to the 3D world in character design and development. The team at Valve is currently researching the development of characters that can emotionally affect the player using the new technology in SoftImage XSi 5.0.

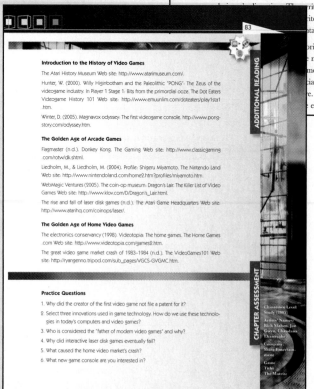

83

ADDITIONAL READING

Introduction to the History of Video Games

The Atari History Museum Web site: http://www.atarimuseum.com/.

Hunter, W. (2000). Willy Higinbotham and the Paleolithic "PONG": The Zeus of the videogame industry. In Player 1 Stage 1: Bits from the primordial ooze. The Dot Eaters Videogame History 101 Web site: http://www.emuunlim.com/doteaters/play1sta1.htm.

Winter, D. (2005). Magnavox odyssey: The first videogame console. http://www.pong-story.com/odyssey.htm.

The Golden Age of Arcade Games

Flagmaster (n.d.). Donkey Kong. The Gaming Web site: http://www.classicgaming.com/rotw/dk.shtml.

Liedholm, M., & Liedholm, M. (2004). Profile: Shigeru Miyamoto. The Nintendo Land Web site: http://www.nintendoland.com/home2.htm?profiles/miyamoto.htm.

WebMagic Ventures (2005). The coin-op museum: Dragon's Lair. The Killer List of Video Games Web site: http://www.klov.com/D/Dragon's_Lair.html.

The rise and fall of laser disk games (n.d.). The Atari Game Headquarters Web site: http://www.atarihq.com/coinops/laser/.

The Golden Age of Home Video Games

The electronics conservancy (1998). Videotopia: The home games. The Home Games.com Web site: http://www.videotopia.com/games2.htm.

The great video game market crash of 1983–1984 (n.d.). The VideoGames101 Web site: http://ryangenno.tripod.com/sub_pages/VGCS-GVGMC.htm.

CHAPTER ASSESSMENT

Practice Questions

1. Why did the creator of the first video game not file a patent for it?
2. Select three innovations used in game technology. How do we use these technologies in today's computers and video games?
3. Who is considered the "father of modern video games" and why?
4. Why did interactive laser disk games eventually fail?
5. What caused the home video market's crash?
6. What new game console are you interested in?

Chapter Assessments

The end-of-chapter material offers a wide variety of assessment tools for the student. The assessments are divided into Practice Questions, Lab Exercises, and Written Assignments or Oral Presentations. Additional Readings are also provided in the form of Web addresses for students wishing to learn more about certain topics.

Using the Book: Supplements for Students and Instructors

Interactive Software

McGraw-Hill is very proud to offer a unique supplement for the *Introduction to Video Game Design and Development* text: interactive software that allows students to access more visual aids to further their knowledge on video game development. This interactive software introduces the student to concepts relative to game modeling, interface development, and UV mapping. It is designed to give an in-depth look at the industry, conceptually enforcing design applications and historical foundation. Students are introduced to a new learning environment through an interactive interface and video tutorials. The video tutorials feature how video game characters and images are created, from a wire frame into a full textured character, using SOFTIMAGEIXSI v.5.0 digital character software. Students see the development process, from start to finish, right before their eyes! The interactive software is available to each student who purchases the text as a CD-ROM.

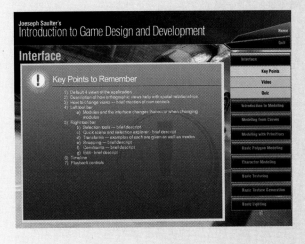

At relevant points throughout the text, a CD icon will appear in the margin that will steer the students towards the interactive software to expand upon the topic presented on that page.

Online Learning Center

The **Online Learning Center (OLC)** is a Web site that follows the text chapter-by-chapter. OLC content is ancillary and supplementary germane to the textbook, as students read the book, they can go online to review material or link to relevant Web sites. An Information Center features an overview of the text, background on the author, and the Preface and Table of Contents from the book. Instructors can access a sample syllabus and PowerPoint presentations. Students see the Learning Objectives and Summaries from the text, as well as useful Web links for other resources on the video gaming industry. Students will also be able to expand their knowledge on the history of video games and their impact on our culture.

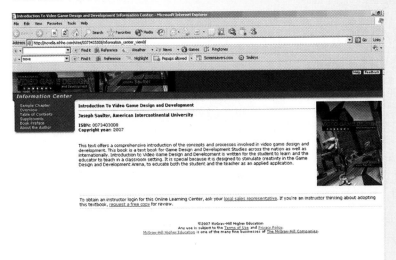

The OLC can be delivered multiple ways – professors and students can access them directly through the text-book Web site through PageOut, or within a course management system (i.e. WebCT, Blackboard, TopClass, or eCollege.)

PowerPoint Presentations

A PowerPoint presentation is available for each chapter. These presentations include the chapter's learning objectives, figures, and tables/charts.

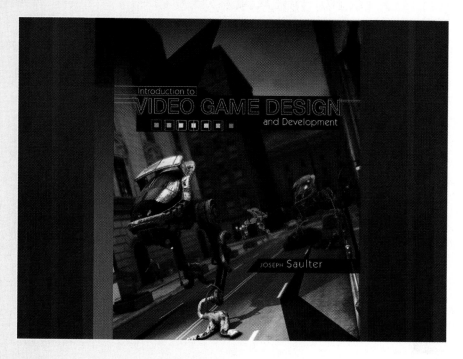

Instructor's Resource CD-ROM

The Instructor's Resource CD-ROM (IRCD) will also be available for instructors. The IRCD will include a test bank, the PowerPoint Presentations, a sample syllabus, and an image bank containing some of the artwork from the text.

PageOut: McGraw-Hill's Course Management System

PageOut is McGraw-Hill's unique point-and-click course Web site tool, enabling you to create a full-featured, professional-quality course Web site without knowing HTML coding. With PageOut you can post your syllabus online, assign McGraw-Hill Online Learning Center or eBook content, add links to important off-site resources, and maintain student results in the online grade book. You can send class announcements, copy your course site to share with colleagues, and upload original files. PageOut is free for every McGraw-Hill/Irwin user and, if you're short on time, we even have a team ready to help you create your site! To learn more, please visit http://www.pageout.net.

Create a custom course website with PageOut, free to instructors using a McGraw-Hill textbook.

To learn more, contact your McGraw-Hill publisher's representative or visit www.mhhe.com/solutions.

Introduction to Video Game Design and Development

Official Selection of the 2005 *Into the Pixel* art exhibition: CCK Tower - New Year's Eve ■ Artists: Danny Tamez, Mark Ecko, Brian Horton, Mike Evans

Company: Atari, Inc. ■ Game Title: Marc Ecko's Getting Up: Contents Under Pressure

Overview of Games, Gameplay, and the Game Experience

As a prelude to any discussion of game design, it is important to establish a fundamental orientation. This chapter defines the concept of a game, explores the behavioral, cultural, and societal motivations behind the playing of games, and identifies what makes a game enjoyable and satisfying.

After completing this chapter, you will be able to:

- Identify the characteristics common to all games.
- Identify the traditional game categories.
- Describe the social and cultural motivations behind game playing.
- Identify the types of people who play computer and video games.
- Classify various player archetypes and their reasons for playing games.
- Summarize the elements of a satisfying and enjoyable gaming experience.
- Describe common mistakes made by game designers that lead to player dissatisfaction.

Pro Tips 1.1

Don Daglow

President and CEO of Stormfront Studios

Daglow's Law of Art and Technology: Creativity expands to fill the visual, aural, and emotional bandwidths of the artistic medium through which it is expressed.

When movies were silent, exaggerated acting and rich black-and-white imagery were used to tell stories. In 1927 "talkies" began, and soon we didn't just have dialogue, we had musicals. Actors' performances became more subtle, and directors used more close-ups. Then new kinds of cameras and dollies were invented, and all the ways that cuts, fades, and pans tell a story changed—methods used to subtly manipulate our emotions in the theater. On and on the process went, completely changing the way we felt when we went to see a good movie. The visual, aural, and emotional "data" all expanded with technology.

The same thing has happened in games, where an odd pattern has also emerged. When we design great new games to take advantage of powerful next-generation consoles, sometimes we realize we didn't need new consoles at all. With simpler graphics and sounds, the essential gameplay—the fun—of the hottest new game often could have been implemented on last year's hardware. What kept us from coming up with the idea last year? We didn't expand our thinking, open ourselves to new ideas, until new hardware came along . . . even though the idea was already viable today!

What Is a Game?

"You can discover more about a person in an hour of play than in a year of conversation."[1]

Games have existed since the dawn of humanity and have become an integral part of modern civilization. This book presents an introduction to game design. However, to examine game design, we must first clarify the use and definition of the word *game*.

Defining *Game*

For our purposes, a game has certain common characteristics.

One or More Players. By definition, a game condition exists only when there is an identifiable player or players. Several types of games can accommodate a single player, such as golf or solitaire; many games require one or more other players, such as tennis or baseball.

---

[1] Plato (n.d.). Retrieved August 18, 2005, from http://www.quotedb.com/quotes/2873.

Set of Rules. A game must have rules that are complete and self-sufficient, and these rules must cover every possible variation of play. Rules should also clarify all the consequences of every possible action. The rules should allow the player to visualize the world of the game and picture what is happening; many games represent a facet of the real world. In the game of Monopoly, for example, the player pretends to buy and sell commercial real estate.

Player Interaction with an Opposing Force. A game must involve conflict, and the player must interact with an opposing force. That force must have objectives that conflict with the player's objectives. This opposing force can be other player(s), the force of "randomization" (a shuffled deck of cards in a game of solitaire, for example), a computer's artificial intelligence, or simply the rules of the game itself. Gameplay must involve interaction between the player and this force, and the eventual outcome of the game must depend on this interaction.

Organized Method of Play. A game must be playable, and the sequence of play should be logical and balanced. Strategies that are more effective should develop as players become familiar with the method of play. In essence, they should be able to learn from their actions and become better players as a result.

Desirable Goals or Outcome. A game must have a goal. It must have one or more possible outcomes that depend on the strategies and choices made by the players during the game; for example, there should be a winner and a loser.

Traditional Game Categories

There are several different categories of games:

- Board games.
- Card games.
- Target games.
- Sports games.

Board Games. Board games have been consistently popular, and the origins of board games date back to ancient times. Over time board games spread to ancient Egypt, Greece, and Rome, through Europe, and eventually to the colonies of the New World. The first people playing board games probably drew grids on the ground with sticks, using pebbles and other common objects as playing pieces. The simple game of Tic-Tac-Toe had its origins in ancient China and almost certainly began in this fashion.

Almost 5,000 years ago durable game boards of wood and clay began to appear. Senet, played in ancient Egypt, is one of the earliest known board games. References to Senet date back to 3100 BCE. Other ancient board games include The Royal Game of Ur from Mesopotamia (2600–2500 BCE) and the Chinese game of Wei-qi, which is over 2,200 years old and is also known as Baduk, Igo, and Go (McAdams, 1995).

Historically board games have fallen into two general categories.

Strategy Games. The objective of a strategy game is to gain control of a larger portion of the game board by using game pieces to block or capture an opponent's pieces (History of board games, 2002). Chess, Risk, and Monopoly are all examples of strategy board games.

Racing Games. The objective of a racing game is to begin at a specific point on the game board and race along one or more paths to reach a specific goal or finish line before your opponent (History of board games, 2002). Chutes and Ladders, Life, and Parcheesi are all examples of racing board games.

Other board games do not fit in these categories. However, most are variations. For example, the objective of the board game Clue is to be the first player to solve a specific puzzle. Although the players are not trying to get to a specific location on the board, this is still a type of racing game.

Card Games. It is likely that the playing of cards originated in China. We know that the emperor Mu-tsung played "domino cards" with his wife on New Year's Eve, AD 969. Card games were introduced to Spain and Italy around AD 1370. The European style of playing cards has origins in a region of Egypt near Mameluke. A Mameluke deck, dated to approximately AD 1400, consisted of 52 cards with four suits: polo sticks, swords, cups, and coins. One of the earliest known references to playing cards in Europe may be a quote from Johannes von Rheinfelden in the 14th century: "Thus it is that a certain game, called the game of cards, has reached us in the present year, namely AD 1377" (von Rheinfelden, 1377).

Figure 1.1 Diversity in the game of cards.

In addition to a deck of cards, card games sometime require a pencil and paper or other equipment, such as a cribbage board, to keep score. We use the traditional 52-card deck for common games like poker and rummy; but other games can use larger decks, more than one deck, or specialized decks. There are four major varieties of card games, and each has its own characteristics.

Playing-Out Games. Each player's move consists of playing out a card from his or her hand to achieve an effect. Play ends when some or all of the players run out of cards. UNO and Mille Borne are good examples of this type of game.

Exchange Games. Each player's move consists of exchanging a card or cards from his or her hand with another player or from a reserve of cards on the table. The objective is usually to collect a certain combination or run of cards, as in Gin Rummy.

Showdown Games. This variety of game involves little or no play of cards. The goal is simply to see which player has the best hand. Some games let you improve your hand by discarding and replacing cards or by arranging your cards in specific orders or groups; Poker and Bridge are games of this sort.

Patience Games. The object of a patience game is simply to sort the deck into order by moving cards in accordance with a specific set of rules. Patience games are usually solitaire games; but when they are played competitively, the object is to see which player is the first to sort his or her cards.

Target Games. Early human survival depended on hunting skill. The hand–eye coordination required for hunting developed at an early age, largely through target games. Certainly the first target games involved the hurling of stones and later primitive weapons like spears and slings. The earliest known use of the bow and arrow occurred approximately 5,000 years ago in Egypt. Although archery competitions took place in China during the Zhou dynasty, 1027–256 BCE, the first organized archery tournament is believed to have taken place in England in 1583 (History of archery, n.d.).

Darts evolved from a simple game played by English archers as early as the 15th century (History of darts, n.d.). They would throw shortened arrows at targets of wood generally made from the bottoms of wine barrels or tree logs–hence the British dart term "log-ends." There are many other examples of target games, including horseshoes, bowling, and marbles. The rules of these games generally assign scores based on the players' accuracy.

Figure 1.2 Doesn't the target look like the sawn-off end of a log?

Sports Games. Games involving physical activity and competition are probably the oldest games, dating back to prehistoric times. Most of these early games, like wrestling and boxing, were essentially simulations of combat. However, some early civilizations developed organized sports that were non-combative. Native Americans, for example, played games resembling modern lacrosse and lawn bowling.

Athletic contests were a large part of social life and religious observance in ancient Greek and Rome. Many modern track and field contests and today's international Olympic Games, originated in these civilizations. In 1894 French educator Pierre de Coubertin proposed that a modern revival of the Olympic Games of ancient Greece might promote peace and understanding between the nations of the world. The first modern Olympics, held in 1896, included only summer events; the Winter Olympics started in 1924. Approximately 300 athletes from fewer than 15 countries attended the 1896 games. One hundred years later, in 1996, the Olympic Games had grown to include more than 10,000 athletes from over 190 countries.

Figure 1.3 Games involving strength and agility are among the oldest known to humanity.

Organized sports declined in popularity after the fall of the Roman Empire but saw resurgence in the 11th century with the introduction of the tournament or joust in England. The English also played early forms of football and various field sports like throwing the bar.

The practice of school and university athletics did not begin until the middle of the 19th century. The practice continued as medical proof of the benefits of exercise began to emerge. Today athletics remains an important part of most educational curricula. Let us examine some of the more popular types of sports games.

Ball Games. In this variety of game, play revolves around an object, often a type of ball or puck. The objective of these games is to score points by achieving a specific goal. This can involve moving the object to a particular location, moving a player to a particular location while holding the object, getting the player to a particular location without being tagged by the object, or simply keeping the object in play until another player fails to do so. Ball games can be team games like football, soccer, or basketball or one-on-one games like tennis or handball. Multiplayer games like golf and bowling are not true athletic games; rather, they are forms of target games.

Combat Games. Combat games like boxing and wrestling involve direct physical contact between players. Other types of combat games offer a safe simulation of combat. Capture the Flag, Paintball, and Laser Tag are all examples of simulated combat games.

Athletic Competitions. We can certainly view athletic competitions as games. Even a solo athlete can compete against a clock or a previously determined distance record.

Why Do People Play Games?

"Your opponent, in the end, is never really the player on the other side of the net, or the swimmer in the next lane, or the team on the other side of the field, or even the bar you must high-jump. Your opponent is yourself, your negative internal voices, your level of determination."[2]

There are several reasons why people play games. Research on computer and video game usage by the Entertainment Software Association (ESA) found that 50 percent of Americans who play computer and video games do so as a form of entertainment (Essential facts, 2005). However, the desire to play games is not limited to television and computer screens, and the reasons for play go beyond entertainment. This section discusses why people play games.

Strategy Games for the Personal Computer

"If you know the enemy and know yourself, you need not fear the result of a hundred battles. If you know yourself, but not the enemy, for every victory gained you will also suffer a defeat. If you know neither the enemy nor yourself, you will succumb in every battle."[3]

There is little doubt that the first computer strategy game was a computer chess program created by mathematician Alan Turing in 1950. Strategy games have come

---

[2] Lichtenstein, G. (1975). Retrieved August 20, 2005, from http://www.houseofquotes.com/authors/Grace_Lichtenstein.htm.

[3] Sun Tzu (circa 500 B.C.). *The art of war.* Retrieved August 14, 2005, from http://www.military-quotes.com/Sun-Tzu.htm.

a long way since then. In this section we describe some of the highlights of the evolution of this popular genre from 1970 through 2005, beginning with a discussion of turn-based strategy games.

Turn-Based Strategy Games. Players take "turns" in "turn-based" strategy games. Typically a player makes a move or series of moves, then the next player has the opportunity to do the same. Chess is an excellent example of a turn-based game. Ideally a turn-based game is easy to learn but takes a long time to master. The best players are always planning several moves ahead with multiple contingencies. Computers are ideally suited to this type of game, and not surprisingly, turn-based computer games have a long and successful history.

Starfleet Orion (1978). Jim Connelly and John Freeman wrote the first computer-based tactical combat game, Starfleet Orion, for the Commodore PET microcomputer in 1978. Connelly was a Dungeons & Dragons fan who enjoyed running the game as the "Dungeon Master" or referee. He bought the PET computer to help him keep track of all the statistics of the game. As tax time approached, he looked for a way to write off the purchase as a business expense, so he set to work on a computer game he might be able to market. His friend and fellow D&D player John Freeman came aboard to assist him. Connelly took care of the programming chores while Freeman took over the creative side of things.

They finished the game before the end of the year and formed their own company, Automated Simulations. The game's platform was the TRS-80 and Apple II. They released a sequel, Invasion Orion, the following year. The company eventually became Epyx and released a number of other hit titles, including the classic D&D adventure Temple of Apshai.

Empire (1978). Caltech student Walter Bright created the first true computer war game, Empire. Bright was a big fan of the board game Risk, and the first version of Empire was a board game he created in 1971 while he was still in high school. The game was impractical in that it used an eight-foot sheet of plywood and the rules were bafflingly complex, but the idea stuck with him.

Bright later discovered some early computer games on the Caltech mainframe, but they were too simplistic for him, and he grew bored quickly. He remembered the old war game he had invented in high school, and it occurred to him that if played on a computer, it could handle the complex bookkeeping automatically. He set to work immediately.

The game was finished in 1978. He presented it to various publishers and collected an impressive stack of rejection letters. Finally, in 1985 a company called Interstel picked up the game and distributed it. Many consider Empire the most influential strategy title ever released.

M.U.L.E. (1982). M.U.L.E. (Multiple Use Labor Element) was a turned-based game released in 1982 by Electronic Arts for the Atari 800 and Commodore 64. M.U.L.E.s are labor robots used to collect resources on distant planets. The game dropped four players onto a planet and gave them a certain amount of time to collect resources with the robots before a ship came to pick them up.

The game's designer, cited as one of the most talented in the history of the industry, was Dani Bunten. Bunten was one of the founding members of Ozark Software, a small group of game developers from Little Rock, Arkansas, and his influence among game developers is legendary. Bunten died of cancer in 1998 at the age of 49.

The game was never a huge hit, but its ingenious gameplay inspired an entire generation of designers. In fact, Will Wright, creator of the best-selling computer game of all time, The Sims, dedicated that game to Dani Bunten.

Real-Time Strategy Games. Computers allowed developers to create strategy games that were not turn-based but rather operated in real time. In a RTS game, there is no time for careful strategy and cautious tactics. Whether the player makes a decision or not, the events of the game continue to play out. The constant time pressure and increased stress level make RTS titles the most challenging of all strategy games.

Dune II (1992). In 1985 Brett Sperry and Louis Castle started designing games out of a garage in Las Vegas. Their humble start-up eventually became the industry giant Westwood Studios. The two developers had some early success with fantasy role-playing titles such as Eye of the Beholder (1990), but Sperry wanted to head in another direction. Sperry was a fan of strategy games, but the slow, turn-based titles on the market bored him. He wanted to create a new type of game, one that combined deep-thinking strategy with split-second decision making.

They released Dune II in 1992. With this title Sperry and Westwood created what would become a classic gaming genre: the *real-time strategy game*. Initially a sequel to the David Lynch film *Dune*, based on the classic science fiction novel by Frank Hebert, the game featured three different armies at war on the desert planet Arrakis. The goal of the game was for the player's "house" to gain control of the planet. To accomplish this, a player used a combination of resource management, construction, and warfare elements. Players would harvest a valuable commodity called "spice" to earn money. The spice allowed a player to build weapons, train soldiers, and harvest more spice. Houses would also attack each other in an attempt to capture additional resources and gain control of the map.

Dune II was very successful, spawning several sequels. However, it also inspired Westwood to develop another game using the same formula. The 1995 Command & Conquer game would later be a runaway hit, breaking multiple sales records.

C&C would also inspire a host of sequels and spin-offs, making it one of the most successful franchises in the history of gaming.

Warcraft (1994). Following the success of Dune II, Blizzard Software released a RTS title in 1994 called Warcraft. This game took real-time strategy out of the realm of science fiction and set it in a "Tolkienesque" fantasy world. The game had the same "harvest, build, fight" gameplay dynamic, but with a different look and feel. Warcraft was not an overwhelming hit, but it sold well enough to spawn Warcraft II in 1995. Warcraft II and Blizzard's 1998 science fiction game Starcraft were both blockbusters, setting up a rivalry between Blizzard and Westwood RTS titles that would continue for years to come.

Total Annihilation (1997). Designer Chris Taylor of Cavedog Games broke new ground with Total Annihilation. On the surface the game looked like a prettier version of Command & Conquer, but the game included a number of innovations that would become standard in later RTS titles.

For the first time players could give their units a string of commands, setting up order queues that they would automatically perform in sequence. Unit AI allowed players to set specific stances so they would not mindlessly chase units that were trying to draw them away from strategic areas. These and other innovations made it possible to formulate elaborate battle plans as complex as the old turn-based titles without giving up the excitement of real-time play.

Simulation and "God" Games. Simulation games are exactly that: simulations of real-life events or circumstances. "God" games take the simulation genre a step further. They allow the player to have control of the simulation in the role of an omnipotent overseer. As these games quickly teach us, being a "god" is not an easy task. These types of strategy games can be quite challenging. We will now look at some of the games in this category.

Kingdom (1970). The mainframe computer game Kingdom, also called Hammurabi, was the first "city" simulation game. The player was given the task of overseeing the economic development of a virtual kingdom in "the cradle of civilization," ancient Mesopotamia. Gameplay involved supplying numeric tax rates and other parameters. The game informed the player of changes in the kingdom's tax revenues, profits, food supplies, birthrates, and death rates resulting from their decisions.

The Game of Life (1970). When British mathematician John H. Conway entered secondary school at the age of 11 an interviewer asked what he wanted to be when he grew up. The son of a laboratory assistant replied, without hesitation, that he intended to be a mathematician at Cambridge. He achieved his ambition in 1964 when he received his doctorate and became a lecturer in Pure Mathematics at the University of Cambridge.

He later became famous outside his field when he created a computer program called The Game of Life in 1970. Sometimes called Life, the program is not actually a game in the conventional sense. There are no players, hence no winner or loser. The user arranges the pieces in a starting pattern, and the program determines everything that follows.

The fascinating thing about Life is that it was impossible to look at a starting position and know, in advance, what would happen as the game progressed. The program mimicked the birth, growth, replication, and death of actual cells. It was impossible to tell if a pattern would die off quickly, form a stable population, or grow forever.

Figure 1.4 Dan Freidman (center) and John Walker (left) Research Development, Entertainment Arts Research.

Conway showed the game to a friend, Martin Gardner. Gardner wrote about the game in *Scientific American* magazine in October 1970. The Game of Life made Conway famous overnight, but it also opened up a completely new field of mathematical research, the field of cellular automata.

Populous (1989). Peter Molyneux was born in Great Britain. His father was the owner of a toyshop, and Molyneux was fond of games from an early age. In the early 1980s he founded a software development company named Taurus. When the company received some free Amiga computers from Commodore, Molyneux, inspired by the graphic capabilities of the machines, began to dabble in game design. He ultimately formed a new game company called Bullfrog Productions.

Molyneux credited his fascination with the idea of "god" games to an experience he had as a child. He found a bustling anthill and began poking it with a stick, then watched in fascination as the ants frantically tried to repair the damage. Overcome by guilt, he gave the colony a cube of sugar. Again, he watched in fascination as they consumed the cube and set about their reconstruction activities with renewed vigor. The feeling of power he felt by playing "god" with the tiny creatures never left him, and Molyneux tried to recapture that feeling when the time came to create a game.

Populous, released in 1989, saw the player taking the role of a deity, trying to win followers as they settled land and grew into a civilization. Players grew more powerful as they attracted more followers. Other deities with their own followers also existed, and the players used their powers to do battle with their opponents while keeping their own followers happy and thriving.

Populous was groundbreaking in many ways. Gameplay took place in real time, yet the player did not have direct influence over followers. The strategy to winning was in influencing events rather than controlling them. The game was a sensation and sold over 4 million copies, making it one of the most successful computer games in history. It also created the genre that would eventually produce the most popular game of all time.

Sim City (1989). In the mid-1980s game designer Will Wright was working on a Broderbund game called Raid of Bungeling Bay. The game involved attack helicopters, and Wright's job was to design the islands where the helicopter battles would take place; to his surprise, Wright found that constructing the islands was more fun than flying the helicopters. At the time, Wright was reading about the work of urban planner Jay Forrester, and Forrester's theories fascinated him.

Wright took the Bungeling Bay editor, added more city elements like automobiles and people, and began to experiment. His idea was to simulate an urban environment, then speed up time to see how things would progress. The concept proved difficult to sell to a publisher, however. It seemed more like an interesting toy than a full-fledged game. Finally Wright was able to release a version of the game for the Commodore in 1987, but the PC and Macintosh markets seemed out of reach. Wright met Jeff Braun in 1987, and Braun was so impressed with the idea that the two formed their own company to publish PC and Mac versions of the game. Maxis released the computer versions of Sim City in 1989.

The game became a classic almost entirely by word-of-mouth. People found the addictive quality of the game irresistible. When *Time* magazine ran a feature on the game it became a bona fide hit, and an avalanche of popular simulation games flooded the market. Wright followed up the success of Sim City with over a dozen sequels and Sim spin-offs, including Sim City 3000, SimAnt, SimEarth, and SimFarm. However, the most popular of all the Sim titles was yet to come.

Civilization (1991). Sim City greatly influenced a young designer named Sid Meier, who cofounded MicroProse Software in 1982. After a string of popular titles including F-15 Strike Eagle, one of the first combat flight simulators, and the popular railroad simulation game Railroad Tycoon, Meier designed a "god" game that would become one of the most honored titles of all time. Civilization, released in 1991, was a game of world exploration and conquest. To win the game, a player had to become the most powerful civilization on earth. Gameplay entailed constructing cities, developing new technologies, and building military forces.

The Sims (2000). After the success of his popular Sim series of games, Will Wright released a new Sim title. In the new game, The Sims, players created a simulated family where they could buy a house, get a job, and micromanage every aspect of their lives in an attempt to stay happy and healthy. The small cartoonlike Sims characters in the game also had personalities. They could be happy or sad, get into fistfights, and even die from hunger. They spoke to each other using a meaningless gibberish known to Sim aficionados as Simlish. The Sims spawned its own series of expansion games, as well as the massively multiplayer game The Sims Online. With more than 7 million copies sold, The Sims series of games became the top-selling PC game of all time.

Hybrid Games. Some games simply do not fit conveniently into a single category. In fact, as the game industry matures, the lines between the genres continue to blur. Some newer games bear examination for their innovation and their influence on future titles.

Tomb Raider (1996). British designer Jeremy Heath-Smith founded Core Design in 1988, beginning with £16,000 and a staff of eight. After a series of successful but generally unmemorable First Person Shooter (FPS) games, CentreGold group acquired the company. Eventually Eidos acquired the company in 1996, releasing the Core Design blockbuster hit Tomb Raider.

This game was one of the earliest hybrids. Part puzzle-solving adventure game and part first-person shooter, the game featured the industry's first female protagonist. The preternaturally well-endowed Lara Croft became a virtual superstar, launching a series of popular games and even a big-budget Hollywood movie.

Thief: The Dark Project (1998). Warren Spector produced the groundbreaking first-person fantasy game Ultimate Underworld for Origin and Blue Sky Productions before accepting the position of executive producer at Looking Glass Technologies. There he developed a moderately successful but groundbreaking hybrid game.

Released as Thief: The Dark Project in 1998, the game was a first-person adventure title, but the main character was a thief who spent his time avoiding combat instead of heading straight into it. In fact, in most circumstances if players found themselves in a combat situation, it was time to load a saved game.

Fans often refer to Thief's action–adventure hybrid, variant genre as a *first-person sneaker*. Despite disappointing initial sales, the game developed a cult following and spawned two sequels.

Deus Ex (2000). Looking Glass Technologies disbanded in 1997, and Warren Spector joined Ion Storm in fall of 1997. In 1999 he took a seat on the company's board of directors. At Ion Storm his team created another groundbreaking title.

Deus Ex was the ultimate hybrid: an action/adventure/first-person shooter/role-playing game. The game was set in a dark, paranoid, near-future world teeming with conspiracies. Players took on the role of anti-terrorist agent for a group called UNATCO. While the character was already set within the context of the game world, players could advance their skills and gain new abilities by using special cybernetic augmentations.

The game was ambitious and influential. There were many different ways to resolve any given situation. Players could rush in with guns blazing or sneak through the shadows, as in Thief, avoiding any conflict. The game had several different endings, depending on the choices the player made.

Grand Theft Auto 3 (2001). Dave Jones established Scottish game developer DMA Design in 1987. In 1998 Take2 and BMG distributed DMA's Grand Theft Auto for the PC and the Sony PlayStation. The game had unsophisticated graphics and a top-down view that made it feel more like an arcade game. Grand Theft Auto 2, distributed by Rockstar Games in the 1990, had slightly better graphics but still had the same top-down perspective and was unremarkable.

In 2001, however, DMA and Rockstar released Grand Theft Auto 3. The combination first-person shooter/driving game featured a rendered 3D city with a completely open environment. There was a linear set of "missions" with a storyline, but the player was also free to go anywhere and do anything–something unheard of in a game until then. The game allowed a player to carjack an automobile; catch a train; or steal an ambulance or a police car. A vast array of deadly and explosive weapons was also available, allowing the player to cause almost unlimited mayhem.

The game and its sequel, Grand Theft Auto: Vice City, sparked controversy for their violent scenes and subject matter. However, there can be no doubt that the nonlinear aspect of gameplay and freedom of choice raised the bar and set a new design standard.

Motivations behind Game Playing

There are many reasons why people play games (Crawford, 1982). The primary social and cultural motivations for playing games are

- Education.
- Fantasy and wish fulfillment.
- Overcoming social restrictions.
- Competition.
- Socialization.
- Exercise.

Education. Nearly half of a child's mental capacity has developed before the age of 4, another 30 percent before the age of 8, and the remaining 20 percent by the time he or she reaches 17. Everything is a learning experience for a child; but in those critical first years, most education comes through play. A simple game of Peek-a-Boo, for example, may teach a child to overcome separation anxiety. The child learns that saying goodbye does not have to be traumatic or permanent. The game of Hide-and-Seek may reinforce that lesson as the child gets older. As children approach adulthood, games continue to teach important life lessons about trust, cooperation, conflict resolution, communication, and even ethics.

Educational games are not limited to children. In recent years major corporations have seen the benefits of organized team-building and motivational games for their employees. These corporate events are becoming increasingly popular. Paintball wars, employee sports leagues, scavenger hunts, and other events stress cooperation and team effort while building camaraderie and trust between coworkers.

However, having fun is not always the objective of educational games. The military has long made use of war games for troop training, and in recent years this practice has emerged into the world of computer simulation games. For example, Mission Rehearsal Exercise (MRE) is a high-tech computer simulation developed for the U.S. military. Its goal is to train soldiers for combat, peacekeeping, and humanitarian missions. In addition, as part of a larger plan to use technology to train the video game generation now entering the service, the U.S. Army released a free computer game as a recruitment tool. Titled America's Army, the game is available on CD, free of charge, at any army recruiting office.

Fantasy and Wish Fulfillment. Another motivation for playing games is that of vicarious experience and fantasy fulfillment (Crawford, 1982). Games can transport players to another world and allow them to temporarily escape the frustrations of everyday life. Like a good novel or an engrossing film, the benefits are undeniable. However, games present an opportunity that these other types of media do not. They allow the player to interact and to become an integral part of the process. The player's actions and choices actually make a difference. The experience is active, not passive.

Overcoming Social Restrictions. Societal mores tell us that lying is an unacceptable behavior in a civilized person. Yet in the game of poker lying, or "bluffing," is a critical and important strategy. It is part of what makes the game enjoyable. In addition, it is entirely acceptable and even encouraged. This is a simple illustration of another motivation. Games give us the opportunity, in a safe and acceptable manner, to overcome many of the restrictions placed on us by society.

It is completely unacceptable to knock a person down and take something from them in everyday life, yet this practice is a key strategy in the game of football. Stealing automobiles is illegal, yet it is virtually impossible to complete a level of the controversial video game Grand Theft Auto 3 successfully without

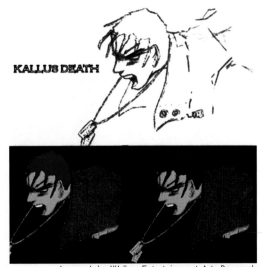

KALLUS DEATH

Image John Walker, Entertainment Arts Research

Figure 1.5 Games provide an outlet for antisocial behavior.

doing so. This same game also encourages the player to commit assassinations and armed robbery and to engage the services of prostitutes.

This is perhaps an extreme example of acceptable antisocial behavior within the context of a game. These are certainly the most distasteful and base of all human emotions, yet games like this continue to grow in popularity. From a simple game of poker to a videogame bloodbath, players enjoy games that permit them to flout societal mores and restrictions without risk.

Competition. The competitive aspect of game playing is another important motivation. The experience of winning can be extremely enjoyable and satisfying. As a result, many types of game competitions and tournaments are especially gratifying.

Players who carry the spirit of competition to an extreme can often make the game playing experience unpleasant for others. For them, winning is not the goal. Beating someone else is of primary importance. Unfortunately, sensitive players will often leave the competitive games dominated by these types of "sharks."

Figure 1.6 Competition can improve performance.

Socialization. A game of Hopscotch on the sidewalk or a pick-up game of basketball at a local playground can also serve an important social function. The game itself is not as important as the social event. A party game like Charades is an excellent example of a game used primarily as a social icebreaker. Today many online gamers use game interfaces in a similar fashion. For some people these games, such as Ultima and Everquest, essentially serve as graphical chat rooms.

Exercise. Of course physical and mental exercise has always been a major motivation for game players. A weekly game of racquetball can do wonders for the health of an avid player. Strategy games like chess can help keep the mind sharp. Even a game in a video arcade can help develop hand–eye coordination.

Video and Computer Game Players

"The opportunities for our industry are vast and exciting. We are growing and broadening our audience, opening new frontiers, developing online and wireless platforms, and creating truly original and unique forms of entertainment."[4]

The desire to play games goes back thousands of years and is part of our nature as human beings. Technological developments have always directly affected the way we play games. Humans will always find a way to have fun with their tools, so board games probably followed closely behind the invention of carving tools. The creation of the computer and the cathode ray tube are no exceptions. Humans quickly found a way to use these new tools to create an entirely new type of game–the electronic game.

Types of Gamers

At first electronic games appealed to a narrow audience. This subculture primarily consisted of computer enthusiasts and science fiction fans. However, more people are experiencing the world of computer and video games. In this section we examine some ways to classify the people who play electronic games.

Classification of Video Game Players. As the appeal of video and computer games broadened, so too did the types of people playing them. Knowing about the categories of players and their reasons for playing is important to game designers. In the following sections we discuss the two major groups of video game players: the core gamer and the casual gamer.

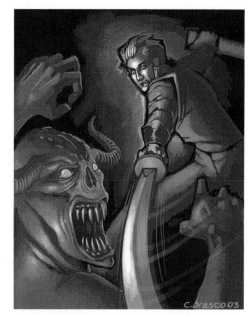

Figure 1.7 Imagery of energy redistribution.

Core Gamer. For core gamers gaming is more than an enjoyable pastime; it is their favorite form of entertainment. They spend most of their leisure time playing games. When they are not playing games, they frequent the local game store, read

[4] Lowenstein, D. (2005). *Essential facts about the computer and video game industry*. Entertainment Software Association. Retrieved August 20, 2005, from http://www.theesa.com/files/2005EssentialFacts.pdf.

game reviews, or post to gaming message boards. Core gamers build fan sites dedicated to their favorite games. They write walk-through and strategy guides. They will save their hard-earned cash to buy the latest video card or the highest-quality monitor.

For core gamers completing, or "beating," a game is paramount. They are much more tolerant of frustrating gameplay because their satisfaction comes from overcoming obstacles. The more difficult and complex the game is, the more satisfaction they receive for having completed it. Core gamers are undaunted by games that demand hundreds of hours of dedicated play. They are also likely to replay a game several times in an attempt to play as nearly "perfect" a game as possible.

Not surprisingly, core gamers are the most vocal of all players. They are most willing to offer developers and publishers their opinions. Consequently game developers seem to spend a large amount of their time trying to please them.

Casual Gamer. Though not quite as vocal, the casual gamer is increasingly important to the game industry. For casual gamers enjoying the game is paramount. If they become frustrated, casual gamers will simply stop playing the game.

Casual gamers demand simplicity at all levels. The game must be easy to install and intuitive to learn. They will play a game for 20 or 30 minutes at a time and expect to have a feeling of accomplishment during that time. The casual gamer will set the game aside for a week or more, and expect it to be a simple matter to resume the game. They are often "outsiders" in the gaming community. They do not have the latest video cards and drivers and do not want to spend hours in character creation or tweaking the statistics of a character before jumping into a role-playing game (RPG).

Pleasing Both Types of Gamers. Satisfying both the core gamer and the casual gamer is one of the most difficult challenges facing the game designer. Since its inception, the game industry has relied on core gamers. They represented a loyal, reliable, and consistent customer base. Game reviewers, almost without exception, are this type of player. In many ways core gamers drive the industry.

However, as the game industry matured, popular breakaway hits like Myst, Doom, and more recently The Sims showed that casual gamers were far more important than anyone had previously suspected. Casual gamers brought the industry out of the "techno-geek" closet and into the realm of mainstream entertainment. In fact, by 2001 video games were outgrossing the U.S. film industry. What does that mean for the industry from a design standpoint? To please both types of gamers, a game must provide

- ☐ Clear objectives and uncomplicated storylines.

- ☐ Rapid opportunities for advancement.

- Frequent and satisfying rewards.

- A simple and intuitive user interface.

- Optional opportunities for extremely high levels of challenge.

- Optional opportunities for extended hours of gameplay.

- A complex yet logical set of rules.

- Optional opportunities for advanced statistical analysis.

These are formidable goals. In fact, many of them seem to be at odds with each other. How can you provide a gameplay mechanism that is simple and intuitive, yet simultaneously highly complex and challenging? These are issues game designers face daily. This dichotomy does not influence every decision, but it is important to acknowledge this fundamental split as an important first step toward understanding the gaming audience from a design perspective. A designer needs to ask who the players are, what sort of gaming experience they are seeking, and what their style of play is. In the next sections we will discuss the characteristics of some common player archetypes.

Player Archetypes. Whether casual or core, different people seem to play games in disparate ways. If they approach a game with a specific agenda, their experience can be quite different. Here are a few of the more common player archetypes:

- The Berserker.

- The Detective.

- The Power-Leveler.

- The Strategist.

- The Socializer.

- The Thespian.

- The Griefer.

The Berserker. For Berserkers, wreaking havoc and mass destruction is paramount. Shooting, stabbing, and setting things on fire form their modus operandi. A Berserker's game focuses on its combat system. Berserkers are not interested in solving intricate puzzles or sneaking quietly past an unsuspecting guard. Berserkers go in with guns blazing, destroying everything in their path; Berserkers are attracted to fast-paced games filled with hostile enemies and breakable objects. Berserkers cannot be bothered with picking locks—they will just break down the door. In general, Berserkers prefer fast-paced games where they can solve most problems through combat and destruction.

Image John Walker, EAR

Figure 1.8 The Berserker.

The Berserker reward system is simple. Give them plenty of enemies, access to ammunition, and the occasional new and interesting weapon. Berserker-style games often feature "power-ups"—surreal floating icons placed strategically throughout gameplay areas. By running over these icons, Berserkers obtain rewards such as temporary abilities, energy boosts, and additional health points. Here are some examples of games that might appeal to the Berserker:

- Doom.
- Duke Nukem.
- Quake.
- Unreal.

Image Craig Brasco, EAR

Figure 1.9 The Detective.

The Detective. The Detective stands at the opposite end of the spectrum. Where the Berserker leaps in, the Detective first listens quietly at the door. Detectives proceed carefully and seek clever ways to outthink the game. Detectives see everything as a puzzle, but when necessary they will involve themselves in combat. However, more often the Detective delights in finding clever ways to avoid conflict. The Detective

- Prefers more deliberately paced gameplay.
- Enjoys logical puzzles and problem-solving exercises.
- Derives pleasure from finding clever ways to solve problems.
- Often seeks to avoid combat.

Games that cater to Detectives will usually proceed at a more deliberate pace. Puzzles, mazes, and the clever use of inventory items are key elements. The best of these games present the player with more than one way to approach any given problem. If there is only one solution to a problem, Detectives will quickly lose interest. Their primary weapon is the application of logic. This presents a particular challenge to the designer. The process of designing logic problems requires considering every possible decision and contingency. Complex decision-making systems can quickly grow to enormous size. Creating a level with intricate puzzles, each with multiple solutions, is much more time-consuming than filling a level with hostile enemies and randomly placed power-ups. Some games that might appeal to the Detective are these:

- Myst.
- Thief: The Dark Project.

- Grim Fandango.
- Syberia.

The Power-Leveler. The Power-Leveler is a different type of player. Generally Power-Levelers are from the core school of gaming. Their mantra is "Give me more!" As a player character, they seek to gain more of everything—more abilities, more weapons, and more items. Power-Levelers can be astonishingly patient. They often play for hours and practice tedious tactics like "camping." This involves finding the level of monster that will provide them with the optimal experience points for their character's level, killing that monster, then remaining in the same spot until the monster "respawns" and killing it again and again. Power-Levelers

Image Craig Brasco, EAR

Figure 1.10 The Power-Leveler.

- Prefer open-ended games.
- Derive pleasure from increasing their character's abilities.
- Need to obtain the best of everything, such as weapons and armor.
- Are willing to endure tedious and repetitive gameplay.

Power-Levelers find open-ended role-playing games like Everquest, Morrowind or Ultima Online attractive. It is not possible to beat an open-ended game. However, some Power-Levelers will complain endlessly about "level caps." For them, reaching the highest possible level the game will allow is not cause for celebration. Power-Levelers must always be able to achieve a higher level. Some games that might appeal to the Power-Leveler are

- Ultima Online.
- Everquest.
- Morrowind.
- Dark Age of Camelot.
- Freelancer.

The Strategist. Strategists are the chess players of the electronic gaming world. More often than not they are from the core school of gaming. They have no desire to immerse themselves in the game world; instead their enjoyment comes from tactics, decision making, and resource management. In many ways Strategists enjoy playing "god." The Strategist

- Prefers games with complex rules.
- Derives pleasure from tactical decision-making.
- Pays high attention to detail.

Image John Walker, EAR

Figure 1.11 The Strategist.

Like many core gamers, Strategists tend to be strict about the rules of the game. Their attention to detail and statistical issues can border on the obsessive. Some games that might appeal to the Strategist are

- Civilization.
- Starcraft.
- Command & Conquer.
- Warcraft.
- Age of Empires.

The Socializer. This player archetype is relatively new but is growing in popularity. From the inception of online chat, text-based role-playing games have been popular. These early games, called MUDs (Multi-User Dimensions), were virtual communities where people would take on fictitious personalities to interact in Dungeons & Dragons–style role-playing games. With the introduction of graphical online games such as Ultima and Everquest, many MUD players moved to these types of games. The Socializer looks at games primarily as a social experience.

(Alternate Ending)

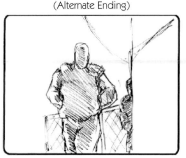

one person appears followed by another

...and another

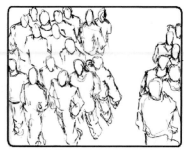

Until a group appears and encircles Kaos and Vic
Storyboard Haji Abdullah, EAR

Figure 1.12 The Socializer.

The curious thing about Socializers is that the other aspects of gameplay, such as leveling, fighting, exploring, and problem solving, are secondary. For Socializers the games are a safe way to interact and communicate with other people in an interesting environment. Real-world relationships and even marriages have grown from social interaction in online games. Today the proliferation of Socializers is creating an entirely new type of online game designed specifically as platforms for social interaction. Some games that might appeal to the Socializer include these:

- The Sims Online.
- There.
- Second Life.

The Thespian. For this type of player, role-playing is everything. Thespians' avatars are a representation not of the player but of the players' alter egos. Thespians derive pleasure from becoming other people for a short time. Often their alter egos are very different from who they are in real life.

A very moral person might choose an immoral alter ego; a tall person might choose to play a dwarf. The player might even choose to play a member of the opposite sex. This archetype is so prevalent that many online role-playing games have set aside special role-playing servers that expressly forbid "O-O-C" (out-of-character) chat. Thespians

☐ Enjoy the role-playing aspects of a game above all else.

☐ See their characters as alter egos.

☐ Enjoy playing characters different from their real-life personae.

☐ Choose to immerse themselves in an alternate reality.

Image John Walker, EAR

Figure 1.13 The Thespian.

Some Thespians frustrate and annoy other players by using faux medieval dialogue sprinkled with thee, thou, and prithee; but most simply enjoy the fun of immersing themselves in an otherworldly environment. Here are some games that might appeal the Thespian:

☐ Ultima Online.

☐ Everquest.

☐ Dark Age of Camelot.

☐ Neverwinter Nights.

☐ Star Wars Galaxies.

The Griefer. Our final archetype is perhaps the most loathsome and despicable of players: the Griefer. Griefers are online gamers whose primary motivation is the infliction of misery on other players. This torment can come in many forms: stalking other players and hurling insults at them; abusing programming bugs to their own advantage; and "kill stealing," the process of lying in wait while other players fight monsters, then leaping in at the last minute and looting any valuables they can find. The Griefer

☐ Has a primary motivation of making others miserable.

☐ Is usually solitary, but in groups can inflict even more damage.

☐ Engages in behavior counter to games' end user agreements.

☐ Can sometimes be permanently banned.

Image Craig Brasco, EAR

Figure 1.14 The Griefer.

Griefers generally work alone; however, organized groups of Griefers can inflict substantial damage. Groups of players can band together and blockade vital areas of a game, demanding payment for allowing other players to pass safely. They can corner the market on vital in-game components and charge ridiculously inflated prices.

Most user agreements forbid these tactics, and players risk banishment from games for using them. But infractions like this are difficult to police in a game with thousands of players. Unfortunately, this is a case where a minority of players can make the experience of gameplay unpleasant for everyone. Some online games that have experienced problems with Griefers include

- Ultima Online.

- Everquest.

- Counterstrike.

- Unreal.

- Battlefield 1942.

TABLE 1.1   Summary of player archetypes.

Player Archetypes	Characteristics	Example Games
The Berserker	Solves problems through combat and/or destruction.	Doom, Duke Nukem, Quake, Unreal
The Detective	Enjoys finding clever ways to solve puzzles and problems.	Myst, Thief: The Dark Project, Grim Fandango, Syberia
The Power-Leveler	Enjoys character abilities.	Everquest, Morrowind or Ultima
The Strategist	Enjoys tactical decision-making.	Civilization, Starcraft, Command & Conquer, Warcraft, Age of Empires
The Socializer	Views games as a social experience.	The Sims Online, There, Second Life
The Thespian	Enjoys role-playing.	Everquest, Neverwinter Nights, Star Wars Galaxies
The Griefer	Makes other players miserable.	Ultima Online, Everquest, Counterstrike, Unreal, Battlefield 1942

Who Are the Game Players?

Demographic changes over the past decade predict that by the year 2050, nonwhite racial and ethnic groups will make up 48 percent of the total U.S. population. Each generation changes our nation, and as the impact of diversity moves through the gaming community, game developers must adapt.

The international gaming community has placed financial hope on the world of video games. Game players spend lots of money to satisfy their interactive entertainment needs. Designers and game developers need to address these desires within their 3D environments, the characters they create, the worlds they design, and the stories they tell. What are the characteristics and expectations of the new breed of gamer? From the research, we find a number of common characteristics ("Essential facts," 2005). Gamers are generally

- Dedicated to playing for unusually long periods.
- Experienced in tactile motor behavior.
- Competitive.
- Aware of interactive technology.
- Pleasure seekers.

Players Come from All Generations and Backgrounds. People of all ages and backgrounds play video games and interact in the same game worlds (see Figure 1.15). The issue of diversity in gaming is a pressing one, and we should view diversity not as a challenge but as an opportunity. The video game industry, with its international appeal and a proven financial record of accomplishment, will benefit economically, educationally, and ethically if it can successfully embrace diversity. As Maya Angelou once said, "We all should know that diversity makes for a rich tapestry, and we must understand that all the threads of the tapestry are equal in value no matter what their color."[5] We will now look at some examples of diverse gaming communities.

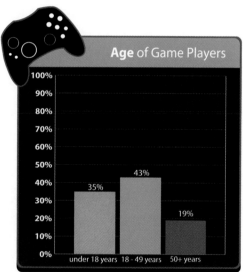

Source: Graph of player age demographics (2005). *Essential facts about the computer and video game industry,* p. 2. Entertainment Software Association. Retrieved August 20, 2005, from http://www.theesa .com/files/2005EssentialFacts.pdf.

Figure 1.15 Age demographics for game players.

---

[5] Angelou, M. (n.d.). Retrieved August 20, 2005, from http://www.brainyquote.com/quotes/ quotes/m/mayaangelo133557.html.

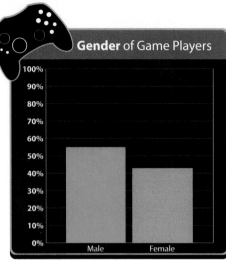

Source: Graph of player gender demographics (2005). *Essential facts about the computer and video game industry,* p. 3, Entertainment Software Association. Retrieved August 20, 2005, from http://www.theesa.com/files/2005EssentialFacts.pdf.

Figure 1.16 Women are becoming valuable consumers of video games.

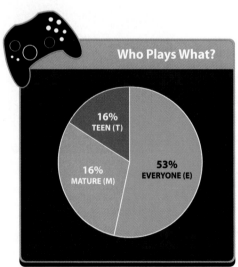

Source: Graph of video game sales by audience (2005). *Essential facts about the computer and video game industry,* p. 4. Entertainment Software Association. Retrieved August 20, 2005, from http://www.theesa.com/files/2005EssentialFacts.pdf

Figure 1.17 Decline in mature players and increase in teen players.

Disabled Players. We seldom talk about people with disabilities as avid game players, but simulations and research projects suggest that accessibility is an area of opportunity for game developers. People with disabilities can play a major role in these new developments. For example, a young man who plays games by using his feet on a hand-held controller is now developing a foot controller for gamers. For deaf gamers there is a captioned version of Half Life under development. We mentioned the America's Army game simulation earlier in the chapter and how the army uses it for developing skills on the front line. There are also new psychological game simulations that are helping our soldiers cope with posttraumatic stress disorder (PTSD) and other disabilities (Zimmerman, 2005).

Female Players. Women make up a huge portion of the gaming population (see Figure 1.16). What games are they playing? What games are they buying and for whom? As heads of households, they continue to play and buy interactive entertainment. Who actually walks through department stores? Women bring a lot to the industry as well as controlling the cash flow of young players.

Mature and Teen Players. As the video and computer game industry develops, it needs a strategic plan based on marketing statistics. According to the Entertainment Software Association, the core mature player is less attractive in terms of generating new revenue. On the other hand, teen gamers are fueling a tremendous market share of the industry (Figure 1.17).

Elements of a Satisfying Game

"My work is a game, a very serious game"[6]

After the release of a video or computer game, it is easy to identify its shortcomings. It is another matter to identify those same problems during the design process and eliminate them. We will now look at some of the major principles of quality game design.

What Makes a Game Satisfying?

The ability of game designers to put themselves in the player's position is perhaps the most important ability in game design. It is important for every designer to ask how will the player react. Empathizing with the player helps designers to create a more enjoyable experience while allowing them to identify potential problems as early as possible in the development process. Let's look at some of the elements that make gameplay satisfying.

Logical Problem Solving. Often in an effort to slow the players' pace and increase the length of a game, designers will place needlessly complex obstacles in their path. Obstacles like these do not rely on typical problem-solving mechanisms, and they merely increase player frustration and dissatisfaction. Next we describe some common examples.

Complex Mazes. A maze of corridors, sewer pipes, or caverns that all look alike is an easy way to keep a player busy for hours. The problem with this type of puzzles is simple: They are not fun.

Pixel Hunts. Another way that lazy designers prolong a game is the dreaded "pixel hunt." This is the process of placing a small but necessary item in a huge, dimly lit area. The object is virtually invisible, and the only way the player can locate it is to slowly and methodically move the cursor over every part of the area until the cursor changes shape, indicating that the object is located.

Game Save Systems. The game save system used by a game is important. In some games players can save their game at any point. If their character is "killed," they can simply reload their last saved game and continue. Other games require the player to return to a specific location before saving, and still others allow the player to save only after successfully completing an entire level or mission. Certain types of games seem to lend themselves to particular game save mechanisms. Choosing the wrong mechanism can result in enormous frustration for the player and ruin

[6] Escher, M.C. (n.d.). Retrieved August 20, 2005, from http://en.wikiquote.org/wiki/M._C._Escher.

the enjoyment of the game. The game save issue is a subject of controversy in the game industry.

Counterintuitive Solutions. Some games require the player to take actions that seem completely illogical and counterintuitive. In certain games combining a grappling hook with a rope may be a logical step to take when attempting to solve a problem. Combining a human skull with a banana peel is not. Yet poorly designed inventory-based adventure games will often contain puzzles like this. Again, the designer's intent is to slow the player's pace and prolong the length of the game.

Trial-and-Error Solutions. Some games have complex puzzles with no easily discernible solutions. Solving these games means using a tedious trial-and-error process. Some jumping puzzles, for example, force the player to try every possible combination of jumps to find the correct combination. This is another obstacle intended to slow the player down.

Player Options. In poorly designed games, the player may be required to solve a problem or puzzle that would appear to have a number of logical solutions but in fact has only one. For example, suppose a player discovers a locked metal door that requires a specific key. The player may have acid, explosives, and even a skeleton key in her inventory, but she discovers, through repeated trials, that none of these tools will open the door. If there were a logical explanation for the failure of these tools, she might be satisfied. However, there is no explanation beyond the designer's decision that only by finding a particular key will the player be able to open the door. In this example the player feels cheated because she examined the problem and tried multiple logical ways to solve it. The player must make the choices that the game demands, and the illusion of free will has been shattered.

Repetition. In some games the player must perform a series of actions repeatedly to make his character powerful enough to continue. This is especially common in poorly designed role-playing games, where the player is forced to wander through the same area fighting the same type of monster again and again to make himself powerful enough to face a more powerful "boss" monster. This is another easy way to prolong gameplay, but it can be incredibly tedious for the player.

Player Trust. It is important that the designer gain and maintain the player's trust during the game. When a player trusts the game's design, she will look upon a given situation as a challenge and not a frustration.

Say, for example, that the player falls into a pit and becomes trapped. If she trusts the design of the game, she will be certain that there is a way out and will take the time to search for it. If she does not trust the design, she might become frustrated and simply revert to a previously saved game. In that case, the solution to the pit puzzle simply becomes "don't fall into the pit in the first place." This might aggravate the player to the point where she stops playing the game and moves on to another, less frustrating game.

Ways to Establish Player Trust. The following are some methods that a designer can employ to earn the player's trust during gameplay:

- Provide clues and hints that, however subtle, are always available to the observant player. The attentive player will quickly realize that clues and hints are rewards that will help during the game.

- Players should be able to see everything they need to see at all times. Graphics and the perspective of the player should support, rather than hinder, gameplay.

- Never force a player into a situation where he will fail regardless of the action he takes. Forced failure is unfair and should never be part of gameplay.

- Always give a player all of the information she needs to complete any given section of the game. The game should never rely on the player having outside information.

- Never trap a player in a dead-end situation that makes it impossible to continue a game.

- Gameplay mechanics should never feel unfair or arbitrary. Nonplayer characters (NPCs), enemies, and monsters should never have an unfair advantage over the player, and the game world should have a consistent internal logic.

High Interactivity. Players *play*—they do not watch. Important actions or decisions should be for the player to make. These should never be a function of the game or the action of a nonplayer character. It is no fun to watch while someone else does something exciting. This is an inherent danger with "cut scenes." They can be used to great effect as a system of rewards and can provide critical information to the player and advance the storyline. However, designers sometimes create a cut scene that is so exciting it leaves players feeling cheated because they want to perform the action themselves. Designers should always ask, "Is this something the player would want to do?" If the answer is yes, then let the player do it.

Reasonable Player Expectations

Players cannot read the designer's mind. In some poorly designed games it often seems as though this is expected. Keep in mind that things that may seem intuitive to the designer, who has been working on the game for months, may not be as obvious to the players.

Clear Goals and Motivations. Players should never feel out of touch. They should always have a clear idea of where they are in the game and why they are there. They should know their abilities and limitations, and most important, they should always be aware of their goals. Ideally the player will always have three goals: an immediate goal, a short-term goal, and the ultimate goal.

Immediate Goals. The immediate goal can be as simple as "avoid the sniper on the hilltop" or "break the computer's security code." The immediate goal is to solve whatever problem the player is currently facing.

Short-Term Goals. The short-term goal is a larger step toward achieving the ultimate goal. Examples of short-term goals might be "deliver the magic scroll to the wizard," "meet the informant near the riverbank," or "establish a military base beyond enemy lines."

Ultimate Goals. The ultimate goal is to complete the objective of the entire game. In a military strategy game this might simply be to "conquer the world." In a role-playing game it might be to "defeat the evil lord and his minions."

Satisfying Rewards. The next element we will discuss is an appropriate and satisfying reward system. As players progress through a game, they will rightly expect rewards for playing well and achieving various objectives. Designers should always be asking themselves, "What is the player going to get for doing this?" There are many ways to reward the player. Here we review the types of rewards.

Entertainment. We have already discussed the use of cut scenes as a reward system. If presented correctly, these can work well. When a player completes a mission, achieves an important goal, or solves a difficult problem, an entertaining, noninteractive cut scene appears. These short, in-game "movies" generally show the players the results of their efforts and introduce the next segment or mission of the game. When combined with the playable storyline, these sequences give players a sense of accomplishment and a feeling of forward momentum.

Revelation. This reward comes in the form of previously unknown and critical information regarding the storyline of the game. In essence, these rewards are interesting and sometimes shocking plot twists. Examples of revelation rewards are an event such as a suspected enemy turning out to be a friend, unexpected help arriving, or a traitor being unmasked.

Nourishment. Players receive nourishment rewards so they can replenish supplies and continue to move forward in the game. Nourishment rewards, strategically placed throughout a game, are an important factor. When used correctly they diminish the player's level of frustration and heighten enjoyment. Examples of nourishment rewards include healing potions, first aid supplies, ammunition, and even NPC (nonplayer character) allies.

Growth. Growth rewards are quite popular in role-playing games. These types of rewards help a player's character to grow more skillful and powerful during the game. These rewards either enhance abilities that the character already has or introduce new abilities. Examples of growth rewards include experience point systems, magic or technological items, and more advanced weaponry.

Privilege. Privilege rewards are rewards of access. These rewards allow a player to enter areas of the game previously closed to them. Such rewards often come in the tangible form of keys, lock picks, or security codes, but they can also be a favor granted by an NPC that allows access to a new area of information. From a design standpoint, privilege rewards are important roadblocks. They keep the player from advancing too quickly and missing some vital and important part of a mission or level. In a well-designed game, these roadblocks will seem logical and necessary. When overused, these same roadblocks can frustrate the player.

Fame. Fame rewards generally do not have any kind of impact on gameplay itself, but their impact should not be underestimated. An NPC general might compliment the player's tactics after a particularly difficult battle, or a group of NPC villagers might praise the player for slaying a particularly troublesome vampire. This simple type of feel-good reward can go a long way toward increasing players' enjoyment of the game.

Nonlinear Gameplay. Whenever possible, the game should present elements of nonlinear game play. Although it is impossible to provide every possible option to players, the designer should attempt to present as many as possible. When players' options are limited, the illusion of free will is shattered, and they may feel that they are shepherded through the game. There are a number of ways to provide nonlinear gameplay. These include

- Branching events.

- Free play mode.

- Emergent gameplay mode.

Branching Events. Branching events give players multiple choices at key points in the game and allow them to pursue several different courses of action. This can be as simple as offering different dialogue options when speaking to an NPC or as complex as allowing players to avoid an entire area of the game.

Branching events are inherently problematic. For example, consider a simple dialogue in which the player has three possible responses, and each of these responses produces three additional responses. If each branch of dialogue is truly distinct, never looping back or borrowing threads from other branches, the amount of dialogue quickly becomes staggering. Five levels of responses would require 729 lines of dialogue. Add one additional response level and the number of lines needed increases to 2,187. Add another level and 6,561 lines are required. This exponential growth factor becomes unmanageable in short order.

A different problem comes with area design. If you give players multiple ways to approach or solve any given problem, they might play through an entire game without ever seeing huge portions of the game world. Attempting to create enough content to make a game truly nonlinear can be like creating three or four games simultaneously.

Free Play Mode. Another popular type of nonlinear gameplay is a "free" mode of play in which players can go anywhere and do anything they like. Grand Theft Auto 3, Mafia, Morrowind, and Freelancer all feature this optional type of game play. Although each game has a story that players can follow, they can also choose to go off and do whatever they please. This adds a sense of realism and considerable "replayability" to the games. It is quickly becoming a popular design decision, although it is expensive and time-consuming and therefore a risk for the developer.

Emergent Gameplay. Emergent gameplay arises spontaneously from the artificial intelligence programming that controls NPCs, enemies, and monsters in a game. Depending on a player's location, choices, and actions, NPCs can respond in surprisingly different ways. The shooter game Half Life was one of the first to use emergent gameplay effectively. A monster might hear the player's character approaching and burst through a door right in front of the character. It might also not hear the character and let him or her pass the door unharmed, then later wander out of the room and stalk the corridor, eventually approaching from behind. This is very different from a scripted event, which always happens in exactly the same way for every player.

Figure 1.18 The 2005 Electronic Entertainment Expo (E3). This annual event is run by the Entertainment Software Association (ESA).

This chapter has presented an overview of the types of games people play and why they play them. Categorizing traditional games is usually done according to the type of game (e.g., board games, card games) and the player's reason(s) for playing (e.g., competition, escape, socializing). Although these classifications also apply to computer and video games, additional factors come into play.

We described two types of video game players: core gamers and casual gamers. Computer and video game designers must tailor their products to satisfy one or both of these audiences. In addition to these high-level classifications, we looked at further classifying players according to the manner in which they play games. A player's archetype may be Berserker, Detective, Power-Leveler, Strategist, Socializer, Thespian, or Griefer; different archetypes are attracted to different types of games.

We also saw that game designers should apply a number of techniques to make gameplay more satisfying for both core and casual gamers. These techniques include creating a consistent and logical game world, providing rewards, and allowing nonlinear gameplay.

The definition of a *game* contains certain characteristics. A game must

- Have one or more players.
- Have a set of rules.
- Involve player interaction with an opposing force that has conflicting objectives.
- Have an organized method of play.
- Have a desirable goal or outcome.

The traditional categories of games include board games, card games, target games, and sports games. The cultural motivations behind game playing are education, vicarious experience and wish fulfillment, overcoming social restrictions, competition, socialization, and exercise.

The primary elements that make a game satisfying for the player include logical problem solving, gaining the confidence of the players, and a high level of interactivity. When these are combined with meeting reasonable player expectations with clear goals, rewards that satisfy, and nonlinear gameplay, the game will be a success.

Why Do People Play Games?

Hawes, A. (1996, January). Jungle gyms: The evolution of animal play. *Zoogoer 25(1)*. Retrieved August 20, 2005, from http://nationalzoo.si.edu/Publications/ZooGoer/1996/1/junglegyms.cfm.

Courtesy of *Into the Pixel*: Chinatown Level Study

Artist:
Rich Mahon, Jon Gwyn, Chandana Ekanayake

Morgan, K. (n.d.). *PSY/BIO 226: Comparative animal behavior: Play.* Norton, MA: Wheaton College. Retrieved August 20, 2005, from http://acunix.wheatonma.edu/kmorgan/Animal_Behavior_Class/Play.html.

Motivations behind Game Playing

Crawford, C. (1982). *The art of computer game design.* Retrieved August 20, 2005, from http://www.vancouver.wsu.edu/fac/peabody/game-book/Coverpage.html.

Game References

Age of Empires. Microsoft, http://www.microsoft.com/games/empires/.

America's Army. The U.S. Army, http://www.americasarmy.com/.

Battlefield 1942. Electronic Arts, http://www.eagames.com/official/battlefield/1942/us/home.jsp.

Command & Conquer. Electronic Arts, http://www.eagames.com/official/cc/franchise/us/home.jsp.

Civilization. Sid Meier, http://www.civ3.com/.

Counterstrike. Valve Software, http://www.counter-strike.net/.

Dark Age of Camelot. Mythic Entertainment, http://www.darkageofcamelot.com/.

Doom. id software, http://www.doom3.com/.

Duke Nukem. 3drealms, http://www.3p://www.3drealms.com/duke3d/index.html.

Everquest. Sony Corporation, http://everquest2.station.sony.com/.

Freelancer. Microsoft, http://www.microsoft.com/games/freelancer.

Grand Theft Auto 3. Rockstar Games, http://www.rockstargames.com/grandtheftauto3.

Grim Fandango. LucasArts, http://www.lucasarts.com/products/grim/default.htm.

Morrowind. Bethesda Softworks, http://www.morrowind.com/games/morrowind_overview.htm.

Myst. Cyan Worlds, Inc., http://www.myst.com.

Neverwinter Nights. BioWare Corp, http://nwn.bioware.com.

Quake. id software, http://www.idsoftware.com/.

Second Life. Linden Research, Inc., http://secondlife.com.

Starcraft. Blizzard Entertainment, http://www.blizzard.com/starcraft/.

Star Wars Galaxies. LucasArts, http://www.lucasarts.com/products/galaxies. Syberia. Microïds, http://www.microids.com/index_en.html.

There. Makena Technologies, http://www.there.com.

Thief: The Dark Project. Eidos Interactive, http://www.eidosinteractive.com/gss/legacy/thief/.

Courtesy of *Into the Pixel*: Yellow Room

Artist: Stephan Martiniere

The Sims. Maxis/Electronic Arts, http://thesims.ea.com/us/index.html.

Ultima Online. Origin Systems/Electronic Arts, http://www.uo.com/.

Unreal. Epic Games/Infogrames Entertainment, http://www.unreal.com/index2.html.

Warcraft. Blizzard Entertainment, http://www.blizzard.com/war3/.

Practice Questions

1. What characteristics are common to all games?

2. Are games important to you? What games do you play?

3. What type of game would you design if given the opportunity?

4. What are the primary cultural and social motivations for playing games?

5. What is the difference between a core and a casual gamer?

6. What type of gamer is most likely to violate a game's end user agreement?

7. What are some elements that can help make a game satisfying for a player?

8. Do you consider yourself a core gamer or a casual gamer? Why?

9. Which player archetypes best describe your motivations for playing games?

Lab Exercises

In this exercise you will discuss why you play games, talk about your style of play, and identify and discuss the different types of players in the class. The goal of this lab is to illustrate, in a practical way, the different types of people who play computer games, their reasons for playing games, and the types of games that appeal to them. Your presentation should address the following questions (approximately 15 minutes in length):

1. How often do you play games, and for how long?

2. What type of games do you most enjoy playing?

3. What games have you played in the last three months?

4. What have you liked and disliked about each game?

Written Assignment

Choose a computer or video game that you played but did not enjoy. Write a short essay (200–250 words) detailing the following:

• What aspects of the game you did not like.

• What you would change to make the game more enjoyable.

MANUSCRIPT REFERENCES

Angelou, M. (n.d.). Retrieved August 20, 2005, from http://www.brainyquote.com/quotes/quotes/m/mayaangelo133557.html.

Bates, B. (2001). *Game design: The art and business of creating games.* Roseville, CA: Prima Publishing.

Crawford, C. (1982). *The art of computer game design.* Retrieved August 20, 2005, from http://www.vancouver.wsu.edu/fac/peabody/game-book/Coverpage.html.

Donnelly, T. (1999). *Terry's Egyptian page: The game of Senet.* Retrieved August 20, 2005, from http://wesheb.tdonnelly.org/esenet.html.

Escher, M.C. (n.d.). Retrieved August 20, 2005, from http://en.wikiquote.org/wiki/M._C._Escher.

Essential facts about the computer and video game industry. (2005). Entertainment Software Association. Retrieved August 20, 2005, from http://www.theesa.com/files/2005EssentialFacts.pdf.

Hallford, N., & Hallford, J. (2001). *Swords & circuitry: A designer's guide to role-playing games.* Roseville, CA: Prima Publishing.

Hawes, A. (1996, January). Jungle gyms: The evolution of animal play. *Zoogoer 25(1).* Retrieved August 20, 2005, from http://nationalzoo.si.edu/Publications/ZooGoer/1996/1/junglegyms.cfm.

History of archery. (n.d.). Retrieved August 20, 2005, from http://www.archery.metu.edu.tr/sitetr/histmain.html.

History of board games. (2002). Retrieved August 20, 2005, from http://wv.essortment.com/historyofboard_rjyw.htm.

History of darts. (n.d.). Retrieved August 20, 2005, from http://www.users.bigpond.com/bullseye/history.htm.

Langdon, K. (1979). *What is a game?* Polymath Systems. Retrieved August 20, 2005, from http://www.polymath-systems.com/games/whatgame.html.

Lichtenstein, G. (1975). Retrieved August 20, 2005, from http://www.houseofquotes.com/authors/Grace_Lichtenstein.htm,

Lowenstein, D. (2005). *Essential facts about the computer and video game industry* Entertainment Software Association, p. 2. Retrieved August 20, 2005, from http://www.theesa.com/files/2005EssentialFacts.pdf.

McAdams, M. (1995). *What is go?* Retrieved August 20, 2005, from http://www.well.com/user/mmcadams/gointro.html.

Morgan, K. (n.d.). *PSY/BIO 226: Comparative animal behavior: Play.* Norton, MA: Wheaton College., Retrieved August 20, 2005, from http://acunix.wheatonma.edu/kmorgan/Animal_Behavior_Class/Play.html.

Plato (n.d.). Retrieved August 20, 2005, from http://www.quotedb.com/quotes/2873.

von Rheinfelden, J. (1377). Retrieved August 20, 2005, from http://playing-cards.us/main.html.

Zimmerman, E. (2005, June 22). The game of their lives: Biofeedback through video helps returning troops fight posttraumatic stress disorder. *San Francisco Chronicle.* Retrieved August 21, 2005, from http://sfgate.com/cgi-bin/article.cgi?f=/c/a/2005/06/22/MNGIUDCK001.DTL&type=printable.

Courtesy of 3D artist Bill Blakesley

CHAPTER 2

Evolution of Video and Computer Games

Any exploration of the science of game development demands an understanding of the evolution of electronic games. A review of the events, innovations, successes, and failures of the past is a valuable step toward understanding the current state of the industry.

After completing this chapter, you will be able to:

- Discuss the history of computer games.
- Discuss the creation of the first electronic games.
- Describe the "Golden Age" of arcade games and describe key events of the era.
- Summarize the key contributions by pioneers of arcade game design.
- Describe the key events in the "Golden Age" of home video games.
- Describe the evolution of home gaming systems.
- Identify the events that led to the industry's "Great Crash."
- Describe the Postcrash Era of Home Games.
- Identify the pioneers of Home Computer Games.
- Discuss Handheld and Portable Games.
- Discuss Wireless Games.
- Describe the Next Generation Consoles.

Pro Tips 2.1

Don Daglow

President and CEO of Stormfront Studios

Entering the games industry today is like entering the movie business in the 1930s and 1940s. In Hollywood during that Golden Age the technology no longer limited to what writers, directors, musicians, and actors could create on-screen . . . only 25 years after the great success of the first major silent movies. If you Google game machines like Atari VCS, Intellivision, and Colecovision, you'll see where games were just 25 years ago—they were even more primitive than an old silent movie! Today in games we have almost unlimited opportunity to create rich experiences, tell different kinds of interactive stories, and create our own Golden Age.

This reality is a sword with two edges, however. As sales of hit games grow into the billions of dollars, so does the complexity of the business. Big budgets mean that many worthy projects are never made for lack of funding. Truly original ideas are less likely to gain a foothold than sequels and titles anchored by major stars. We can choose to let these things discourage us, or we can remember that these same kinds of challenges faced the filmmakers of the 1930s . . . who today are remembered for inventing many of the visual storytelling methods we find so compelling in modern films. Today's teams will be remembered generations from now for ways in which they influenced entertainment . . . we just have to do work that will earn those memories downstream.

Introduction to the History of Video Games

**"Daring ideas are like chessmen moved forward; they may be defeated, but
they start a winning game."**[1]

The history of video and computer games is long and complex. Every significant advance in gaming technology drew upon earlier successes and innovations. To understand the evolution of this technology, let's go back to the beginning of the era and look at some important early milestones.

First Electronic Games

**"The present invention pertains to an apparatus [and method], in conjunc-
tion with monochrome and color television receivers, for the generation,
display, manipulation, and use of symbols or geometric figures upon the
screen of the television receivers for [training simulation, for] playing
games [and for engaging in other activities] by one or more participants.**

---

[1] Goethe, J.W. (n.d.). Retrieved August 20, 2005, from http://www.thinkexist.com/English/Topic/x/Topic_313_2.htm.

The invention comprises in one embodiment a control unit, an apparatus connecting the control unit to the television receiver and in some applications a television screen overlay mask utilized in conjunction with a standard television receiver. The control unit includes the control, circuitry, switches and other electronic circuitry for the generation, manipulation and control of video signals."[2]

First Video Game. In 1959 at the Brookhaven National Laboratories, William A. Higinbotham, a physicist, decided to create an exhibit for the laboratory's annual Visitor's Day. Higinbotham noticed that guests quickly grew tired of static displays and baffling equipment; they wanted something that was educational but fun.

With the help of coworker David Potter, Higinbotham used the lab's small analog computer to plot the trajectory of a moving ball and display it on an oscilloscope screen. They added a simple graphic of a net and factored in wind speed, gravity, and bounce. Visitors could then play a simple game of tennis using two controllers. The machine did not keep score and the screen was only five inches in diameter, but Tennis for Two was the most popular exhibit. The following year Higinbotham updated Tennis for Two with a larger screen and added variable gravity settings that simulated play on other planets. He decided not to pursue it any further, dismantled the project, and never thought to patent the idea.

In 1961 the Massachusetts Institute of Technology (MIT) purchased Digital Equipment Corporation's new state-of-the-art computer, the PDP-1. The refrigerator-sized unit was revolutionary for its time and featured a cathode ray graphics display. The new machine was of particular interest to a group of computer and sci-fi fans who called themselves the Tech Model Railroad Club. Three of the club members, Wayne Witanen, J. Martin Graetz, and Steve Russell were fans of the space opera novels of E.E. Doc Smith, and they decided to use the computer to create a science fiction game.

The results of their efforts was Spacewar!, which featured two spaceships, depicted as simple needle and wedge shapes on a field of stars. Players used a pair of primitive control boxes to fly the ships and fire missiles. There was a "black hole" in the center of the screen with realistic gravitational effects, as well as a "hyperspace" button that would make a player's ship vanish and then reappear at a random point on the screen.

The group finished the game in April 1962, and it made its public debut at the MIT annual Science Open House. It was such a hit that the group implemented a scoring system to keep players from monopolizing the controls. Spacewar! became the standard demo for the PDP-1 and came installed on all future units. Educational facilities

---

[2] Winter, D. (2005). Original patent filed by Ralph Baer for the first home video game apparatus. Retrieved August 20, 2005, from http://www.pong-story.com/sanders.htm.

Figure 2.1 Mindstorm video game console.

could request copies of the game via the ARPAnet, the precursor to today's Internet.

Unlike Higinbotham, Russell, Martin, and Witanen patented the game. However, it could run only on a refrigerator-sized computer that cost more than $120,000. A commercial application seemed impossible. Later the code would be in the public domain, and Spacewar! became the most copied game concept in history.

Magnavox Odyssey - 1972. Designed by Ralph Baer in 1966 and assisted by Bill Harrison and Bill Rusch of Sanders Associates, a military electronics firm. The Odyssey was introduced on January 27, 1972 at a price of $100.

First Home Video Game System. In 1966 an engineer working for Sanders Associates, a New Hampshire electronics company, began a proto- type for a revolutionary new type of machine that would allow people to play games on their television sets. Ralph Baer did not realize that future generations would label him the Thomas Edison of video games.

Two years later, in January 1968, Baer filed his first patent on the concept. In October of that same year he demonstrated his "Brown Box" video game unit. The prototype could play Ping-Pong, football, volleyball, and, with a specially designed light gun, target games. The games used colored transparent Mylar overlays that would stick to the television screen via static electricity. Sanders set up demonstra- tions with all the major television manufacturers. RCA, General Electric, Philco, Sylvania, Magnavox, and Motorola all expressed interest but did not invest in the game unit.

One member of the RCA team, Bill Benders, was impressed with Baer's unit. After leaving RCA and joining Magnavox, he called the team in for another demonstration in 1971. This time Magnavox licensed the technology. Magnavox released the first Odyssey video game system the following year. A special tele- vision broadcast hosted by Frank Sinatra introduced the unit to America, and 100,000 units sold between August and December of 1972.

Father of Modern Video Games. As an undergraduate at the University of Utah, Nolan Bushnell spent most of his time playing Spacewar! on the university's PDP-1.

During the summers he worked as the manager of a local arcade. As he watched teenagers stuff quarters into pinball machines, it occurred to him that a game like Spacewar! could be a huge moneymaker if there were a way to run it on a less expensive machine.

Creating an arcade version of the game became an obsession. When Bushnell graduated with an engineering degree in 1968, he moved to California and went to work in the computer graphics division at Ampex, the company that invented videotape. He left Ampex in 1971 to work on the game full-time and completed his Spacewar! clone, Computer Space, that same year. Nutting Associates, a manufacturer of coin-operated trivia games, agreed to distribute it. Fifteen thousands units were constructed, but the game was ultimately a failure. The controls were just too complex for players who had never seen a computer game. Bushnell felt that he was on the right track, but he needed a game with a simpler design, something that anyone could pick up and play immediately.

Bushnell attended the Magnavox Profit Caravan trade show in May 1972. There he saw Baer's Odyssey game for the first time. He spent over half an hour playing the Ping-Pong game and left with an entirely new motivation. He quit his job at Nutting and formed his own company along with two other former Ampex employees. They originally called the company Syzygy but discovered the name was already in use. Instead Bushnell suggested the name "Atari." He was a big fan of the Japanese strategy game Go, and *atari* is that game's equivalent of a "check."

Al Alcorn was one of Atari's first employees. He decided to join the company when Bushnell described their first proposed project, a driving game. However, Bushnell decided that they would first release a simple tennis game. Bushnell had unrealistic ideas about audio for the game. He wanted effects like a roaring crowd, but this was impossible given the current technology. Instead Alcorn amplified the beeps and bleeps that were already part of the game's circuitry. In describing the sound made when the ball hit one of the paddles, he hit upon the perfect name for the game, Pong.

Although Bushnell's first effort, Computer Space, had an impossibly long and complex set of instructions, Pong had but a single line: "AVOID MISSING BALL FOR HIGH SCORE." Bushnell was right. The simplicity of the game made it irresistible. Pong became a huge hit in arcades. Bushnell originally intended the game to be a stepping-stone, a way to raise additional capital to create games. However, it sold 8,500 units in the first year at $1,200 each, while each unit had

Figure 2.2 Atari Pong.

a production cost of approximately $500. This minor stepping-stone would carry Atari for the next two years.

Atari PONG - 1975. Designed by Al Alcorn, Bob Brown, and Harold Lee. Released under the Sears Telegames brand name, PONG went on sale at 900 Sears stores across the country in January, 1975, and was the number one hit that Christmas season. The machine gave Atari a reputation for quality home games as well as arcade machines.

The Golden Age of Arcade Games

"Design is the creation and modification of the rules governing a gaming system. The quality of the overall system of rules is the result of balancing the rules against one another. The process of balancing a game is merely the creation and modification of rules while continually evaluating the effectiveness of the resulting system. This view of design suggests that good design happens through an inherently iterative process."[3]

Nolan Bushnell started Atari in 1976 with an investment of $250. Two years later he would sell the company to Warner Communications for $28 million. Pong's success caught the attention of other manufacturers who rushed to take advantage of the new video game fad. Dozens of Pong imitations hit the market. In this section we will see how this success spawned innovations in early arcade game design.

The Arcade Era Begins

In 1974 Atari's Joe Keegan left with several other key designers to open their own company, Kee Games. The company appeared to be Atari's first real competitor. Their game Tank was a simpler variation of Spacewar!, involving two tanks going head-to-head on a battlefield while avoiding land mines. The game was the first to use read only memory (ROM) chips to store graphics memory, giving it a more complex look than all the Pong variations. It became the biggest hit of the year.

However, there had been no mutiny. Kee Games was actually a covert subsidiary of Atari. Bushnell had set up the new company to circumvent an "arcade distribution" issue that had been an industry standard since the pinball era. Distributors demanded exclusive rights to a company's games, and Atari was no different. But Tank was so successful that every distributor wanted it. Bushnell had managed to change the rules overnight. Later Kee Games and Atari would merge, legally re-forming the company, with Keenan as company president.

---

[3] Cook, D. (2002). *Evolutionary design: A practical process for creating great game designs.* Retrieved August 12, 2005, from http://www.lostgarden.com/evolutionary_game_design2.htm.

Although Atari was the first to use ROM to store graphics, other innovations (and challenges) in game design during this period included these:

- *First simulated color game (1972):* Atari's Pong-inspired Breakout was the first to use color overlays on the screen to simulate color graphics. The game was very successful and sold 15,000 units.

- *First game to use a microprocessor (1975):* Japan's Taito Corporation used a microprocessor to enhance the graphics and achieve more varied and randomized gameplay in its Gun Fight game.

- *First controversial video game (1976):* Exidy's Death Race 2000, based on a low-budget film by Roger Corman, had players use cars to run down stick figure pedestrians to score points. The game infuriated parents, and one community in Texas attempted to ban the game. The controversy was also the subject of a segment of the *60 Minutes* television show.

Figure 2.3 Atari Video Computer System (VCS) – 1977.

Designed by: Joe Decure, Harold Lee, and Steve Meyer. Better known as the Atari 2600, the Atari VCS was the most popular videogame console of its day. Available until 1990, the VCS was on the market longer than any other system in history. The VCS was released in October 1977, at a retail price of $199.95. The heart of the system was a 1.19 MHz 8-bit Motorola 6507 microprocessor. The machine contained 256 bytes of RAM to produce on-screen images.

Early Arcade Game Technology. From 1971 through 1973, 11 manufacturers released 30 titles. In 1974 and 1975, this increased to 57 titles. In 1976 the Golden Age of arcade games began with the release of over 53 titles in a single year. A factor in this growth was the use of emerging technology in arcade games. In this section we will examine the changes in early arcade game technology, including the first games to use sound, color, and microprocessors.

Introduction of Vectorbeam Graphics (1977). MIT graduate Larry Rosenthal was another future designer whose life changed because of the Spacewar! game. He saw the game on a tour of the MIT campus as a freshman candidate in 1968. Rosenthal based his master's thesis on the concept that an inexpensive hardware platform could run the game. Later he set to work to make this dream a reality.

Rosenthal created his own processor board with inexpensive TTL logic chips and a black-and-white CRT Vectorbeam display of his own design. This display could render straight lines between points; solid or rounded shapes were not possible, but the resolution was incredible. The images were much crisper and brighter than the heavily pixelated games of the time.

Rosenthal demonstrated the system to several companies, including Atari, that were not interested. The industry rejected his demands for a 50/50 split of all profits and the right to license all future use of his Vectorbeam monitor. However, a struggling producer of Pong knock-offs in El Cajon, California, showed some interest, and Cinematronics offered to distribute the game on Rosenthal's terms.

The timing could not have been better for the release of the Space Wars game in 1977. The George Lucas blockbuster *Star Wars* was breaking records at the box office, and science fiction had never been more popular. Space Wars sold 30,000 units and remained one of the top 10 moneymaking arcade games for three years. Rosenthal's Vectorbeam graphics instantly became the hottest new trend in video games.

First Game with "Attract Mode" and "High Score" (1978). The Taito Corporation of Japan manufactured Pachinko games, a sort of cross between slot machines and pinball, until 1978. Then Taito engineer Toshiro Nishikado decided to design the company's first video arcade game.

Three sequels had followed Atari's Tank, and they had all been popular. The most recent of these, 1977's UltraTank, allowed a single player to battle the computer. Nishikado's initial idea was a similar game in which the player faced off against an unending row of advancing tanks. However, the technology of the time could not create a large amount of convincing tanks that would all turn and move smoothly, so he replaced them with rows of cartoon alien invaders. The electronic guts of the game consisted of two circuit boards, one that generated the graphics and controlled gameplay, and another that contained sound effects circuitry and an audio amplifier. Like Breakout, the game simulated color using green and red transparent overlays.

The game introduced several features that would soon become standard. It was the first arcade game to include an entertaining "attract mode"—an intermission show that played between games. The little cartoon aliens would zip around the screen, fixing typographical errors by shooting the extra "C" in the game's instruction to "INSERT COIN" and flipping around an inverted "Y" in "PLAY SPACE INVADERS." It was also the first game to introduce the concept of a "high score." Previous titles either had a set time limit or continued forever if a player survived. Space Invaders would keep track of players' scores and display the current record, giving players an incentive to play again and again.

Space Invaders was an instant sensation in Japan. In fact, it was so popular it caused a shortage of 100-yen coins. Many shopkeepers removed their inventory and became Space Invaders parlors. The giant speakers broadcasting the "thump-thump-thump" sound effects of the marching invaders lured customers into the stores. People played the game outside arcades and game parlors. Space Invaders was the first machine to appear in restaurants and other public places. When restaurant owners complained that their customers were playing instead of eating, Taito even created a line of cocktail tables with the game built into the tabletop.

Bally Midway released the game outside of Japan, where the phenomenon was repeated. Space Invaders broke all arcade records in the United States. The game began appearing in department stores, restaurants, laundry facilities, and other mainstream venues. Countless imitations and several sequels followed. The game, in its various arcade and home video incarnations, earned more than $500 million.

First Game with "Top Ten Score" (1979). After the success of Cinematronics' Space Wars, Atari was quick to adopt the Vectorbeam technology. Its first vector game was the moderately successful Lunar Lander. The game put the players at the controls of an Apollo-style lunar landing module. The object was to battle the forces of friction, gravity, and momentum and safely touch down on the jagged, uneven surface of the moon. Despite its success, Lunar Lander's production stopped mid-year when Atari was flooded with orders for another vector game, Asteroids. The game would unseat Space Invaders as the reigning arcade champion.

Lyle Rains, Atari's 27-year-old vice president of engineering, was developing a new gaming technology called "Cosmos." In the search for the next popular game, Atari's new project was to utilize holograms as part of gameplay. However, the technology was not feasible. The Cosmos prototypes simply used holograms as a backdrop for a series of traditional video games. Atari canceled the project.

One of the titles under development for Cosmos was a Space War clone called Planet Grab. The two-player game had spaceships engaged in a dogfight amid a field of static asteroids. The ships had to fire on each other while avoiding or destroying the asteroid obstacles. Rains thought the game had potential and took it to Atari designer Ed Logg.

Logg also saw some potential and began developing it as a single-player vector graphics game. In Logg's version of the game, the asteroids were not static; they moved around the screen. When fired upon, the larger asteroids would break up into numerous smaller asteroids, each with a different trajectory. Intermittently, two enemy flying saucers would appear, firing on the player and breaking up the larger asteroids. Destroying the saucers earned the player extra points.

Logg created the first Asteroids prototype in two weeks. He created a second prototype because he could not pull the other employees away from the game long enough to continue his work. It was obvious he had created something special. Whereas Space Invaders was the first game to track high scores, Asteroids was the first game to allow players to enter their initials on a top 10 list. The list would periodically appear on the game's screen during its attract mode, along with a pre-programmed example of gameplay. The opportunity to achieve fame in the arcade was irresistible, and players lined up to wait their turn.

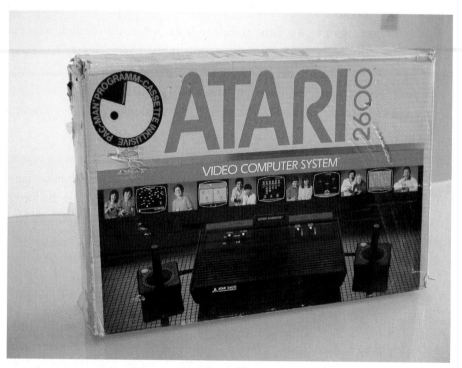

Figure 2.4 Atari 2600 Video Computer System.

Asteroids was such a success that some arcade owners installed larger coin boxes to contain the flood of quarters. Demand for the game was so high that

Atari discontinued Lunar Lander to focus on producing Asteroids units. More than 70,000 Asteroids machines shipped, making it the largest run of any coin-operated game to date. When the 50,000th unit rolled off the production line, it was fitted with a special gold cabinet and presented to the game's creator, Ed Logg. Logg went on to create a string of successful games for Atari, including Centipede (with designer Donna Bailey), Millipede, Gauntlet, Xybots, and Steel Talons.

First Color Video Game (1979). Nakamura Manufacturing was a merry-go-round manufacturer founded in 1955. In 1974 the company shortened its name to Namco and purchased the Japanese subsidiary of Atari. In 1979 it made history by producing the first arcade with true color graphics instead of the traditional color overlays.

Galaxian was a variation of Space Invaders, but this time the enemy ships could break formation and swoop down at the player while dropping their bombs. The game was a huge success and spawned numerous sequels including 1983's Galaga.

First Game with Speech (1980). Taito's Galaxian clone, Stratovox, was the first game to feature synthesized human speech. The object of the game was to prevent the abduction of planetary colonists by alien invaders. The synthesized speech involved alien taunts and the colonists' pleas for help. However, because speech synthesis required so much memory, these taunts and pleas were limited to four simple phrases, "Help me!", "Lucky!", "Very good!", and "We'll be back!"

Figure 2.5 Philips Odyssey 2100 System.

First Video Game Superstar (1980). Toru Iwatani was a designer for Namco, the company that released the first color video game, Galaxian. Iwatani wanted to create something different from the shoot-em-up games and Space Invader clones that were on the market. He had an idea for a cartoon game with an animated pizza running through a maze, eating other foods. A missing slice would be the pizza's "mouth." When it came time to actually program the game, technological limitations forced him to scale back his vision, and the pizza became a solid yellow circle with the same wedge-shaped mouth.

For its initial Japanese release, the game's name was Puckman, a take on the English word *puck* and the Japanese phrase *paku-paku,* which, loosely translated, means "flapping mouth." They changed the name to Pac-Man for the game's North American release.

Space Invaders had already established the animated attract mode that was currently a standard in arcade games. However, Pac-Man added a new twist. As players reached certain levels of play, they received animated cartoon intermissions featuring Pac-Man and the four ghosts that chased him around the maze.

The game was a sensation on both sides of the Pacific. Namco shipped 100,000 units to the United States. With its cartoonlike characters and nonviolent gameplay, Pac-Man appealed to children and adults alike. In addition, remarkably, the game seemed to appeal to women, a demographic that previous video games had been unable to reach.

An avalanche of merchandising followed. Like the peace sign of the 1960s and the smiley face of the 1970s, the Pac-Man symbol was everywhere. There were Pac-Man T-shirts, trading cards, lunchboxes, beach towels, and board games and even a Pac-Man breakfast cereal. In 1981 two unknown songwriters named Buckner & Garcia released the novelty single "Pac-Man Fever." The game so permeated American pop culture that it appeared on magazine covers as diverse as *Time* and *Mad* magazines.

No fewer than 10 arcade sequels followed. Midway developed and released the second, Ms. Pac-Man, in 1982. It sold 115,000 units, becoming the biggest-selling arcade game to date. Pac-Man sequels included Pac Man World and Pac-Man Adventures in Time. Only three video games are on display in the Smithsonian Institution: Pong, Dragon's Lair (the first laser disk game), and Pac-Man.

First Platform Genre (1981). The first game in the "platform" genre was 1981's Space Panic from Universal Games. Platform games usually involve a series of horizontal platforms with ladders that interconnect. In the case of Space Panic, the enemies were evil, chomping "space apples." The hero, armed with only a shovel, had to dig pits to trap and bury the apples. Universal later went on to produce the popular "Mr. Do" franchise. The company disbanded in 1985, but platform games became an industry standard. And the king of all platform games was yet to come.

In 1963 the Nintendo Playing Card Co. changed its name to Nintendo, Co. Ltd., and began producing electronic toys. In 1977 the company released a six-game home video game system called "The Color TV Game 6" that sold well in Japan. Game designer Shigeru Miyamoto joined the company that same year.

Soon Nintendo moved into the arcade market, releasing several unremarkable titles. Miyamoto worked on Radarscope, a Galaxian knockoff, and Nintendo built more than 20,000 units; but the game did not sell. There were already too many similar titles on the market. Nintendo had a warehouse full of useless Radioscope game cabinets, and Miyamoto worked to create a new game that would fit in them.

Miyamoto discovered the idea for his new game while watching a late-night rerun of the movie *King Kong*. His idea was to create a "beauty and the beast"–themed video game. The object of the game would be to rescue a damsel in distress from the clutches of a giant cartoon ape. Miyamoto designed every aspect of the game and even created the music.

He chose the name Donkey Kong because one of the definitions of *donkey* in his Japanese-to-English dictionary was "stubborn, wily, and goofy." Pauline, the female character in the game, probably received her name in tribute to the old damsel-in-distress serial *The Perils of Pauline*. The hero did not have a name initially. Miyamoto just called him Jumpman. This character was a squat little figure with a mustache, cap, and bulbous nose. Miyamoto added overalls simply because they highlighted the arm movements of the tiny pixelated character. The cap and overalls gave him the appearance of a carpenter or plumber.

Nintendo premiered the game in 1981 at the Amusement Machine Operators of America trade show. The company's American sales representatives were not overly enthusiastic about Donkey Kong. It sounded like the punch line to a bad joke. However, opinions changed once they tried the game. Donkey Kong was more successful than Nintendo could have possibly hoped. The company sold all the remaining Radarscope cabinets and had to construct tens of thousands more. It was the number one game in 1981.

Although the name Jumpman was on the original game cabinets, the American distributors began calling the hero Mario because he resembled the owner of the warehouse where all the Radarscope cabinets had been stored. Somehow the name caught on and soon became common knowledge.

Mario went on to become one of the most familiar characters in video game history. In addition to two direct Donkey Kong sequels, Mario starred in a number of spin-off games. For 1983's Mario Bros. he received a brother named Luigi in honor of the owner of a pizza parlor near the Seattle headquarters of Nintendo.

This game positively identified Mario's profession. He and Luigi were plumbers, fighting off various nasty creatures that emerged from drainpipes.

Super Mario Bros. followed in 1985 and introduced a new type of platform game, the "side-scroller." There were a number of Super Mario Bros. sequels including Super Mario World, Mario Party 2, and Super Mario Kart. A seemingly unending string of arcade sequels, console games, and handheld games that continues to this day followed it. The Mario franchise, along with the popular role-playing series The Legend of Zelda, helped to make Nintendo the successor to the Atari throne.

Laser Disk Boom (1981). Despite a few successful titles like Stern Electronics' Berzerk, Williams Electronics' Defender in 1980, and Vid Kidz's Robotron in 1982, by 1983 the arcade industry's revenues began to sag. According to some industry analysts, a full third of the existing arcades had closed by the year's end.

The previous year, game designer Rick Dyer had an intriguing concept for a new type of game. His idea was to use the new laser disk technology to create a game with movie-quality images that the player could control. He took the idea to Cinematronics, the company that introduced vector graphics with 1977's Space Wars. Like all developers of that time, Cinematronics was desperately searching for the next breakout concept that would revive the failing industry and agreed to produce the game.

They called the game Dragon's Lair. The player would take on the role of the bumbling cartoon knight Dirk the Daring. The object of the game was to rescue Princess Daphne from the clutches of an evil, fire-breathing dragon. However, standing between Dirk and the titular lair was a castle full of tricks, traps, and cartoon monsters. By negotiating a specific set of moves with a joystick and an action button, the player would lead Dirk through each of these perils and move deeper into the castle toward his ultimate goal.

A new animation studio run by the legendary Disney animator Don Bluth created the game's high-quality animation. The work, done in secret, cost over a million dollars. Bluth's staff finished the animation in May 1983, and the game premiered the following month. Dragon's Lair opened at selected arcades across the country. The game cost arcade owners a whopping $4,300 a unit and demanded a previously unheard-of 50 cents per player. But the game was a sensation. The novelty of the game, coupled with the scarcity of machines, made it an instant legend. Many arcade owners installed extra monitors on top of the game cabinets so gathering crowds could watch the gameplay. At the height of Dragon's Lair's popularity, a game in a well-trafficked area could earn as much as $1,400 a week, nearly 10 times the take of the average arcade game.

Like Pac-Man and Mario, Dragon's Lair inspired a vast line of commercial tie-ins and licensed products, including lunch boxes, T-shirts, and the obligatory

Saturday morning cartoon show. The frenzy also inspired other game developers to rush their own laser disk titles to market. Several of the arcade laser disk games released in 1983 and 1984 included Albegas (Sega/Bally/Midway), Cube Quest (Simutek), Dragon's Lair (Cinematronics/Starcom), Star Rider (Williams), and Time Traveler (Sega).

The huge and unexpected demand for laser disk players from arcade developers caused laser manufacturers like Philips, Hitachi, and Pioneer to quickly deplete their stocks. This affected all of the manufacturers, most of which had huge back orders. In addition, there were technical problems with the new technology. The laser disk players would often overheat or slip out of sync.

Unlike Dragon's Lair, the other rushed-to-market laser releases did not have the same high-quality animation or interesting design. After the novelty wore off, players did not find the games challenging enough. Even Dragon's Lair did not require any true strategy or skill. Ultimately it was an exercise in memorization and repetition.

By mid-1984 the laser disk fad was over and, after the cancellation of Dragon's Lair II and a big-budget laser disk game based on the movie *Legend,* arcades began to close across the country. This, with the crash of the home video market, caused investors to balk.

The Golden Age of arcade games was over.

Figure 2.6 Sega Mega Drive II

Golden Age of Home Video Games

"The computing power in those days was very primitive and power problems were huge (remember, there were no laptops then). The cost of technology was a lot different then as well—much more expensive. The technology is now closer to being available and financially feasible to making robots a more commonplace occurrence in our everyday lives."[4]

As we discussed earlier in the chapter, the arcade phenomenon originated with Ralph Baer's Odyssey home game, which inspired Atari's Pong, the first arcade hit. However, while Pong launched the Golden Age of arcade games, another phenomenon was taking place in living rooms across the world: the home video game explosion. In this section we will examine the Golden Age of home video games and the events leading to the "crash" in 1984.

The Growth of Home Video Games. The home video game market mirrored the growth of the arcade game market. A number of vendors entered this lucrative

Figure 2.7 Prinztronic Tournament Ten TV Game System.

---

[4] Bushnell, N. (2001). *Interview, Nolan Bushnell*. Retrieved August 20, 2005, from the Good Deal Games.com Web site: http://www.gooddealgames.com/interviews/int_bushnell.html.

market, producing the first generation of home video games. These ranged from the early Fairchild Channel F systems to the success of the Atari 5200. We will now examine this generation of game consoles.

Home Video Game Explosion. Atari took notice of the success of Baer's Odyssey. The company created a home version of Pong because of the success of the arcade game. In 1975 the Pong home game sold at Sears department stores under the name Sears Tele-Games. By the end of that year the unit was Sears's best-selling item. The following year Coleco released its home video game, Telstar Video Table Tennis. At $49.95, the Coleco version was half the price of the Sears machine, and it became a huge seller.

Between its arcade success and the Sears Pong unit, Atari's annual sales grew to $40 million by 1975. Warner Communications purchased it the following year for $28 million. Joe Keenan remained as company president, and Bushnell became the company CEO. With an infusion of capital from Warner, Atari began developing the home video unit that would change everything.

Programmable Home Games. Fairchild Electronics introduced the first programmable video game system, Channel F, in 1976. The system was programmable because the user could play an unlimited number of games by inserting special ROM cartridges called Videocarts. In all, Fairchild released 21 different game cartridges, each retailing for $19.95. The game unit alone retailed for $169.95.

In 1976 RCA also released a programmable system. The RCA Studio II was less expensive than the Fairchild unit, but its monochrome graphics were as primitive as those in Pong. RCA discontinued the system in 1979 after poor sales. Atari's programmable home unit, the Atari VCS, released in 1975, was more expensive than the Channel F system. The initial sales were unimpressive and Atari lost millions. Bushnell finally left the company in 1978.

Meanwhile at the arcades, business was booming. Games like Asteroids and Space Invaders were huge hits. In 1980 Atari became the first home video game producer to license an arcade title. When Atari released Space Invaders for the VCS, millions of consumers rushed out to buy the home unit based on that title. Atari wisely included variations on the original arcade game, giving players options like moving bunkers and invisible aliens. There was even a two-player mode.

Atari dominated the home market for the next two years. An updated version of the VCS called the Atari 2600 sold more than 25 million units. Consumers bought more than 120 million game cartridges of over 200 games from 40 different manufacturers. In 1979 a group of Atari designers left to form their own company.

Activision became the first third-party video game software developer. Atari sued and lost, signaling the start of an open market for third-party developers.

First-Generation Home Video Game Systems. Here are the major home video game systems developed and released during the Golden Age of home games:

◻ *Magnavox Odyssey (1972):* Ralph Baer's original "brown box" started a completely new industry. The Odyssey's retail price was $100. Constructed using transistors and diodes, the unit could produce only simple graphics. Magnavox used Mylar overlays to simulate more complex game elements. The unit shipped with the overlays, two controllers, six game cards, play money, playing cards, roulette and football playfield, a foldout scoreboard, poker chips, and a pair of dice.

◻ *Sears Telegames's Pong (1975):* Atari's Pong, distributed through Sears, was a best-selling item for the Christmas season in 1975.

◻ *Fairchild's Channel F (1976):* Fairchild's system was the first to use ROM cartridges that allowed consumers to purchase and play an unlimited number of games on the system.

Figure 2.8 Norda TV Game System.

- *Atari Video Computer System (1977):* Later known as the Atari 2600, the Atari VCS was available until 1990, making it the longest-selling system in history. The VCS featured a 1.19 MHz 8-bit Motorola 6507 microprocessor and 256 bytes of RAM.

- *Mattel Intellivision (1980):* The Intellivision unit had better graphics than the Atari VCS, but it ran more slowly. The Intellivision unit also featured the "PlayCable" service, a 24-hour system that delivered games to the unit via cable TV.

- *Colecovision (1982):* Coleco's home unit was very popular. It contained 48K of random access memory (RAM) and a 3.58 MHz 8-bit microprocessor.

- *Atari 5200 SuperSystem (1982):* When Atari released its 400 and 800 home computers, both had game cartridge slots and joystick ports. The Atari 5200 was essentially an Atari 400 computer without the keyboard.

- *Milton Bradley/GCE Vectrex (1982):* The Vectrex featured a 9-inch Vectorbeam monitor and a Motorola 68A09 8-bit microprocessor. It brought arcade-quality vector graphics to the home market and had a small but loyal following.

Home Video Market's Great Crash

The downward spiral and eventual crash began with the high-profile release of a popular arcade game for the Atari 2600. In 1981 Atari made a deal to produce a home version of the blockbuster game Pac-Man. The game, developed quickly and rushed into stores, was a disaster. The home version replaced the original blue-on-black graphics with an orange-on-blue color scheme. The bouncy theme music was gone, as was the familiar "wukka-wukka-wukka" chomping sound effect. Instead the game opened with a teeth-grating siren, and the player "gobbled" dots in the maze to an annoying twanging sound.

The release underscored just how far behind the technology for home games had fallen. Arcade games had begun to use magnetic floppy disks as a storage medium. The ROM chips of the home games simply were not able to produce the same quality graphics that players had come to expect. The game, panned by critics, sold well below expectations. However, Atari's next release was an even bigger disaster.

After the losses suffered by the failed Pac-Man, the company decided to create an original game based on popular licensed property. The just-released blockbuster film *E.T.: The Extraterrestrial* seemed a natural choice. The licensing rights for the film were expensive, so the game had to be a huge success to realize any profits.

The game, designed in five weeks to ship in time for the 1982 Christmas shopping season, was a dull and virtually unplayable fiasco. Atari produced 5 million cartridges and sold fewer than 1 million. Atari wound up with so many unsold games that the company buried millions of cartridges in a New Mexico landfill.

On December 7, 1982, Atari officially announced that 2600 sales did not meet predictions. Warner Communications stock plummeted 32 percent in a single day. Consumers, stung by the disappointing Pac-Man and E.T. releases, stopped buying games. Many third-party developers went out of business, and games from those companies sold at large discounts. Games that had retailed for as much as $60 the previous year were drastically discounted, some selling for as little as 99 cents. Companies that were still in business simply could not compete.

Atari made one last effort to regain its former glory with the release of the Atari 5200 SuperSystem, but it was already too late. The final blow came in 1984 when Warner Communications sold Atari's consumer division. Even as Dragon's Lair and the laser disk games were giving the arcade industry one last gasp of air before they eventually drowned, the home video game market died. It would be several years before the Japanese company Nintendo would revive it.

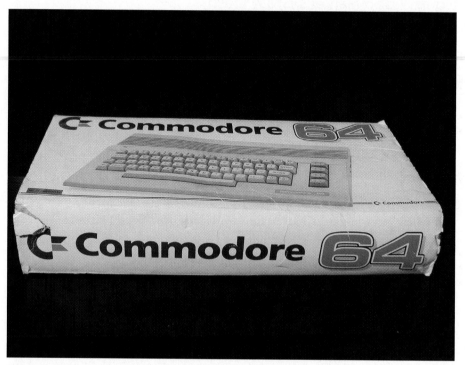

Figure 2.9 Keyboard for the Commodore 64 Personal Computer.

A comparative timeline of early arcade, video and home computer events and innovations.

TABLE 2.1   Comparative timeline of "firsts" in arcade, video and home video games.

Video and Arcade Games			Home Video Games			
1962 - 1972	Early Games	Tennis for Two, Spacewar! Computer Space				1962 - 1972
	Arcade Games	Pong Tank	Magnovox's Odyssey	Home Games		
	Simulated Color Game	Breakout				
1973 - 1983	Vectorbeam Graphics	Space War Lunar Lander	Pong Home Game Coleco's Telestar Video Table Tennis	Home Games		1973 - 1983
	Color Video Game	Galaxian	FaiChannel F Studio II	Programmable Games		
	Game with Speech	Stratovox	Atari 2600	Home Systems		
	Attract Game and High Score	Space Invaders	Mattel Intellivision Colecovision			
	Top Ten Score	Asteroids	Atari 5200 Milton Bradey			
	Superstar	Pac-Man				
	Platform Genre	Space Panic Donkey Kong				

Postcrash Era of Home Games

"You have to find something that you love enough to be able to take risks, jump over the hurdles and break through the brick walls that are always going to be placed in front of you. If you don't have that kind of feeling for what it is you are doing, you'll stop at the first giant hurdle."[5]

Now let's examine the revival of the home video game market. We'll look at the game companies that emerged during this period and pay special attention to the

---

[5] Lucas, G. (1999, June 19). Academy of achievement interview. Retrieved August 18, 2005, from http://www.achievement.org/autodoc/printmember/luc0int-1.

pioneers of game design. We'll also discuss the technologies that contributed to the revival of the video game market and to the development of the next generation of consoles.

The Revival of Home Video Games

Most distributors and retailers lost interest in video games following the crash of the home video market. However, one Japanese company decided to remain in the market. This decision marked the beginning of a new age for the home console market.

Figure 2.10 Super Nintendo Entertainment System.

Sole Survivor: Nintendo. In 1980 the Golden Age of home video games was still in full swing, and the market share of former playing card manufacturer Nintendo was growing. Its home unit, the Color TV Game 15, was selling well in Japan, and Shigeru Miyamoto's Donkey Kong was an international arcade phenomenon. That same year Nintendo engineers began to develop a new home console system that was more advanced than anything else on the market. Like the popular Atari 2600, the new system would feature interchangeable game cartridges, but it would provide better performance at a much lower cost.

Nintendo's new console was finished the following year and released in Japan as the Famicom, or Family Computer. The system sold for the equivalent of $100, less than half the price of any competitor's console. Nintendo first approached Atari at the 1983 Consumer Electronics (CES) trade show to distribute the new console outside Japan. Atari initially agreed to distribute the Famicom; however, an Atari representative at the show saw an unauthorized demonstration of Donkey Kong on Coleco's new Adam home computer and incorrectly assumed that Nintendo had signed a covert deal with Atari's competitor. Based on this faulty information, Atari canceled the deal that could have saved it as a game console company.

Nintendo decided to distribute the system on its own. It redesigned the Famicom, changing its original red-and-white case to a smaller case in an industrial gray. They also changed the name, avoiding terms such as *computer, video,* and *game* in favor of the Nintendo Entertainment System (NES). The deluxe version came bundled with accessories (a light gun and a plastic robot that could interact with games) and the popular arcade hits Super Mario Brothers and Duck Hunt. The NES made an immediate and undeniable statement: It was *not* an Atari clone.

The NES, released in the United States in 1985, outsold its competitors by a 10-to-1 margin. By the time Nintendo discontinued the NES, it had sold over 20 million units in the United States. Nintendo had taken Atari's place as the market leader and single-handedly revived the home video game market.

Figure 2.11 Super Nintendo Control Set.

Sega: Contender to the Throne. In 1951 David Rosen moved from the United States to Japan and founded an art export company named Rosen Enterprises. Toward the end of that decade Rosen Enterprises began to export coin-operated games and instant photo booths to the United States. In 1965 the company merged with a jukebox manufacturer and changed its name to Sega, a contraction of "Service Games."

In the early eighties Sega released several third-party home game cartridges of arcade games such as Frogger and Zaxxon. An arcade game cartridge created by another company (Third Party) was inserted into the Sega game console. Once inserted the Sega console would play the arcade game. During 1986 and 1987 the company had a string of arcade hits including Out Run, Shinobi, and After Burner. These games provided Sega with the funds to begin developing its own home system and gave it a series of familiar arcade titles to release on that system.

When Nintendo revived the home video game market following the crash of 1984, Sega took notice. Atari, Mattel, Coleco, and the other major players of the early eighties had either given up on the market or gone out of business. When the NES became a success, it had no competitors. Sega was determined to change that.

Sega released the Mark III game system in Japan as a direct competitor of the Nintendo Famicom. After Nintendo's NES became a huge smash, Sega released its unit in the United States, renamed the Sega Master System. Although the new system was technically superior to the NES, it was too late. Nintendo dominated the market and had made deals with most of the third-party developers that prevented them from creating games for competing systems. The lack of titles, coupled with Nintendo's head start, doomed the Sega system. Sega discontinued the Master System but did not pull out of the market.

Figure 2.12 Sega 16-bit Mega Drive System.

Pioneers of Home Computer Games

"A computer terminal is not some clunky old television with a typewriter in front of it. It is an interface where the mind and body can connect with the universe and move bits of it about."[6]

As we discussed earlier, the evolution of arcade games began with a space combat game written on the PDP-1 computer at MIT in 1961. We will now review a different evolutionary path beginning in the same era–the home computer game. This chapter looks at some of the game genres that became popular and the designers for games in those genres ranging from Gregory Yob's Hunt the Wumpus to the current generation of multiplayer online games such as Everquest and Asheron's Call.

Text-Based Adventure Games

Years after Spacewar! became an underground hit, a role-playing game played with pencil and dice became a popular pastime on university campuses across the United States. Dungeons & Dragons players would create fictional characters with specific attributes and skills; then one player, known as the Dungeon Master, would act as the referee and guide the other players though an adventure. A roll of the dice determined the outcome of events during the adventure, such as the results of combat and the effectiveness of magic spells.

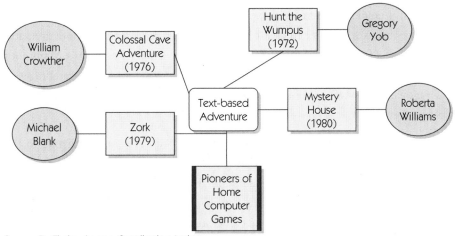

Source: Dr. Thelma Looms, Contributing Author.

Figure 2.13 Pioneers of Home Computer Games – Text-based Adventures.

---

[6] Adams, D. (2000). *Mostly harmless*. New York: Del Rey. Retrieved August 20, 2005, from http://en.thinkexist.com/quotation/a_computer_terminal_is_not_some_clunky_old/261301 .html.

At about this time the mainframe computers at major educational facilities across the United States joined in a network for cooperative resource sharing. ARPAnet, sponsored by the U.S. Department of Defense, introduced the concept of e-mail and became the forerunner of today's Internet. These two seemingly unconnected popular trends saw the rise of an entirely new type of computer game, the text-based adventure game. Let's look at a few designers of the games in this new genre.

Gregory Yob (Hunt the Wumpus, 1972). In 1972 Gregory Yob programmed a simple text adventure at the University of Massachusetts, Dartmouth. The game involved moving through a series of interconnected caves searching for a fictional creature called a Wumpus. In each room the player would receive clues about what was happening in the adjoining caves. Hunt the Wumpus spread quickly over ARPAnet and became a huge hit. In 1975 *Creative Computing* magazine published the code, and to this day several versions of Hunt the Wumpus are still available online.

William Crowther (Colossal Cave Adventure, 1976). "You are in a splendid chamber, thirty feet high. The walls are frozen rivers of orange stone. An awkward canyon and a good passage exit from the east and west sides of the chamber."[7]

The Boston firm Bolt, Beranek, and Newman Inc. (BBN) created much of the technology that made ARPAnet possible. In 1976 a BBN employee created the first true text-based adventure game on the firm's PDP-10. Willie Crowther and his wife Pat, also a BBN employee, were avid spelunkers. Crowther sometimes used the BBN computers in his spare time to create maps for the Cave Research Foundation, and Pat was part of the team that discovered the link between Kentucky's Mammoth and Flint Ridge caves. Crowther's other love was the role-playing game Dungeons & Dragons. These two passions merged when Crowther began work on Colossal Cave Adventure.

The game involved exploring a vast labyrinth of caves and returning to the starting point with as much treasure as possible. Once again, access to the BBN database via ARPAnet made the game popular at universities all over the country. It was then discovered by a graduate student at Stanford named Don Woods. Woods saw incredible potential in the game but also realized it contained bugs and glitches. Crowther had programmed the game for fun over a weekend and had never properly finished it.

---

[7] Crowther, W. (1976). *Colossal cave adventure.*

Figure 2.14 Microsoft Xbox 360 System.

Woods contacted Crowther and obtained the original code. He cleaned it up, added new elements, and reposted the new version on the Stanford computer. The game grew even more popular as the new version spread via ARPAnet. Eventually a version of the game, retitled simply as Adventure, appeared for personal computers in 1981. Crowther and Woods both endorsed it as the official version.

The next popular text-based game, and the first to become a commercial hit, originated with another group of programmers at the Massachusetts Institute of Technology, Marc Blank, Joel Berez, Tim Anderson, and Bruce Daniels. The group played Colossal Cave Adventure and was inspired to create a game. Zork was different from its precursor, however. Mark Blank created a new type of text parser that allowed the computer to understand the player's commands. Colossal Cave Adventure could only handle two-word commands like "go north" and "eat food." Blank's parser, which he called ZIL (Zork Interactive Language), could understand complete sentences.

The team completed the game in 1979 and immediately recognized its commercial potential. They formed their own company, which they called Infocom. In 1980 Infocom collaborated with Personal Software to release Zork 1 for several first-generation home computers, including the Apple 1. The game was successful and led to the development of the sci-fi game Starcross and the sequels Zork II and Zork III.

Roberta Williams (Mystery House, 1980). The cofounder of Sierra Online, Roberta Williams, discovered the world of adventure games when her husband bought a copy of Colossal Cave Adventure for their new computer. In 1980, frustrated by the lack of additional games to play, Roberta worked with her husband, a computer programmer, to write a game for the Apple II. In less than a month they produced Mystery House, a game that included simple graphics in addition to the text descriptions. They formed a company, Online Systems, to distribute their game and, after receiving many orders, began work on a second game, The Wizard and the Princess.

After moving to a small community in the foothills of the Sierra Mountains, they changed the company's name to Sierra Online. Sierra Online became a huge success and grew from a home-based business into a major developer of interactive entertainment with more than 130 employees. In addition to their enormous success with games for the home computer, Sierra developed several classic arcade games, including Frogger and Jawbreaker.

Graphic Adventure Games

The success of Mystery House set a new standard and launched an entire new genre of games. We now look at some of the key developments, game designers, and games in this genre.

Richard Garriott (Akalabeth, 1979; Ultima, 1980). Richard "British" Garriott was still in high school when he began creating computer games. He convinced school officials to let him use the school teletype to connect to a remote computer and used it to write 28 small games based on the Dungeons & Dragons game. When he finished his 29th game at the age of 19, he had a summer job at a local computer store. When his boss saw the game, he encouraged Garriott to make copies and sell it in the store.

He changed the title to Akalabeth, an obscure name from J.R.R. Tolkien's *Lord of the Rings* novels (with a slight change in spelling to avoid copyright issues). Although Garriott created the game for his own amusement and had never intended to sell it, one of the 15 copies sold at the store found its way to a software publisher in California. In 1979 California Pacific Computer (CPC) published the game and sold 30,000 copies. Garriott earned a $5 royalty on every game sold. The game that took six weeks to create earned Garriott $150,000.

In 1980 Garriott created a similar but much more ambitious game he originally called Ultimatum. Later he discovered that there was a board game with the same name, so he shortened his game's name to Ultima. After a disagreement with CPC over Akalabeth royalties, Garriott took Ultima to Ken and Roberta Williams, who released the game under the Sierra banner. The first sequel, Ultima II, followed in 1982. The following year Garriott would start his own company, Origin Systems, to distribute Ultima III.

In the mid-eighties conservative watchdog groups began to target Garriott's beloved Dungeons & Dragons role-playing game, labeling it immoral and dangerous to the youth of America. In response, Garriott broke through the typical "kill stuff and get treasure" adventure game paradigm with the release of Ultima IV. The game included a cause-and-effect system of morality. For instance, if you plundered and killed indiscriminately, your character would pay a price. Shopkeepers might not deal with you, and villagers might run from you in fear. On the other hand, the player received rewards for honesty, valor, and humility. This was previously unheard of in computer games. This idea became a defining principal in future Ultima releases. In all, there were nine titles in the Ultima series and a number of spin-off series including Worlds of Ultima and Ultima Online.

LucasArts (Manic Mansion, 1982; Monkey Island, 1990). In 1982 *Star Wars* director George Lucas dedicated a new division of his LucasFilm production company to developing computer games. After several successful arcade-style games for the Atari 2600, Apple II, and Commodore 64, LucasFilm Games (which would later become LucasArts) released an adventure game that would revolutionize the home video market.

Maniac Mansion introduced a new point-and-click interface that was user friendly and light-years beyond traditional text parser interfaces. The game engine's developer, Ron Gilbert, called his creation SCUMM (Script Creation Utility for Maniac Mansion). The game interface featured text action icons that allowed the player to interact with objects and characters and perform various actions without typing in commands.

Maniac Mansion and the second SCUMM release, Zak McKracken, were rather unsophisticated, but 1990's The Secret of Monkey Island featured inventory-based puzzles, dialogue options with multiple replies, higher-quality graphics, and a unique brand of humor that made it an instant classic. Developers at LucasArts went on to create a series of memorable games including Day of the Tentacle, Full Throttle, and the amazing Grim Fandango, as well as a series of Monkey Island sequels.

Rand and Robyn Miller (The Manhole, 1987; Myst, 1994). When Rand Miller wanted to produce a computer game for children, he asked his brother Robyn to illustrate it in Apple's HyperCard. Their collaboration led to the creation of Cyan Games.

The Manhole was a "what-if" game for children. The player would chase a rabbit down a manhole and discover a wonderful fantasy world beneath the streets of the city. The game, one of the first on CD, won an award from the Software Publishers Association award in 1987 for best new use of a computer. The Manhole was the first of their children's worlds including Cosmic Osmo and Spelunx.

In 1991 Rand and Robyn began working on a game for adults. With the addition of an artist (Chuck Carter) and an audio engineer (Chris Brandkamp), they built an interactive fantasy world filled with puzzles they called Myst. It was a game world different from anything anyone had ever seen. Originally implemented in HyperCard for the Macintosh, Myst came with almost no instructions except a brief message in the game manual. The game itself began with a brief cinematic introduction showing how the player came to be in Myst.

Interaction in the game world was a model of simplicity. Players navigated by clicking in whatever direction they wished to move. Clicking on items would activate or move them. The rest was up to the players. Myst became the best-selling graphic adventure game in history; Myst and its sequels (Riven, Myst III, and Uru) have sold over 10 million copies worldwide, earning over $250 million in revenue.

Computer Role-Playing Games

As computer games became more sophisticated, a split in the adventure game genre occurred. The adventure game genre came to refer to games like Myst that featured exploration and puzzle solving with little emphasis on character or combat. Another genre of games that is closer to the Dungeons & Dragons pencil and dice game are the computer role-playing games or CRPGs. Here are some of the pioneers in this genre.

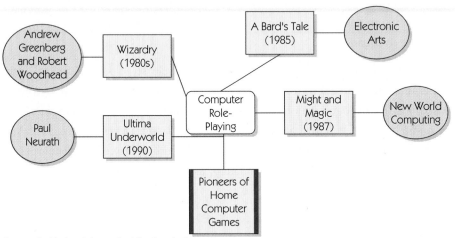

Source: Dr. Thelma Looms, Contributing Author.

Figure 2.15 Pioneers of Home Computer Games – Computer Role-Playing

Andrew Greenberg and Robert Woodhead (Wizardry). In 1980 Andrew Greenberg started writing a Dungeons & Dragons–style game on the computer for his friends. The result, written with his friend Robert Woodhead, was Wizardry 1. The game had simple wire-frame graphics but was one of the first graphical role-playing games. They took the game to a Boston computer show where Sir-Tech Software, a software company run by one of Greenberg's friends, picked it up.

The first version, for the Apple II, was a D&D–style dungeon crawl. The player led a party of up to six adventurers through a massive dungeon, fighting monsters, solving puzzles, and finding treasure. The game was turn-based, and players entered commands through the keyboard. Wizardry inspired seven sequels, the last released in 2001.

Electronic Arts (A Bard's Tale, 1985). Electronic Arts released A Bard's Tale in 1985. Like Wizardry, the game had a faux 3D perspective and multiple characters, but it also had many innovations. A Bard's Tale added texture to walls of dungeons and allowed players to adventure indoors as well as out. (Most of the gameplay took place in a city called Skara Brae.) For the first time players could import characters from a competing game, including both Ultima III and Wizardry. The popular game spawned two sequels and became legendary in gaming circles. There is an online petition circulating for a fourth game in the series.

New World Computing (Might and Magic, 1987). In 1984 New World Computing released the first game in the Might and Magic series. Might and Magic, Book 1: The Secret of the Inner Sanctum was the first computer RPG to feature a first-person perspective and combined cartoonlike graphics with offbeat humor. The popular series inspired eight sequels and numerous spin-offs.

The role-playing game of the year in 1991, Might and Magic III was the first game of its type to feature an automatic mapping system, which would become a CRPG standard. In all, the Might and Magic series has sold more than 5 million units worldwide.

Paul Neurath (Ultima Underworld, 1990). The 1990 Ultima Underworld: The Stygian Abyss could be the ancestor of all modern first-person 3D games. Although published by Origin (Richard Garriott's company) under the Ultima name, Blue Sky Productions, a small game developer in Salem, New Hampshire, actually created the game. Paul Neurath, a Dungeons & Dragons player who learned computer programming at college during the 1970s, formed Blue Sky. The other key developers were Doug Church and Warren Spector, who would later go on to separately develop well-known games like System Shock, Thief, and Deus Ex.

While working on a sci-fi game for Origin called Space Rogue, Neurath got the idea to create a first-person, real-time 3D fantasy game. He created an astonishing demo that was little more than a character walking through a 3D-texture mapped dungeon. No one had every seen anything like it. He signed a deal with Origin in 1990 and took over two years to complete the game. Released in 1992, Ultima Underworld: The Stygian Abyss met with remarkable success. The game sold over half a million copies and won numerous awards, becoming one of the most influential games produced by Origin.

Massive Multiplayer Role-Playing Games

In the early days of the Internet, gamers began playing online games inspired by the old text-based adventure games. These games, called MUDs (multi-user dungeons or more generically, multi-user dimensions), were online environments where multiple users could log on and interact. Some MUDs were similar to online chat systems, where you could interact only with other logged-on players. Others were interactive game worlds you could explore.

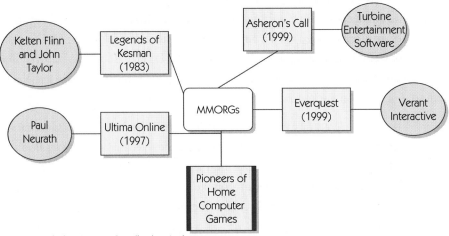

Source: Dr. Thelma Looms, Contributing Author.

Figure 2.16 Pioneers of Home Computer Games – MMORG

Just as with the old-style single-player text adventures, there could be creatures to fight or treasure to collect; but in the online environments players could do this in the company of other players. Some MUDs even allowed players to change and expand the environment. In this section we will look at several early online graphical games that were the precursors of massive multiplayer online role-playing (MMORPG) games.

Legends of Kesman (1983). In 1982 Kelten Flinn and John Taylor created the text MUDs Dungeons of Kesmai and Island of Kesmai. In 1983 they started the first graphical online game role-playing game, Legends of Kesmai, as part of the America On Line (AOL) service. They later transferred the game to the Gamestorm network, and the game shut down when Electronic Arts (EA) purchased Gamestorm in 1999. It was a simple combat game that was obsolete by the time EA shut it down. Many of the players migrated to EA's Ultima Online.

The Big Three. Other early online graphical games include AOL's version of Neverwinter Nights (1991–1997), 3DO's Meridian 59 (1995–2000), and Dark

Sun Online (1996–1999). Meridian 59 came closest to going mainstream of all the games of this period. At its peak it boasted 30,000 paying players. Dark Sun Online was part of the fee-based gaming network TEN. However, none of the games found a loyal audience. The first successful online RPG was yet to come. Ultimately three massive multiplayer online role-playing games emerged as the most popular titles.

Ultima Online (1997). With a loyal following of Ultima fans already in place, it was no surprise that Ultima Online was a hit. Despite a rocky start, the online game's community quickly grew to more than 100,000 subscribers. Despite its dated 2D graphics and isometric perspective, Ultima Online had an unmatched level of interactivity. Its skill system allowed players to be tradespeople or artisans and earn a living without ever having to fight. It also let players buy and decorate their own homes.

Everquest (1999). Everquest, released in 1999, quickly surpassed Ultima Online as the most popular online game. With more than 330,000 active subscribers, developer Verant and distributor Sony hit on the perfect mix of features: first-person perspective, colorful graphics, and well-designed, class-based character development. Verant continues to release expansions for the game, so the imaginary game world of Norrath gets bigger all the time. The game's addictive qualities and the infamous level treadmill mentality it seems to promote have been widely publicized. Fans eagerly await the imminent release of Everquest 2, a revised, state-of-the-art version of the game set years in Norrath's future.

Asheron's Call (1999). Microsoft released Asheron's Call later that same year. Microsoft does not release subscriber statistics, but the game's Massachusetts developer, Turbine Entertainment, estimates there are somewhere around 100,000 players.

Though Asheron's Call had a smoother launch than either Ultima or Everquest, it never generated as much publicity. However, Asheron's Call differs from other online games in that it updates its story line monthly. Far from being a static world, Dereth changes over time. Turbine's team creates new and original content every month. This feature might not bring in vast quantities of subscribers, but Asheron's Call can boast the best subscriber survival rate: Asheron's Call players tend to be loyal.

Of all the online games, Asheron's Call seems to have a jump on the next generation titles with the release of Asheron's Call 2: Fallen Kings in November of 2002. Time will tell if this head start will give Turbine and Microsoft an advantage in the MMORPG market.

Handheld and Portable Games

"Since new developments are the products of a creative mind, we must therefore stimulate and encourage that type of mind in every way possible."[8]

In the history of gaming 1977 was a big year. In the arcades, the vector beam game Space War! was a big hit. Atari released its VCS home system, later known as the 2600, which would become the longest-selling home system ever. The Golden Age of home games was just beginning. Another industry milestone occurred in the same year: the introduction of the portable video game.

History of Handheld Game Systems

This section reviews the history of handheld gaming systems from 1977 to the present. We will look at the innovations in handheld systems beginning with a discussion of the Milton Bradley Comp IV and ending with the Sony PSP.

Milton Bradley's Comp IV (1977). In February 1977 at the annual Toy Fair in New York, board game manufacturer Milton Bradley announced the formation of Milton Bradley Electronics, its new electronic toy division. Milton Bradley Electronics also unveiled its first product there.

Comp IV was the first electronic game that did not require a television set to play. A logic game challenged the player to determine four (or five) random numbers in as few guesses as possible. The game was quite popular, and the titles for the games released in Great Britain and Japan were Logic 5 and Pythagoras, respectively.

Mattel's Handheld Sports Games (1977). In March of that same year, Mattel Toys introduced a line of handheld sports games. Mattel's Hockey, Basketball, and Football games were a huge success. Oddly enough, Richard Chong, the designer of the football game, was not a sports fan, and he gave the game only a 90-yard playing field.

The Mattel games used simple red LEDs (light-emitting diodes) to crudely simulate gameplay. The game had no true graphics. However, three years later Nintendo would revolutionize the handheld industry by introducing the first games that used LCDs (liquid crystal displays).

Microvision (1979). Milton Bradley released Microvision in 1979. Jay Smith, who would later create the Vectrex home vector graphics unit, designed the unit.

---

[8] Carver, G. W. (n.d.). Retrieved August 12, 2005, from http://www.brainyquote.com/quotes/authors/g/george_washington_carver.html.

The Microvision had the distinction of being the first programmable handheld game. The idea was to combine the portability of the Mattel games with the interchangeable cartridges of the Atari VCS. The unit met with some initial success, but with a small library of games and poor screen resolution, Microvision discontinued the product. Later Nintendo would prove that the Microvision concept was ahead of its time.

Nintendo Game and Watch Series (1980). Nintendo released a series of games under the Game and Watch name beginning in 1980. The games were immediately popular, showing up in schoolyards and playgrounds around the world. The graphics were crude by today's standards, but they were certainly recognizable.

Despite the inevitable slew of copycats, the Game and Watch series secured Nintendo as the leader in the handheld games market right away. Eventually Nintendo would introduce the most popular handheld console of the 20th century.

Adventure Vision (1982). Entex released the Adventure Vision system in 1982. The small tabletop unit game used interchangeable cartridges. A version of the popular arcade game Defender shipped with the unit. There were only three other titles in the Adventure Vision library—Space Force, Super Cobra, and Turtles.

The game mimicked a video display by using a vertical row of 40 red LEDs and a spinning mirror. The game displayed with a total screen resolution of 150×40 and in a dimly lit environment because of the low refresh rate and screen flicker. Limited titles and the low-resolution display resulted in poor sales (fewer than 100,000 units), and the Adventure Vision went off the market within a year.

Nintendo Game Boy (1989). In 1988 Nintendo released the Game Boy, a handheld 8-bit black-and-white system that accepted interchangeable cartridges. The game sold for $99 and shipped with the blockbuster puzzle game Tetris. Gumpie Yokoi created the unit; over a decade and a half later, the Game Boy series of handhelds has been by far the most successful of all time.

By 1993 sales of the original Game Boy were beginning to slow. To revive sales Nintendo released an add-on unit called the Super Game Boy in 1994. The device allowed gamers to play Game Boy cartridges on the SuperNES home console. Super Game Boy revived interest in the system and kept Game Boy alive.

Game Boy Color, released in 1998, was an inexpensive unit that was backward compatible with existing Game Boy titles. It featured a color screen and extended battery life. The color system immediately attracted swarms of third party developers, and a flood of game titles joined the already extensive Game Boy Library. By 2000 Nintendo had sold more than 110 million Game Boys. The following year, as beloved Nintendo icons Donkey Kong and Mario celebrated their 20th anniversary,

Nintendo released its next generation handheld, the Game Boy Advance. The latest systems are the Game Boy Advance SP (Special Project), released in 2003, and the Game Boy DS (Dual Screen), released in 2004.

Sony PSP (2005). Sony entered the handheld game market in 2005 with the introduction of the PSP (PlayStation Portable). Intended as a combination portable gaming system and multimedia device, the PSP plays games and movies from small optical disks in a proprietary Sony format called UMD (Universal Media Disk). Players can also transfer pictures, music, and video to the PSP using removable memory sticks.

As a gaming platform, Sony intended the PSP to provide the experience of a Sony Playstation2 in a handheld form. The system has virtually the same processing power as a PS2 and has a very high screen resolution for a handheld unit (480×272); it can display over 16 million colors. The PSP also supports stereo sound and can be connected to a PC using either a USB (universal serial bus) 2.0 connection or an 11 megabit wireless network (802.11b). Dozens of games were available on the system's release date with over a hundred more in various stages of development. See Table 2.2 for a comparison of handheld game systems both past and present.

TABLE 2.2   Comparison Matrix of Handheld Game Systems (1977-2005).

Systems	Features			
	LED	LCD	Color LCD	Cartridge
Milton Bradley's Comp IV (1977)	✓			
Mattel's Handheld Sports Game (1977)	✓			
Microvision (1979)	✓			✓
Nintendo Game and Watch Series (1980)		✓		
Entex Adventure Vision (1982)	✓			✓
Nintendo Game Boy (1989)		✓	✓	✓
Sony PSP (2005)			✓	✓

Wireless Games

"**We've arranged a civilization in which most crucial elements profoundly depend on science and technology. We have also arranged things so that almost no one understands science and technology. This is a prescription for disaster. We might get away with it for a while, but sooner or later this combustible mixture of ignorance and power is going to blow up in our faces.**"[9]

Research firm Informa indicates that the global market for mobile entertainment will be worth $42.8 billion by 2010. "Mobile music, mobile games, mobile gambling, and adult content will be the royal content" (David, 2005). The opportunities for game designers will grow with the industry. Strategic game design and development that take advantage of the growing market can help make a game design team successful in this lucrative market.

Beginning of Wireless Games

The latest trend in gaming really has not reached the United States yet. It began, as many gaming trends have, in Japan. Affordable Internet access has grown slowly there, and a large portion of the Japanese population have come to depend on their cell phones as their primary means of accessing the Web. Downloading games for cellular telephones has become popular and common.

In Japan monthly subscription services are the most popular way to play wireless games. One popular service, called G-Mode, offers a selection of more than 60 games, and subscribers choose three games to play in any given month. Hudson Soft is a service that allows subscribers to download an unlimited number of games.

It is likely that wireless games could be successful in the United States. In 2001 four companies in the wireless industry (Ericsson, Motorola, Nokia, and Siemens) created the Mobile Games Interoperability (MGI) Forum to define specifications for mobile gaming (Olavsrud, 2001). More recently a number of wireless providers, including Sprint PCS and Verizon, have begun marketing campaigns designed to introduce wireless gaming in the United States. Many cell phones provide limited built-in gaming capabilities, and Nokia introduced the N-Gage, a combination phone and mobile gaming platform, in 2003. The N-Gage received mixed reviews when it was announced (Davis, 2003). Although Nokia has sold over a million N-Gage units, only time will tell if wireless gaming will become as popular in the United States and Europe as it is in Japan.

---

[9] Sagan, C., & Druyan, A. (1995). *The demon haunted world: Science as a candle in the dark.* Random House. Retrieved August 12, 2005, from http://www.quotegarden.com/technology.html.

Next Generation Consoles

"Man is a gaming animal. He must always be trying to get the better in something or other."[10]

Game consoles continue to evolve. From the early Atari and Nintendo units to the latest systems from Microsoft and Sony, game consoles have made major advances. In this section we review the capabilities of the latest generations of game consoles and their impact on gaming.

Game Consoles in the 21st Century

The current generation of game consoles provides capabilities that early game designers could only dream of. From graphics to gameplay, today's consoles provide a more realistic and immersive experience for players and add the ability to compete against other players from around the world.

The next phase of home video game development introduced the consoles that are popular today, including the Microsoft Xbox, the Nintendo GameCube, and the Sony Playstation 2. All three manufacturers have announced the systems that will replace the current generation: the XBox 360, the Revolution, and the Playstation 3.

Sony's PlayStation 2. In March 2000 Sony released the PlayStation 2 in Japan and sold a record million units in just two days. The demand for the unit was so great that not everyone who had preordered the PS2 received one.

That same year, at the Electronic Entertainment Expo (E3) trade show, Sony announced several changes to the American version of the PS2. It would include DVD drivers as part of the system, and the memory cards (required for game saves) were not included in the base system. The unit also did not include a modem or hard drive. These sold separately as optional peripherals. These changes reduced the price of the unit to $299.

The PS2 went on sale in the United States on October 26, 2000. At Sony's Metreon store in San Francisco, customers began lining up over 24 hours in advance. More than a thousand people came to buy one of the machines, but nearly half of them went home empty-handed. The scarcity of available units gave the PS2 almost legendary status. On some Internet auction sites the units were selling for as much as $1,000. By the following spring 10 million PS2s had been sold internationally.

In 2001 Microsoft and Nintendo launched their own next generation consoles, but despite the fierce competition, PS2 sales continued at rapid pace. By the end of 2001 there were 6 million PS2 systems in North America alone.

---

[10] Lamb, C. (1775–1834). Retrieved August 20, 2005, from http://en.thinkexist.com/quotation/man_is_a_gaming_animal-he_must_always_be_trying/260522.html.

Microsoft Xbox. At San Jose's GDC (Game Developer's Conference) in March 2000, Microsoft Chairman Bill Gates announced that Microsoft was entering the home video game market. In his keynote address, Gates revealed that when the Microsoft Xbox was released the following year it would feature a 32-bit Intel Pentium III processor, a Nvidia graphics processor, 64 MB of RAM, an 8 GB hard drive, an internal modem, and a network interface that would support broadband Internet access.

In January 2001 at the Consumer Electronics Show in Las Vegas, Gates demonstrated the production version of the Xbox. He also promised that no fewer than 12 (and as many as 20) games would be available when the product launched. Microsoft officially released the Xbox in the United States in November 2001 with a Japanese release planned for February 2002. The unit retailed for $299, placing it in direct price competition with Sony's PS2.

Nintendo's GameCube. There was speculation that Nintendo would unveil its next generation console at the Electronic Entertainment Expo (E3) in May 2000. Instead the company introduced the latest version of the N64 and its new Game Boy Color handheld unit. In July Nintendo announced that it would release its new console, known by the code name "Dolphin," in 2001.

In August 2001 the GameCube was unveiled at the Japanese trade show Space World. It was literally a cube, and rather than using DVDs or CDs as a storage medium, it utilized a new, smaller optical disk designed by Matsushita. The smaller disks were ideal for consoles and handheld units, and Nintendo hoped that the media would become an industry standard.

Nintendo released the GameCube in Japan on September 13, 2001, with the U.S. release in November. The retail price was $199, making the GameCube $100 less than either the Xbox or PS2. On the first day of sales in the United States Nintendo sold a reported $98 million in consoles, games, and accessories.

Next Generation Game Consoles

The release of the Xbox Shepard's in a new era of game design and development. We have mixed reactions but for sure the launch of the new game console sets a new paradigm for game developers across the board. As for the gamer we have an extremely well developed computer console with a wireless handheld controller. This new device blurs the line between the hard core computer gamer and the video game console user. One of the truly exciting experiences is the fact that this unit is designed to interface with your TV. The HD quality of the graphics elevates this extremely popular device to a whole new level. In the years to come when developers learn to harness the power of this new development tool we will see video games that embrace the new technology and give the gamer new challenges to overcome. Gamers crave more power, more graphic capability, swifter controller manipulation, and more powerful games. They demand more from developers in the 3D arena and deeper thrills. Gamers seek subversive interactive entertainment and are unsatisfied with games that do not challenge them to play harder and longer. Gamers have become educated controller masters, experts at play, and are devoted to games and the time they spend playing them. Gamers have proven that they will pay billions for interactive entertainment. We will look at the specs and see what the new Xbox 360 has to offer. See Table 2.3.

TABLE 2.3	The Technology in the Next Generation Game Consoles.	
Microsoft Xbox 360	**PlayStation 3**	**Nintendo Revolution**
3 custom IBM PowerPC CPUs	Cell Processor	Custom ATI graphics processor
Custom ATI graphics processor	256 MB XDR DRAM	512MB flash memory (2 slots)
512 MB GDDR3 RAM	256 MB GDDR3 RAM	GCN discs
DVD-ROM	Custom Nvidia graphics processor	Proprietary new 12cm discs
Detachable 20GB hard drive	Blue-Ray DVD Drive	802.11b and 802.11g, Wi-Fi wireless
Ethernet	Removable hard drive	Wireless controllers
HDTV support	Gigabit Ethernet	
Surround Sound output	HDTV support	
Wireless controllers	802.11b and 802.11g, Wi-Fi wireless	
	Surround Sound output	
	Wireless controllers	

Figure 2.17 Sony PlayStation 3.

Next Up: PlayStation 3

It's thought that PlayStation 3 will usher in the new generation of game consoles with a powerful punch. The official specs from Sony are shown in Table 2.3. A collaborative team from IBM, Sony, and Toshiba created a unique cell processor. The mix includes NVIDIA and SCEI for the graphic card design along with a 54GB hard drive, making a powerful computer-based operating system that merges high-quality HD entertainment content with electronic gaming capabilities. The realistic capabilities of 3D game content developed by leaders in the industry are expected to bring a new age to the game world with an anticipated release date of spring 2006.

The arcade and home video game markets prospered during the mid 1970s through the mid 1980s. Advances in gaming technology (such as use of micro-processors and color displays) drove the Golden Age for both arcades and home machines. The creation of the first electronic video games began in laboratories and on college campuses with the development of programs such as Tennis for Two and Spacewar!. The Golden Age of arcade games built on these early programs. Games such as Asteroids, Space Invaders, Donkey Kong, and Pac-Man were instrumental in the popularity and growth of video arcades. Arcade machines incorporated some of the latest developments in computer technology ranging from microprocessors to laser disks. The change to laser disks helped bring about the "Great Crash" as players grew dissatisfied with poor-quality content and poor gameplay. Combined with the downturn in the home video market, the Golden Age of video games ended.

This chapter has presented an overview of game consoles and game genres beginning after the game industry crash in the 1980s and continuing to the present. Game consoles have evolved from the NES and Sega Master System through the Microsoft XBox, Nintendo GameCube, and PlayStation 3. The capabilities provided by personal computers and consoles have increased dramatically. Improvements in processing power, graphics resolution, storage capability, and sound allow game designers to create virtual worlds for users.

Games evolved as well. Starting with simple, single-player, text-based adventures such as Hunt the Wumpus, games have added features and capa-bilities so that it is now possible for players to enter virtual worlds and com-pete with thousands of other players from around the planet in games such as Asheron's Call, Everquest, and Ultima Online. With the success of these games, massively multiplayer games have flooded the market. These include science fiction titles including Earth & Beyond, Anarchy Online, Eve, Neocron, and Star Wars Galaxies; nongenre titles like The Sims Online; and many others. Only time will tell which games will survive and which will become footnotes in the history of the industry.

The following lists summarize the key facts and concepts discussed in this chapter:

- The first electronic games included

    - Computer Space.

    - Odyssey.

    - Pong.

    - Spacewar!.

    - Tennis for Two.

Courtesy of *Into the Pixel*: Chinatown Level Study

Artist:
Rich Mahon, Jon Gwyn, Chandana Ekanayake

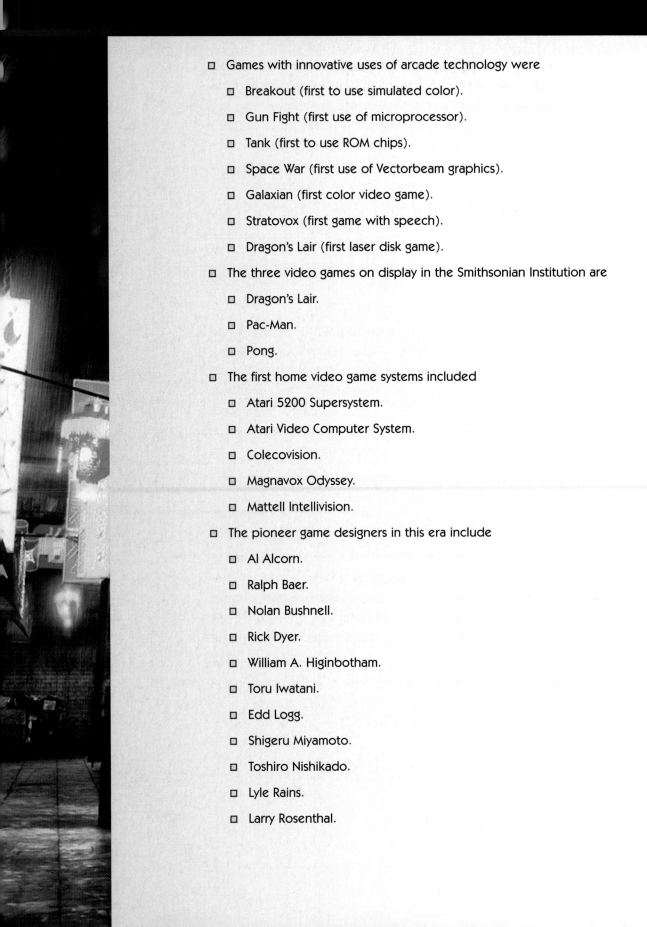

- Games with innovative uses of arcade technology were
  - Breakout (first to use simulated color).
  - Gun Fight (first use of microprocessor).
  - Tank (first to use ROM chips).
  - Space War (first use of Vectorbeam graphics).
  - Galaxian (first color video game).
  - Stratovox (first game with speech).
  - Dragon's Lair (first laser disk game).
- The three video games on display in the Smithsonian Institution are
  - Dragon's Lair.
  - Pac-Man.
  - Pong.
- The first home video game systems included
  - Atari 5200 Supersystem.
  - Atari Video Computer System.
  - Colecovision.
  - Magnavox Odyssey.
  - Mattell Intellivision.
- The pioneer game designers in this era include
  - Al Alcorn.
  - Ralph Baer.
  - Nolan Bushnell.
  - Rick Dyer.
  - William A. Higinbotham.
  - Toru Iwatani.
  - Edd Logg.
  - Shigeru Miyamoto.
  - Toshiro Nishikado.
  - Lyle Rains.
  - Larry Rosenthal.

Introduction to the History of Video Games

The Atari History Museum Web site: http://www.atarimuseum.com/.

Hunter, W. (2000). Willy Higinbotham and the Paleolithic "PONG": The Zeus of the videogame industry. In Player 1 Stage 1: Bits from the primordial ooze. The Dot Eaters Videogame History 101 Web site: http://www.emuunlim.com/doteaters/play1sta1 .htm.

Winter, D. (2005). Magnavox odyssey: The first videogame console. http://www.pong-story.com/odyssey.htm.

The Golden Age of Arcade Games

Flagmaster (n.d.). Donkey Kong. The Gaming Web site: http://www.classicgaming .com/rotw/dk.shtml.

Liedholm, M., & Liedholm, M. (2004). Profile: Shigeru Miyamoto. The Nintendo Land Web site: http://www.nintendoland.com/home2.htm?profiles/miyamoto.htm.

WebMagic Ventures (2005). The coin-op museum: Dragon's Lair. The Killer List of Video Games Web site: http://www.klov.com/D/Dragon's_Lair.html.

The rise and fall of laser disk games (n.d.). The Atari Game Headquarters Web site: http://www.atarihq.com/coinops/laser/.

The Golden Age of Home Video Games

The electronics conservancy (1998). Videotopia: The home games. The Home Games .com Web site: http://www.videotopia.com/games2.htm.

The great video game market crash of 1983–1984 (n.d.). The VideoGames101 Web site: http://ryangenno.tripod.com/sub_pages/VGCS-GVGMC.htm.

Practice Questions

1. Why did the creator of the first video game not file a patent for it?

2. Select three innovations used in game technology. How do we use these technologies in today's computers and video games?

3. Who is considered the "father of modern video games" and why?

4. Why did interactive laser disk games eventually fail?

5. What caused the home video market's crash?

6. What new game console are you interested in?

Courtesy of *Into the Pixel*
Yellow Room

Artist: Stephan
Martiniere

Lab Exercises

In this exercise you will visit a local video arcade and use the experience to compare old and new video games. You will play both current and, if available, classic arcade games. While you are at the arcade, take note of the games that are available to play. (If there are no arcades in your town, you might want to Google "retro games" to research these types of arcade games.)

1. Identify any trends you noticed in the types of games available at the arcade. Were any classic games in the arcade? If so, why do you think those games still appeal to players?

2. Pick a newer arcade game and play it several times. Did you enjoy it? Explain why or why not. What type of player do you think might like the game? What might make it more appealing for you?

3. Upon returning, use the remainder of the lab to discuss the various games in the arcade.

4. Discuss the new game consoles and what you like or dislike about the products. What new games are you currently playing on the new generation consoles?

Written Assignment

Choose a designer, game company, or game franchise from the Golden Age of home video games and compare the next generation game platforms. Write a 750-word essay about the history, game designers, and their impact on the future of game development. Please use new references rather than those used in the chapter.

Adams, D. (2000). *Mostly harmless*. New York: Del Rey. Retrieved August 20, 2005, from http://en.thinkexist.com/quotation/a_computer_terminal_is_not_some_clunky_old/261301.html.

Adams, R. (n.d.). *The colossal cave adventure*. Retrieved August, 12, 2005, from http://www.rickadams.org/adventure/.

The Atari History Museum Web site. (n.d.). http://www.atarimuseum.com/.

Bates, B. (2001). Game design: The art & business of creating games. Roseville, CA: Prima Publishing.

Bonsor, K. (n.d.). How GameCube works. *Howstuffworks*. Retrieved August 20, 2005, from http://entertainment.howstuffworks.com/gamecube.htm/printable.

Bonsor, K. (n.d.). How Xbox works. *Howstuffworks*. Retrieved August 20, 2005, from http://entertainment.howstuffworks.com/xbox.htm/printable.

Brand, S. (1972). SPACEWAR: Fanatic life and symbolic death among the computer bums. *Rolling Stone* [Electronic source]. Retrieved August 12, 2005, from http://www.wheels.org/spacewar/stone/rolling_stone.html.

Bushnell, N. (2001). Interview, Nolan Bushnell. Retrieved August 20, 2005, from the Good Deal Games.com Web site: http://www.gooddealgames.com/interviews/int_bushnell.html.

Carroll, J. (1994). Guerillas in the Myst. *Wired Magazine, 2(08)* [Electronic Version]. Retrieved August 12, 2005, from http://www.wired.com/wired/archive/2.08/myst.html.

Cassidy, W. (n.d.). GOTW:ASTEROIDS by William Cassidy. http://www.classicgaming.com/rotw/asteroids/.

Chance, G. (1994). History of home video games. Retrieved August 12, 2005, from http://videogames.org/html/.

Cook, D. (2002). Evolutionary design: A practical process for creating great game designs. Retrieved August 12, 2005, from http://www.lostgarden.com/evolutionary_game_design2.htm.

Cuciz, D. (n.d.). *The history of MUDs*. Retrieved August 12, 2005, from GameSpy.com Web Site: http://www.gamespy.com/articles/january01/muds1/index.shtm.

Davis, T. (2003, December 5). Nokia N-Gage, The Register, Retrieved August 14, 2005, from http://www.theregister.co.uk/2003/12/05/nokia_ngage/.

The electronics conservancy (1998). Videotopia: The home games. Retrieved August 20, 2005, from the Home Games.com Web site: http://www.videotopia.com/games2.htm.

Flagmaster. (n.d.). Donkey Kong. Retrieved August 12, 2005, from the Game of the Week, Game Museum, Classic Gaming Web Site: http://www.classicgaming.com/rotw/dk.shtml.

Gallear, M. (2004). *The computer role playing game genre*. Retrieved August 20, 2005, from http://www.geocities.com/TimesSquare/Arena/8461/crpg1.html.

Garaetz, J. M. (1981). The origin of Spacewar! *Creative Computing*. [Electronic source]. Retrieved August 12, 2005, from http://www.wheels.org/spacewar/creative/SpacewarOrigin.html.

Goethe, J.W. (n.d.). Retrieved August 20, 2005, from http://www.thinkexist.com/English/Topic/x/Topic_313_2.htm.

The great video game market crash of 1983–1984 (n.d.). Retrieved August 20, 2005, from the VideoGames101 Web site: http://ryangenno.tripod.com/sub_pages/VGCS-GVGMC.htm.

Green, C. (2002). Pac-Man. Retrieved August 12, 2005, from the Salon.com Web site: http://www.salon.com/ent/masterpiece/2002/06/17/pac_man/?x.

Groff, D., & Steele, K. (2005, February 15). When multimedia was black and white. *Smackerel*. Retrieved August 20, 2005, from http://www.smackerel.net/black_white_03.html.

Hallford, N., & Hallford, J. Swords & circuitry: A designer's guide to computer role-playing games. Roseville, CA: Prima Publishing.

Courtesy of *Into the Pixel*: Enzo in Florence

Artists: Ben O'Sullivan, Gren Atherton, Mark Sharratt, Matt Watts

Hart, S. (1998). A brief history of home video games. Retrieved August 12, 2005, from http://www.geekcomix.com/vgh/.

Herz, J. C. (1997). *Joystick nation: How computer games ate our quarters, won our hearts, and rewired our minds.* New York: Little, Brown.

The history of Nintendo. (n.d.). Retrieved August 12, 2005, from the Nintendo Land Web site: http://www.nintendoland.com/home2.htm?history/index.htmany History.

Inventor of the week: Roberta Williams (2002). Retrieved August 12, 2005, from Inventor of the Week Web site, Massachusetts Institute of Technology: http://web.mit.edu/invent/iow/williams.html.

Kent, S. (2001). *The ultimate history of video games: From Pong to Pokemon—The story behind the craze that touched our lives and changed the world.* Three Rivers, MI: Three Rivers Press.

King, B., & Borland, J. (2003). *Dungeons & dreamers: The rise of computer game culture from geek to chic.* Emeryville, CA: McGraw-Hill/Osborne Media.

Lamb, C. (1775–1834). Retrieved August 20, 2005, from http://en.thinkexist.com/quotation/man_is_a_gaming_animal-he_must_always_be_trying/260522.html .Liedholm, M., & Liedholm, M. (2004). Profile: Shigeru Miyamoto. Retrieved August 12, 2005, from the Nintendo Land Web site: http://www.nintendoland.com/home2.htm?profiles/miyamoto.htm.

Lucas, G. (1999, June 19). *Academy of achievement interview.* Retrieved August 18, 2005, from http://www.achievement.org/autodoc/printmember/luc0int-1.

Mallison, P. (2002). *Games that changed the world: Ultima underworld.* http://www.tiscali.co.uk/games/features/2002/04/16/gamesthatchangedtheworldultimaunderworld.html.

Miller, M. (2005, April 1). A history of home video game consoles. *informIT.* Retrieved August 20, 2005, from http://www.informit.com/articles/printerfriendly.asp?p=378141.

Mukenhoupt, C. (2005). Retrieved August 12, 2005, from http://www.wurb.com/if/game/442.

Olavsrud, T. (July, 2001). Four Wireless Firms Form Mobile Gaming Forum, Retrieved August 14, 2005, from the internetnews.com Web site: http://siliconvalley.internet.com/news/article.php/795621

The origin museum. (2004). Retrieved August 12, 2005, from. http://originmuseum.solsector.net/.

Perrson, H. (n.d.). *Sierra Online: A history.* Retrieved August 12, 2005, from http://www.lysator.liu.se/adventure/Sierra_On-Line,_Inc.html.

Richard Garriott & origin systems (n.d). http://www.mcgrawhill.co.uk/mh_community/images/0072224282%20_118_123.pdf.

The rise and fall of laser disk games. (n.d.). Retrieved August 12, 2005, from the Atari Game Headquarters Web site: http://www.atarihq.com/coinops/laser/.

The rise and fall of vectors. (n.d.). *Syzygy Magazine* [Online source]. Retrieved August 12, 2005, from the GoodDeal Games.com Web site: http://www.gooddealgames.com/articles/Rise_Fall_Vectors.html.

Stephenson, J. (n.d.). *World builder: A conversation with Robyn Miller*. Retrieved August 12, 2005, from The Riven Unofficial Web Site: http://members.aol.com/jamesstep2/robyn/robyn1.html.

Sheff, D. (1993). *Game over: How Nintendo conquered the world*. New York: Random House.

Sony PlayStation 2. Dark Watcher's Console History. Retrieved August 20, 2005, from http://darkwatcher.psxfanatics.com/console/ps2.htm.

Turner, B. (2002). Nintendo. Retrieved August, 12, 2005, from The Planet Nintendo Web site: http://www.planetnintendo.com/community/nintendo/.

Tyson, J. (n.d.). How Playstation 2 works. *Howstuffworks*. Retrieved August 20, 2005, from http://www.howstuffworks.com/ps2.htm/printable.

VIDEOTOPIA: The exhibit of the true history of video games. (1997). Retrieved from the Videotopia Web Site: http://www.videotopia.com/.

WebMagic Ventures. (2005). The coin-op museum: Dragon's Lair. Retrieved August 20, 2005, from the Killer List of Video Games Web site: http://www.klov.com/D/Dragon's_Lair.html.

Wikipedia: Hunt the Wumpus. (n.d.). Retrieved August 12, 2005, from Wikipedia The Free Encyclopedia Web site: http://www.wikipedia.org/wiki/Wumpus.

Winter, D. (2005). Magnavox odyssey: The first videogame console. Retrieved August 12, 2005, from http://www.pong-story.com/odyssey.htm.

Winter, D. (2005). Original patent filed by Ralph Baer for the first home video game apparatus. Retrieved August 20, 2005, from http://www.pong-story.com/sanders.htm.

Courtesy of 3D artist Harshdeep Borah

CHAPTER 3

Game Components: Part One

An understanding of the various design components of a game, in particular the user interface (UI), is vital to any study of game design and technology. The goal of this chapter is to provide an overview of the functions of the user interface and other important design components, including game input, game output, player perspective, player options, and player education.

After completing this chapter, you will be able to:

- Explain the fundamental elements in a user interface.
- Discuss the importance of input and game control mechanisms.
- Discuss the importance of output and game world feedback.
- Identify the various player perspective options and their use in different game genres.
- Identify the various types of options available to the player via a game's interface menu.
- Discuss the importance of educating the player.
- Classify the various methods used to educate the player.
- Identify the various types of game tutorials.

President and CEO of Stormfront Studios

Daglow's Law of Data Storage: No matter how large the capacity of a device may be, game designers will create titles that are too large to fit within it.

At Intellivision in 1982 we went from writing 4K game cartridges to having 8K cartridges. (No, that's not a typo...an entire game was smaller than a one-page English paper in Microsoft Word is today!) We said, "Wow, how are we ever going to fill all that space?" A year later we had 16K carts and were having trouble cutting games back to fit in them.

When CDs came along, we said, "Wow, all that space...if we use half the disk it'd be incredible!" But then we started adding pictures and movies and building games that wouldn't fit on one disk.

When DVDs came along...I guess you know The Rest of the story already, don't you?

User Interface Fundamentals

"Form follows function."[1]

The ultimate goal of a game designer is to create a good game. However, there are no recipes to follow and no magic formulas to help the designer to achieve that goal. As with any creative endeavor, a designer must draw from experience as a player, knowledge as a designer, and, much of the time, simply intuition (Rouse, 2001). Most quality games possess several key components. We will start by looking at some of these critical elements, beginning with the user interface.

User Interface Components

One of the most critical and difficult tasks a designer must face is creating a game's UI. The screen layout must be aesthetically pleasing because the player will work with it for hours. However, the layout must also be intuitive. A needlessly complex UI will cause the player to become frustrated. A simple, intuitive interface will increase user enjoyment of the game.

There are two primary factors to consider when creating a user interface:

☐ Input (actions taken by the player).

☐ Output (feedback from the gaming world).

---

[1] Sullivan, L. H. (n.d.). Retrieved August 12, 2005, from the WordNet 1.7.1 database, Princeton University.

Input. Controls are the player's link to the game world, and well-designed controls are vital to a player's enjoyment of a game. If the controls are not intuitive, the player feels separated from the game world, and feelings of immersion are shattered. The actions that the player takes most often should be the simplest to access using a keyboard, mouse, or game controller.

Computer Mouse. The computer mouse is a particularly effective input device. All computer users, even those who have never played a game, are already comfortable with the point/click/drag/drop functions of a mouse. Consequently, a game that uses a mouse as its primary control device is nonthreatening and easy to start. The most popular computer game of all time, The Sims, relies on mouse commands almost exclusively.

Most of the important functions in The Sims interface require just a single mouse click on graphical icons in the lower left corner of the screen. The game groups the few functions that require more than one click in pop-up windows. A user can play the entire game with one hand.

Another example of a game with a well-designed interface is Blizzard Entertainment's Diablo 2. The game is so easy to learn that it is not necessary to read the manual. A single click on an icon will open windows with character information, inventory, and quests. Moving the mouse cursor around the screen will pop up identifying text over anything the player can examine, pick up, or fight. The interfaces of Diablo 2 and The Sims are also excellent examples of aesthetically pleasing designs. Each is in keeping with the style, tone, and genre of the game. However, striking this sort of balance of form and function can be difficult to achieve.

Sugmas Toning by Liquid Moon Studio

Figure 3.1 The game controller is the player's link to the game world.

Keyboard. A complex set of keyboard controls may cause novice and casual gamers to become discouraged. In a mainstream game like The Sims or Diablo, adding a complex control scheme might alienate a large portion of the potential audience. However, other games, by their nature, target a specific audience of advanced and core gamers. These types of gamers often favor a more complex set of controls.

Many designers attempt to please both core and casual players by offering different control options. Some games not only have simple click-on-icon/mouse-driven controls for novices, but also have shortcut commands that allow experienced gamers to trigger specific actions with the touch of a key. Other games actually have mappable keyboards, allowing gamers to program their own set of "hot" keys.

Many first-person shooter (FPS) games use a standardized set of keyboard controls. While the player's right hand is using the mouse to look around and aim,

Jupiter by Liquid Moon Studio

Figure 3.2 Real time strategy (RTS) Diversity in Gaming.

the left hand controls character movement. Some early shooters used the directional cursor keys for movement, but their location on the right side of the keyboard made this awkward. Now many FPS games utilize four keys on the far left side of the keyboard: W, A, S, and D.

The use of the W key causes the player to move forward, the S key in reverse, and A and D to the left and right, respectively. A game may often use other keys in the same vicinity. A player uses the Q and E keys to lean or strafe to the left and right. The R key (to the right of the E key) is often RELOAD. The C key (below and to the right of the D key) is usually CROUCH. A player generally uses the space bar to JUMP. The popular WWII shooter Medal of Honor: Allied Assault uses these keys as default settings.

Console Game Pad. Whereas the early consoles had clunky control boxes or old-style joysticks, newer consoles have ergonomically designed game pads. These pads have more buttons than the old controllers but far fewer than a computer keyboard. Because console games are now as sophisticated as PC games, this reduction in control options can limit the designer's choices considerably. This is not necessarily a bad thing: It forces the designer to focus on the options that are most important to gameplay. But it does present problems for some genres.

A standard convention in real-time strategy (RTS) games is to use the point and click/drag/drop functions of a mouse to make command decisions and allocate resources. Creating an RTS console game is inherently problematic because game pads cannot replicate these functions. The PlayStation 2 release Army Men, an RTS game, overcame this limitation well. By moving the cursor to an area and tapping the controller's "circle" button the player could select all the units in that area. Moving over one particular unit and holding down the same key selected all the units of that type. A player could add more units to a selected group by using the "square" button, and the "triangle" button returned the player to the previous selection.

Not all console games have simple control schemes. In fact, the popular console title Metal Gear Solid 2 had an extremely complex set of controls. The left pad controlled movement. The right pad allowed the player to look around in first-person view. Four side buttons controlled weapons, crouching, crawling, climbing, punching, and actions like opening doors. The first left button (L1) was the target lock. Second left (L2) selected inventory items and allowed the player to lean around corners in first-person mode. These complex controls were difficult to master, even for an advanced player, but they provided a level of interaction that was previously unmatched in console titles.

One advantage that game pad controllers have over keyboards is their compact size. A keyboard and mouse require the gamer to sit at a desk or a table. Handheld game pads allow players to lie on a sofa or stretch out on the floor. Duel controllers allow two players to compete on the same screen. Wireless game pads are also available, freeing the gamer even further.

Other Control Devices. A variety of other input devices for computer and console games are also available, and many double as optional controllers for specific game genres. Joysticks work well with flight simulation and space combat games, while steering wheel controllers help to make driving games more immersive.

Many of these devices, and some game pads, are equipped with force feedback features. Force feedback causes the pad, joystick, or steering wheel to vibrate at key moments during game action. This can simulate the revving engine of an automobile, the rumbling of a tank, or the shockwave caused by exploding artillery shells. A game must be programmed for force feedback effects.

The underwater action title Sub Culture is an excellent example of innovative force feedback use. This open-ended game has players trading goods and engaging in combat in an underwater world. Force feedback adds an additional layer of immersion, rocking the submarine during collisions and explosions.

Output. The second important factor to consider when designing a game's UI is output: the feedback that the player receives about the conditions of the game world. Typical feedback might include the player character's current health or the amount of ammunition left in a weapon. During gameplay the game engine is usually keeping track of a massive amount of information, but not all of this is necessary for the players to know.

A well-designed UI will present the most relevant information to the players in an instantly recognizable form. However, a good output system should also become invisible to the players. One glance at the screen should immediately place players within the gaming world and tell them what they need to know quickly and efficiently. Some commonly accepted methods of game output are the graphic user interface (GUI) displays, visual representation, and audio output.

GUI (Graphical User Interface) Displays. The most common output device is the graphical user interface (GUI). This incorporates graphical information that frames the view of the game world or provides transparent heads-up display (HUD) graphics that overlay the screen. The trend in modern games is to make the GUI as unobtrusive as possible to display a larger view of the game world, but the common picture frame style of GUI has also served a different purpose. Many older game engines were not able to render a convincing full-screen image. Aesthetically pleasing GUIs would block a large portion of the screen, shrinking the game world window.

Game Cheats 3.1

A relatively recent development is the creation of keyboards specifically intended for gaming. These keyboards use interchangeable sets of keys to provide controls for different functions. While the default keyset is not gaming specific, keysets are available for several games including Battlefield 2, Doom 3, Everquest 2 and World of Warcraft. An example of a fully customizable "keyboard" is the Ergodex DX1 Input System. The DX1 allows a player to position up to 25 keys anywhere on a base and specify the function of each key. The DX1 can use as many, or as few, keys as the player desires and complex sets of functions can be assigned to each key.

The best GUIs keep things as visual as possible. In Diablo 2 the player's hit points (units of health) and mana levels (units of power needed to cast magical spells) were represented as large globes in the lower corners of the screen filled with red and blue liquid. As these units diminished, the level of liquid dropped. When restored by resting or by drinking potions, the levels went up. With a single glance players instantly knew where they stood with regard to these vital statistics. This is extremely important, especially in fast action. If players stop for even a moment to check statistics, their characters could easily die.

The recent PlayStation 2 action/shooter/driving game The Getaway was remarkable because it did not have a GUI. The game screen was simply a third-person view of the game world. There was nothing to indicate the player's health or ammo supply and no way to access any kind of inventory. There was no way to change weapons because the player could not carry more than one in each hand. In addition, if a player wanted to use a two-handed weapon, he or she had to drop everything.

Although this ambitious design was admirable, it caused some unusual design decisions. Most action games have some sort of healing mechanism. Occasionally players will stumble on an object that will restore all or part of their health. In a modern game this might be a first aid kit. In a fantasy game healing potions are often used. However, in a game with no inventory options or visible health displayed, the designers had to come up with a different way to simulate injury and healing.

In The Getaway the game represented a player's injuries by showing the player's avatar (the graphical representation of the character) bloodied, beaten, and out of breath, eventually slowing to a limping crawl. To heal, the player had merely to lean against a wall for some time. In a game where the developers went to great lengths to make things as realistic as possible, many players saw this as an illogical contrivance. Even in the best of worlds it simply was not believable that leaning against a wall could accelerate the healing of bullet wounds.

Visual Representation. Despite its shortcomings, The Getaway represented an excellent example of another type of output—visual representation. The battered visual representation of the player's avatar in the game left no doubt about the seriousness of the character's injuries, so no health bar was required. Games can represent other data in a similar visual fashion.

When a specific item or weapon is equipped and the player can see it in the avatar's hand, this conveys information about the item's size, appearance, and possible usage. No pop-up window or text is required. If the player has been buffed (a role-playing term indicating that a spell has been cast), giving special enhancements or protections, these might be represented by a glowing aura around the avatar. When the light fades, it is obvious to the player that the spell has worn off.

Audio Output. Audio cues can also give the player important information. The Command & Conquer series of real-time strategy games uses audio cues to great effect.

Figure 3.3 Defining player perspective through character development.

A distinctly feminine computer voice known as Electronic Video Agent (EVE) keeps the player apprised of events going on off-screen, on other portions of the map, with announcements like "Your base is under attack" or "Unit lost." The units themselves respond with audio snippets, identifying their function when selected ("Harvester, ready to roll") and confirming that they have received an order when one has been given ("On the move" or "Understood").

When done well, these audio snippets can provide vital information to the player while adding flavor and character to the game. This can be surprisingly effective. The popular commando unit from the original Command & Conquer had just six short lines of dialogue. In the midst of combat the unit would shout sardonic wisecracks like "I got somethin' for ya!" and "That was left handed!" However, the unit was so popular with players that years later the unit starred in the first-person shooter game Command & Conquer: Renegade.

Another common output issue, especially in a game that requires stealthy sneaking past enemies, is letting the player know where those enemies are. The World War II–based escape game Prisoner of War used a visual output system—a sort of radar screen in the lower left corner of the GUI—to show the player where the guards were. This was a simple solution but a poor design decision. It might have worked well in a high-tech environment in which the player had a handheld radar unit that would provide screen help; but in a period game like POW it seemed anachronistic and illogical. How would a prisoner with no inventory items be able to see this radar screen?

Stealth games like Thief and the No One Lives Forever series solved the same problem brilliantly by using audio output. As the players snuck about they could actually listen for guards conversing, walking in their direction, whistling, mumbling, or clearing their throats. This worked remarkably well because it immersed players in the game world almost immediately. In fact, the No One Lives Forever titles had such clever ambient dialogue that players felt encouraged to sneak, rather than fight, just to overhear conversations that were at once informative and genuinely humorous.

Defining the Player Perspective

"Let's call it retro-futurism. Science fiction, post 9/11, has offered little by way of alternative visions of the future beyond more of the same. Perhaps the only way forward is to retrace our steps."[2]

In gameplay development the shift in perspective from third person to first person has changed the player's view of the world. These changes create an environment with varying content for the player to discover. In this section we look at the wide range of opportunities and challenges the game designer must address in the development of games in various genres.

Types of Player Perspectives

One of the earliest decisions a designer must make is to determine what the player's perspective will be during gameplay. Often the genre of the game determines the type of perspective, but a designer must also consider other elements. Table 3.1 describes the most common player perspectives.

First Person. Action, shooter, and simulation games often use first-person perspective, which provides the most immersive gameplay experience. It puts players right in the middle of the action, giving them a real sense of "thereness" in the game world.

With first-person perspective players essentially see the game through the characters' eyes. Games like this, at least in single-player mode, do not actually provide an avatar that represents the player. Instead players might see the muzzles of their weapons or their hands on a steering wheel. In a first-person game the enemies and monsters are generally the largest and most graphically detailed. This can create a frightening and tension-filled gameplay experience.

Some inventory-based and puzzle-solving adventure games use first-person views to immerse the player in the world of the game. However, unlike many FPS titles, the goal of this immersion is to foster feelings of wonder and exploration rather than tension and fear. Often in these types of game there is no visible hand or weapon. Instead a point-and-click mouse interface handles the interactions with

---

[2] Jenkins, H. (2004). *Henry Jenkins on the retro future*. Retrieved August 12, 2005, from the Institute for the Future Web site: http://future.iftf.org/2004/10/henry_jenkins_o.html.

TABLE 3.1 — Types of player perspectives.

Perspective	Game Experience	Example
First Person	Players view the game through the eyes of a character Provides an immersive experience	Duke Nukem, Doom 3, Halo, Medal of Honor: Allied Assault, Myst, Syberia
Third Person	Players exist within the game world; less immersive Focus on navigating a player's avatar through the game world	Grand Theft Auto 3, Final Fantasy, Lord of the Rings: Return of the King, Prince of Persia, Tomb Raider
Top-Down	Player has a global view of the game world Focus on the big picture to manage the combat units in a strategy game	Command & Conquer: Generals, Frogger, Grand Theft Auto, Legend of Zelda, Total Annihilation
Side-scrolling	Fast-paced; action is viewed from side-view camera angle Does not show as much information about the game world	BlowOut, Duke Nukem: Manhattan Project, Super Mario, Prince of Persia
Isometric	Player has a global view of the game world Provides concise view of three dimensions for strategic positioning	Civilization II, Diablo III, Neverwinter Nights, Sim City, The Sims, Ultima, Warcraft

the environment. For example, a pointing hand or arrow might indicate that the player can move in a particular direction. A small magnifying glass might indicate that the player can examine something more closely. A gear might mean that the player can use an item in the game.

Third Person. In a third-person game players can actually see the characters they are playing from an outside perspective. Sometimes the game presents an over-the-shoulder view, but often camera angles will change depending on the players' movements and actions.

Third-person perspective offers better control over the player's avatar and presents a wider variety of possible actions. This is especially important in games where hand-to-hand combat is part of the action. Martial arts flips, jumps, punches, and kicks simply do not work from a first-person perspective.

Because of the wide variety of possible movements, third-person games are well suited to game pad controllers. Computer mouse-and-keyboard versions of these games are often clumsy and difficult to manage. The third-person perspective has other disadvantages as well. Third-person gameplay can often feel distant and disengaged from the game world. Constantly changing camera views can also present annoying clipping problems. For example, if the player's back is against a wall, the camera view might be stuck behind the avatar, blocking the player's view of the scene. Despite its shortcomings, third-person perspective is still quite popular among many players and developers.

Top-Down. Top-down games have two-dimensional graphics viewed from directly above. With the advent of 3D graphics, this perspective has fallen out of favor in recent years. Most top-down titles have been strategy games, but a few adventure and driving games have also adopted this perspective. In fact, the first two titles in the popular Grand Theft Auto franchise were both top-down, whereas Grand Theft Auto 3 adopted a third-person view.

Side-Scrolling. Side-scrolling games are those in which the player travels from left to right (or in rare cases, right to left) but actually remains in the center of the screen while the playfield shifts or "scrolls" to compensate for the player's movement. Gameplay can involve shooting and destroying targets or simply navigating through the game world.

The first side-scrolling games were arcade titles like Super Mario Brothers. As the use of 3D graphics increased, these simple titles migrated to smaller handheld console titles; but recently side-scrolling games have made a comeback with high-profile releases like Duke Nukem: Manhattan Project and BlowOut. These newer titles have added some 3D graphics and greater movement options to side-scrolling games.

Isometric. Isometric perspective games provide a tilted three-quarter view from above the playing field. This style gave 2D games a three-dimensional appearance and became a popular choice for many real-time strategy and role-playing titles.

The isometric perspective gives players a better view of a large area, enabling them to fight larger groups of enemies in a strategic way. This wider view is also important for role-playing games like Baldur's Gate 2 that allow the player to control an entire party of adventurers.

One disadvantage to using an isometric perspective is that enemies and monsters appear as small figures with little detail. The close-up intensity and immersion provided by first- and third-person games is missing. For some genres like strategy and role-playing titles, this perspective was the only viable choice, but recent advances in graphics technology have changed this dramatically.

Variable Perspectives. The latest series of 3D strategy and role-playing titles have taken advantage of the new 3D acceleration technologies and created games that let the player change perspective during gameplay. RTS games like Warcraft III and

Intry by Liquid Moon Studio

Figure 3.4 Types of player perspectives; what's your perspective?

RPGs such as Neverwinter Nights and Dungeon Siege allow the player to view the scene from an isometric perspective, zoom in close, or rotate the scene to view it from any angle in stunning clarity.

Other games use different perspectives for different activities. Some even allow the player to switch from third to first person using a keystroke. For example, in Grand Theft Auto 3, designed in a third-person perspective, the player can switch to the top-down perspective of the first two versions of the game. The massively multiplayer online RPG Everquest allows the player to choose first-person, third-person, or top-down view.

Game Menu Options

"Most designers start off as programmers or artists. . . . From my perspective, I was making my own games, programming them, doing all the artwork, the production, level design, and everything because I didn't have anybody else to do it for me. That background helped give me the perspective it takes to pull a product together and have a creative vision for it. Being a designer is about having a creative vision and adhering to it."[3]

In this section we examine the types of options provided by game menus. The challenge facing the game designer is to allow players to tailor the characteristics of a game to suit their preferred style of play. The design and development of the game should provide options that reflect the players' perspective. Designers use menus to present these options and give each player the opportunity to choose the visual style, the sounds, and the general conditions that will be in effect during the game.

Types of Menu Options

Most games have a menu of options available to the player upon loading a game. Table 3.2 shows some commonly available options.

Tutorial. Some games give the player an optional training level or mission that is not part of the game proper. Upon loading the game, the player can choose between playing the tutorial and jumping straight into the game. We will discuss tutorials at length in the next section, which describes methods for educating the player.

New Game. This option loads the first level of a new game.

Save Game. This option varies; some games provide a Save Anywhere option. This type of save is generally presented as part of the game's main menu. The player can exit to the main menu at any point during the game and save the action. If players die or perform a regrettable action, they can reload the game and pick up

---

[3] Colayco, B. (2005). *So you're a game designer*. Retrieved August 12, 2005, from the Gamespot Web site: http://www.gamespot.com/features/6129276/index.html.

TABLE 3.2   Examples of game menu options.

Category	Sample Menu Options / Features
Configuration	*Audio, Controls, Video*: Players can adjust how the game plays, looks and sounds
Education/Help	*Stand-Alone and In-Game Tutorials*: Provide instruction and assistance before, and during, gameplay
Game Play	*Load, New and Saved Game*: Allows the player to resume or restart the game or replay a favorite level

from the last save. Some games even provide a Quick Save option, allowing players to save with a single keystroke. Many players, especially those from the casual school of gaming, prefer a Save Anywhere option because this option is the most forgiving.

Other games do not allow the player to save at all. Instead the game interface automatically saves when the player reaches a certain point in the game (often at the end of a mission or upon the completion of a mission objective.) This type of mechanism makes a game much more challenging, but it can also force the player to repeat large portions of a game many times to advance to the next level. Core gamers often welcome this type of challenge, but novices and casual gamers can become frustrated by this quickly. A third type of game save mechanism is the Checkpoint Save, which is commonly used in console games. With this style of game, the player must find a specific location or object in the game world in order to save the game.

The game saving issue has become controversial in the game industry. Many players and designers have adopted the view that a Save Anywhere option is a form of cheating. However, having a Save Anywhere feature does not require a player to use it. Core players will always have the option to delay saving their games until the end of a level, but not providing this feature will almost certainly cause some novice and casual gamers to go elsewhere.

Developer Io Interactive released the game Hitman without a Save Anywhere feature. The game was popular with core gamers, and many praised this design decision. However, the game was also heavily criticized for the same reason, and sales suffered. Later, when Io released Hitman 2, the company added a Save Anywhere option. The sequel became a best seller.

Load Game. This option allows players to reload the game if their character dies or to reload an earlier saved game if they wish to try a different set of actions.

Quit. This option allows players to exit the game completely. Most games also give players the option to save the game before quitting, or to abort quitting—a vital option if the player chooses the quit option accidentally.

Video Configuration. Video options have become increasingly important in recent years. Game developers are under increasing pressure to produce higher-quality graphics and dramatic lighting effects so that gamers can take advantage of the newest system and graphics cards. However, many players cannot afford to upgrade to state-of-the-art hardware. Consequently, games must support many different systems with different capabilities and resolutions. The video options menu allows players to tailor the game for their systems. Video settings can have a dramatic effect on the speed and quality of a game's graphics. Some common display settings adjust the display resolution, color depth, texture detail, and gamma correction.

Resolution. The resolution setting determines the level of detail used when graphics appear on a screen. The typical default resolution (which works well for an average computer monitor) is 800 × 600, but today's games can utilize resolution of 1600 × 1200 or higher if the system will allow it. The resolution represents the number of horizontally and vertically displayed pixels on the screen. Higher resolutions require more processing power and memory and can often lower a game's frame rate (the number of complete image scans contained in one second of play), causing a choppy or stuttered image.

Color Depth. Color depth, which is usually either 16-bit or 32-bit, is the maximum number of distinct colors displayable at one time. A 16-bit setting can display 65,536 colors, while a 24-bit setting can display 16,777,216 colors. The higher setting can adversely affect a game's frame rate.

Texture Detail. Most games come with a low, medium, or high setting for texture detail. The various settings depend on the system specifications and the desired frame rate. Some games also allow more advanced settings, allowing the player to choose a type of texture filter or specific texture details for models, terrain, effects, and shadows.

Gamma Correction. Gamma correction is simply an adjustment to the brightness of the game's graphics. This control is ostensibly included to allow gamers with faulty monitors to brighten or darken the image when the monitor's own brightness control is not working correctly. However, gamma correction can give a player an unplanned advantage. When a player is in a dark area without an in-game light source (like a torch or flashlight), it is often possible to adjust this control in order to see.

Audio Configuration. Audio controls are generally much simpler than video controls, and usually involve setting the volume levels for different audio categories.

Earth 3D by Liquid Moon Studio

Figure 3.5 3D Models before the texture.

These can include music, sound effects, or dialogue. Sometimes the audio configuration will also require that the player specify the system's sound card or speaker configuration.

Controls Configuration. The game controller is an input device used to control the video game on a game console or personal computer. Depending on the system, the controller can be a keyboard, mouse, joystick, steering wheel, game pad, or any of the other input devices that are available. Players can alter the configuration of the input device to match their preferences in the game application. This ability to configure the controller gives gamers the power to customize the way they will play the game. For example, in many recent games, players can customize the keyboard commands to suit their own style of gameplay.

Methods for Educating the Player

"The short answer is that designers of good games have hit on excellent methods for getting people to learn and to enjoy learning. The longer answer is more complex. Integral to this answer are the good principles of learning built into successful games."[4]

The level of gameplay depends on the player's ability to learn the game: A player comes with a history of developed skills. There are challenges every time a player opens a new game. Playing skills are developed through the cognitive behaviors and learning patterns developed by the designer. In this section we look at the educating patterns of gameplay and discuss the various methods used by game designers.

Educating the Player

Most games come with instruction manuals. The truth is that the vast majority of players do not want to read a set of instructions before playing a new game. Most players jump right in and start playing. A designer must consider this from the beginning. If players find a game too complex, they are not likely to continue playing. This presents the designer with an important problem to solve. How do you educate the players and keep them entertained at the same time?

---

[4] Gee, J. P. (2005, June). Learning by design: Good video games as learning machines. *E-Learning, 2(1)*. Retrieved August 12, 2005, from http://www.wwwords.co.uk/pdf/viewpdf .asp?j=elea&vol=2&issue=1&year=2005&article=2_Gee_ELEA_2_1_web&id=67.177.228.243.

One way is to make the interface so intuitively obvious that players do not need training on how to play the game. It becomes a simple matter of using common sense. As we have discussed, games like Diablo and The Sims have achieved this level of simplicity. However, many games by nature have a learning curve. A talented designer can make this educational period interesting and enjoyable. You can accomplish this in a number of ways by using

- Real-world conventions.

- Accepted computer conventions.

- Standard gaming conventions.

- Game tutorials.

Real-World Conventions. This is the simplest and most obvious way to give the player a head start from the outset. Imagine, for example, that a player purchases a new game and loads it without reading the manual. She immediately finds herself standing before a giant, salivating monster on the attack. The game's interface uses F2 to draw a weapon and Alt-P to attack. The player does not know this and is concerned only with a hostile enemy and the fact that she is in danger. She clicks on the monster, rushes into its gaping maw, and is devoured immediately.

Now the player can reload the game, probably a number of times, and go through a potentially frustrating trial-and-error process to find the proper attack command. Alternatively she can pick up the game's manual and search through it for the proper keystroke. Whatever their choice, players will eventually learn the proper commands to allow them to continue playing, but they may already feel cheated. The players tried to put up a defense, but the game penalized them for failing to initiate what should have been an intuitive action.

Now imagine that instead of a random keystroke, there is a button on the game interface with a picture of a sword or a gun. The players' first instinct would be to click on the button because in the real world, a gun or a sword is a weapon for self-defense. When they click on the button, an avatar draws a weapon and attacks the monster. The players learned how to initiate the attack, but now the learning experience is different: The game rewards them for intuition and quick thinking. Instead of an exercise in frustration, the players' education has become fun.

Using real-world experiences when designing a game can greatly increase players' enjoyment. Logical choices become the best choices.

Accepted Computer Conventions. As we described earlier in the chapter, nongamers are comfortable with standard point-and-click and drag-and-drop mouse functions. A game can incorporate other standard computer conventions in its design. For example, a game can support standard methods for opening, closing, and resizing windows. In addition, many software applications have tool tips, which are small blocks of text that pop up when the cursor moves over a button or item on the screen.

These familiar ways to display information can be readily adapted to a game's interface, giving the player instant and intuitive control over many game functions.

Standard Gaming Conventions. Standard game conventions are less intuitive, especially for the novice player. However, many of these conventions grew out of the real world and computer conventions, and when used consistently they can be helpful. The commonly used directional controls employ the W-A-S-D keyboard scheme, but many other keyboard and mouse controls are commonly used in a wide variety of games.

The following list shows some of the characters in a standard keyboard mapping:

Left mouse button	Select.
Right mouse button	Brings up list of options for this item.
Directional arrows	Move in selected direction (alternative to W-A-S-D).
C	Crouch or crawl.
R	Reload weapon.
ESC	Pause and go to main menu.
P	Pause game.
M	Display map of area.

There are other types of standard gaming conventions as well. A creature identified in green text is generally friendly, or at least, nonhostile. Red text denotes a hostile creature. Bright text will often denote an active state or the selection of an item. Flashing text is often a warning that the state of an object, spell, or creature is about to change. These conventions are not universal, but they are so common that designers can give their players an extra edge by adopting as many as the game will allow.

Game Tutorials. Finally, the most obvious method of educating the player is directly via a game tutorial. There are generally two types of tutorials—in-game and stand-alone.

In-Game Tutorials. Several games use in-game tutorials to educate players. Generally this involves a first level, mission, or scenario that leads players through a series of actions that teaches them the primary functions of the game interface. At first players perform the simplest tasks: moving through the game world, jumping, or accessing inventory. As the scenario progresses, they are likely to be given some sort of combat challenge or encounter.

An in-game tutorial that has good design components will go to great lengths not to disturb the atmosphere of the game. The designer should present information unobtrusively because the game's narrative has already begun. Sometimes this is as simple as pop-up text providing hints. Other times a nonplayer character (NPC) can serve as an instructor or mentor.

The FPS game No One Lives Forever 2 used an ingenious tutorial device in its opening level. The game had the player assuming the role of secret agent Kate Archer. A big part of gameplay involved various James Bond–style gizmos and gadgets. In the opening sequence, Kate's introduction to one of these gadgets was a robotic mynah bird that appeared from time to time, perched on a fence or a tree limb. Her commander used the robot to watch her moves and communicate with her during the mission. Consequently, the bird appeared at key moments with important information regarding gameplay. This imaginative plot device made the tutorial seem natural and part of the story.

The introductory, or educational, portion of a game should be fun and engaging, but it should never be too difficult. The player is the hero of the game. As such, he should enter feeling empowered and in control. The initial challenges should feel genuine but never life-threatening. As the gameplay progresses, the danger will increase. By the time players face a challenging opponent or scenario, they are used to the game. Now the increased danger is not a frustration, but rather a challenge that the player can overcome.

Stand-Alone Tutorials. The second type of tutorial presents information outside the game world. For example, the game might display a special training level or mission as an option on the main menu of the game. Upon loading the game, the player can choose between playing the tutorial and jumping straight into the game. Medal of Honor: Allied Assault is an example of a game with a stand-alone tutorial. Upon starting a new game, the player has the option of entering basic training. The voice of a NPC drill instructor will then lead the player through an obstacle course, demolition exercises, and target practice to familiarize her with the basic mechanics of play.

There is a danger with this type of tutorial. Some players will view it as an electronic instruction manual. They might think that because the tutorial is not part of the actual game it is not worth their time. Like the paper manual, they might ignore it and jump straight into the game. These players might end up walking away in frustration. However, for some games, a stand-alone tutorial can be an asset. If the game is a sequel to an already published title and the gameplay mechanics are similar, some players might not need a tutorial. It may be frustrating or insulting to require an experienced player to participate in a tutorial.

A stand-alone tutorial is an excellent way to provide entertaining, interactive education for players before they enter the game proper, but the designer must never assume that all players will take advantage of it. A game developer's first mission is to consider how long it will take players to learn a game, giving the players ample time to become familiar with the game and rewarding them for their early efforts.

D_Koei by Liquid Moon Studio

Figure 3.6 Character development and game play increase the player's emersion.

SUMMARY

Understanding the different components of a game is essential to designing a game that is intuitive and enjoyable to play. The game designer must choose the best way to present the mechanics of gameplay to players. This chapter provided an overview of the functions of the user interface and the other components used in a game design. How the designer plans the user interface influences how players will interact with a game, and it is important to take components such as graphical displays and input and output devices into consideration. It is also essential to remember that an important part of a game's design is educating the user.

The key facts and concepts covered in this chapter included the two primary factors necessary to consider when designing a game interface: the actions taken by the player and the feedback gained from the gaming world. The game designer needs to understand how the player views critical components such as the computer mouse, the keyboard, and the game pad controller. The designer also needs to understand the commonly accepted methods of game output such as the GUI, visual representation, and audio output. Knowledge of the common types of player perspective (first-person, third-person, top-down, side-scrolling, isometric, and variable) is also important.

The tutorial is one of the most important options that game interfaces give the player, but the designer also needs to let the player choose a new game, save an existing game, load the game, quit the game, and have some control over video and audio configuration. The common video configuration display settings include resolution, color depth, texture detail, and gamma correction. Audio configurations usually affect volume levels for different audio categories and may require that the player specify the system's sound card.

The two basic types of game tutorials are tutorials programmed within the game itself and stand-alone tutorials that the player can read before and during the game. There are several other effective strategies to educate the player: applying real-world conventions, where the player clicks on an icon that makes sense in the context of the game; the use of accepted computer conventions; and the use of standard gaming conventions.

ADDITIONAL READING

Courtesy of *Into the Pixel*: Chinatown Level Study

Artist:
Rich Mahon, Jon Gwyn, Chandana Ekanayake

Game research: Perspective. (2002). Retrieved August 12, 2005, from http://www.game-research.com/perspective.asp.

Irving, R. (2002, April). *Lost along the way: Design pitfalls on the road from concept to completion.* From the Gamasutra Web site: http://ludumdare.com/articles/?link=v&arid=14. (Requires username and password to access page.)

Kremecek, M. (n.d.). *The interface part I: Mapping the player*. Retrieved August 12, 2005, from the GameDev.net Web site: http://www.gamedev.net/reference/design/features/ui1/.

Kremecek, M. (n.d.). *The interface part II: Feeding the player*. Retrieved August 12, 2005, from the GameDev.net Web site: http://www.gamedev.net/reference/design/features/ui2/.

Mandel, B. (2001). *Viewing perspective and game genres*. Retrieved August 12, 2005, from the Adrenaline Vault Web site: http://www.avault.com/articles/getarticle.asp?name=perspectives.

Rouse III, R. (2001). The elements of gameplay. In *Game design theory and practice*. Dallas, TX: WordWare Publishing, Inc. [Electronic version.] Retrieved August 12, 2005, from http://www.gamasutra.com/features/20010627/rouse_01.htm. (Requires username and password to access page.)

Rouse III, R. (2001, May). The console and PC: Separated at birth? *Computer Graphics, 35(2)*. ACM Siggraph. [Electronic version.] Retrieved August 12, 2005, from http://www.paranoidproductions.com/gamingandgraphics/gg5_01.html.

Sánchez-Crespo, D. R. (1999, November). *Learn faster to play better: How to shorten the learning cycle*. Retrieved August 12, 2005, from the Gamasutra Web site: http://www.gamasutra.com/features/19991108/dalmau_01.htm. (Requires username and password to access page.)

Saving... Please acknowledge lack of skills. (n.d.). Retrieved August 12, 2005, from the Gamespy.com Web site: http://www.gamespy.com/legacy/editorials/saving.shtm.

Practice Questions

1. Why is the computer mouse an effective game input device, especially for novice or casual players?

2. What is visual representation? How does a game designer use it as an output device to deliver information about the game world?

3. What are the advantages and disadvantages of using a first-person perspective in a game?

4. Why has the issue of the saving a game become so controversial in the game industry in recent years? What is your opinion about this issue?

5. Why is it important for a game to educate the player at its outset? What are the advantages and disadvantages of the education methods described in the chapter?

CHAPTER ASSESSMENT

Courtesy of *Into the Pi* Yellow Room

Artist: Stephan Martiniere

Lab Exercises

A game designer must understand the importance of the game's components and the use of intuitive game controls. The goal in performing this lab exercise is to explain how to play a game by showing a sketch of your user interface.

Each student computer should have the following free demos installed:

• Zork 1 (available at http://www.csd.uwo.ca/Infocom/Download/zork1.zip).

• Neverwinter Nights (available at http://nwn.bioware.com/downloads/demo.html).

Choose one of the games included with the course materials.

1. Play the game for 15–20 minutes and then make a detailed sketch of the user interface.

2. Note the player's options and the function of each controller (such as on-screen buttons and cursor symbols). Be as detailed as possible. The goal is to provide enough information to describe the workings of the game to someone who has never seen it.

3. Using only the sketch of the UI you created, describe the game you chose to a classmate who is not familiar with it. Be as clear and concise as possible. Now have your classmate describe a different game to you.

4. Play the game your classmate described to you, giving special attention to the UI. Makes notes about the experience. You will write a report on the experience as part of your written assignment.

Written Assignment

Write a short essay (100–200 words) that describes your experience with the lab exercise.

• How easy or difficult was it to make your classmate understand the various interface functions of your game?

• How clear was your classmate's description of his or her game?

• How difficult was it to play the game based on that description?

• Did the UI seem intuitive or needlessly complex? Explain your answer.

Courtesy of *Into the Pixel*: Ryu Hayabusa

Artist: Tomonobu Itagaki, Hiroaki Matsui

MANUSCRIPT REFERENCES

Bates, B. (2001). Game design: The art and business of creating games. Roseville, CA: Prima Publishing.

Colayco, B. (2005). So you're a game designer. Retrieved August 12, 2005, from the Gamespot Web site: http://www.gamespot.com/features/6129276/index.html.

Game research: Perspective. (2002). Retrieved August 12, 2005, from http://www.game research.com/perspective.asp.

Gee, J. P. (2005, June). Learning by design: Good video games as learning machines. E-Learning, 2(1). Retrieved August 12, 2005, from http://www.wwwords.co.uk/pdf/viewpdf.asp?j=elea&vol=2&issue=1&year=2005&article=2_Gee_ELEA_2_1_web&id=67.177.228.243.

Hallford, N., & Hallford, J. (2001). Swords and circuitry: A designer's guide to role-playing games. Roseville, CA: Prima Publishing.

Howland, G. (2002, February). The interface's impact on gameplay. From the Ludumdare.com Web site: http://ludumdare.com/articles/?link=v&arid=14.

Irving, R. (2002, April). Lost along the way: Design pitfalls on the road from concept to completion. From the Gamasutra Web site: http://ludumdare.com/articles/?link=v&arid=14.

Kremecek, M. (n.d.). The interface part I: Mapping the player. Retrieved August 12, 2005, from the GameDev.net Web site: http://www.gamedev.net/reference/design/features/ui1/.

Kremecek, M. (n.d.). The interface part II: Feeding the player. Retrieved August 12, 2005, from the GameDev.net Web site: http://www.gamedev.net/reference/design/features/ui2/.

Mandel, B. (2001). Viewing perspective and game genres. Retrieved August 12, 2005, from the Adrenaline Vault Web site: http://www.avault.com/articles/getarticle.asp?name=perspectives.

Rouse III, R. (2001). The elements of gameplay. In Game design theory and practice. Dallas, TX: WordWare Publishing, Inc. [Electronic version.] Retrieved August 12, 2005, from http://www.gamasutra.com/features/20010627/rouse_01.htm.

Rouse III, R. (2001, May). The console and PC: Separated at birth? Computer Graphics, 35(2). ACM Siggraph. [Electronic version.] Retrieved August 12, 2005, from http://www.paranoidproductions.com/gamingandgraphics/gg5_01.html.

Sánchez-Crespo, D. R. (1999, November). Learn faster to play better: How to shorten the learning cycle. Retrieved August 12, 2005, from the Gamasutra Web site: http://www.gamasutra.com/features/19991108/dalmau_01.htm.

Saving... Please acknowledge lack of skills. (n.d.). Retrieved August 12, 2005, from the Gamespy.com Web site: http://www.gamespy.com/legacy/editorials/saving.shtm.

Courtesy of *Into the Pixel*: Enzo in Florence

Artists: Ben O'Sullivan, Gren Atherton, Mark Sharratt, Matt Watts

Courtesy of 3D artist Bill Blakesley

CHAPTER 4

Game Components: Part Two

Understanding the various design components of a game is vital to any study of game design and technology. This chapter completes our discussion of this subject by examining visual design components like lighting and special effects, the technical components that make up a game engine, and narrative components like dramatic structure and character development.

After completing this chapter, you will be able to:

- Describe the importance of lighting and special effects in a game, and identify some of the commonly used types of these effects.

- Describe the use of animation in games.

- Discuss the use of video in games.

- Describe the software used by modelers and texture artists.

- Define and discuss the term *game engine*.

- Describe the basic elements of narrative structure in games.

- Describe the importance of character development in games.

Virgile Delporte

Vice President of Sales & Managing Director, Americas for Virtools Canada Inc.

In the last few years the game development industry has seen some dramatic changes. Among others due to the complexity of the gaming consoles, game development has become more and more complex, requiring many more people to collaborate over an average rather long period of 18–24 months. Game engines and dedicated render engines have started to emerge, providing the groundwork for game programmers to build their games on. The most successful game engine/middleware, widely adopted by game developers, was Renderware by Criterion (previously owned by Canon)—thanks to their great support for the PlayStation 2.

Today the bottleneck for large game production is definitely not the rendering engine but rather is the management of huge amounts of data and working with a rapid development environment, allowing the very fast validation/invalidation of game ideas.

Virtools has actually been around since 1999, and we took a different approach to game development from the other game engines/middleware. Rather than considering the ultimate game development bottleneck would be the real-time 3D engine, we thought we should offer user-friendly software to dramatically speed up the development of interactivity by providing a visual programming interface and ready-to-use functions, which virtually would allow the development of 3D games and other highly interactive applications without a line of code.

Visual Components

"The details are not the details. They make the design."[1]

Components that affect the "look" of a game are increasingly important as graphics technology becomes more sophisticated. Let's review some of these critical elements.

Lighting and Special Effects

The use of lighting and special effects in a game can have a huge impact on the experience of gameplay. Not only do these effects help to immerse the player in the game world, but they can also provide valuable feedback to the player in the form

---

[1] Eames, C. (n.d.). Retrieved on September 26, 2005, from the ThinkExist Web site: http://en.thinkexist.com/quotation/the-details-are-not-the-details-they-make-the/371679.html.

of visual representation. In this section we examine the types of effects commonly used in games today.

Image created by Bill Blakesley

Figure 4.1 Various textures of light.

Lighting. Lighting in a game world can be extremely important. The proper use of lighting can bring life to a 3D environment and reveal important information about the objects in it. It is one of the easiest and most effective ways to add realism to a game.

The game Quake was the first to use "lightmaps" to create realistic lighting effects. A lightmap is a type of gray-shaded texture map that overlays the other textures in a game to simulate shadows from light sources (Table 4.1).

TABLE 4.1	Types of lighting effects used in game design
Type	**Example Effects**
Ambient Lighting (fills an entire scene, no position or direction)	• Glow in the sky around a city • Blue ambient light to set the mood for a player entering a cold area
Diffuse Lighting (directional, even illumination)	• Heavy overcast day • Light on a playground scene
Source Lighting (light from particular source)	• Flickering light of a torch • Car headlights
Specularity (light causes a hotspot)	• Shiny bit on an apple • Highlight off the faceplate on a space suit

Source: Dr. Thelma Looms, Contributing Author.

However, lightmaps are static. Later games introduced dynamic lighting: Shadows would change and react to moving light sources, which would correctly illuminate objects in the game environment. This introduced another level of realism.

Figure 4.2 An example of ambient lighting.

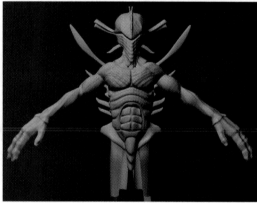

Figure 4.3 An example of diffuse lighting.

Figure 4.4 An example of source lighting.

What are the common types of lighting and their effects on rendered objects in the game environment?

Ambient Light. Ambient is a general flood of light that fills a given area. Ambient light (Figure 4.2) illuminates objects but gives no clue as to the source of the light. A moonless twilight is a good example of ambient lighting. Objects are visible, but they do not cast distinct shadows.

Diffuse Light. Objects lit by diffuse light (Figure 4.3) receive illumination from a specific direction. Diffuse lighting is constant. The position of the viewer will not change the way lighting affects an object. A sunlit day is a good example of diffuse lighting: The direction of illumination depends only on the sun's angle in the sky.

Source Lighting. As the name suggests, this type of lighting comes from a particular source within the environment (Figure 4.4). This could be the flickering light of a torch, a square of moonlight cast by an open window, or even a wandering searchlight. Moving source lighting, such as a flaming projectile lighting up dungeon walls as it flies toward an enemy, can be a particularly spectacular effect.

Specularity. Specularity, or specular reflection, is the amount of light reflected from an object's surface (Figure 4.5). Specularity depends on where the light hits the surface and the position of the viewer. Display calculations must take into account the locations of the camera and the player's avatar to render the reflected highlights properly.

Depth Cueing Effects. Fog effects are one of the simplest ways to add realism to a game by giving the illusion of an atmospheric haze or mist. The effect is usually achieved through a process called *depth cueing*. The farther away a game object is, the hazier and darker it becomes. The game Soldier of Fortune 2 used fog effects extensively.

Fog effects can be integral components of gameplay. The fog effects used in the horror survival game Silent Hill hid enemies and created a sense of tension and dread. Because players could see only within a small area lit by their flashlights, the sudden emergence of a creature was startling.

Depth cueing can help simulate underwater environments. The game Aquanox combined it with other special effects to create a believable and realistic underwater environment.

Shadows. Shadows are another critical visual component. Not only do shadows add a sense of realism to an environment by creating an additional sense of depth, but they can also have a tremendous impact on the mood and atmosphere of a game. The eagerly awaited Doom 3 has some of the most advanced shadow effects ever rendered, creating a truly terrifying and immersive environment.

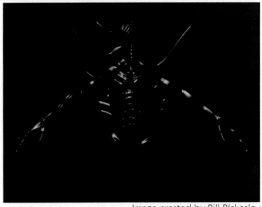

Image created by Bill Blakesley

Figure 4.5 An example of specularity.

There are a number of ways to create shadows in a game. The simplest is to add polygons to the bottom of an object, creating a false shadow. This kind of shadow is actually a part of the object itself and does not have any bearing on the direction that the light is coming from. In recent years, increasingly complex algorithms have created dynamic shadows that react realistically to moving objects and light sources in the game environment.

Shadows can also be an important part of gameplay. The games Splinter Cell and No One Lives Forever 3 allowed the player to sneak stealthily through shadows, avoiding guards and other enemies. The enemy AI actually behaves differently if the player's character is standing or crouching in a shadowy area.

Optical Conventions. Over the years certain optical conventions from the arts of still photography and filmmaking have found their way into the world of game design. These familiar conventions are optical artifacts that came from standard photographic techniques. By mimicking these conventions while rendering game graphics, designers have found an easy way to add a certain photorealistic element to their games. In this section we discuss some of these conventions.

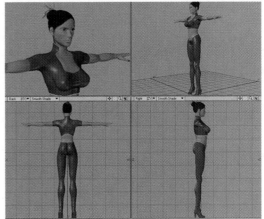

Image created by Ola Gardner

Figure 4.6 3D Model character development for game play.

Motion Blur. Motion blur is a photographic effect that is a direct result of a slow shutter speed. Capturing a fast-moving image or background on film distorts the image. In still photography and motion pictures, motion blur has come to represent dynamic motion.

The human eye creates this same effect. The retina of the eye retains an image for one-tenth of a second before moving on to another image. This phenomenon, known as *persistence of vision,* allows the eye to see motion pictures and video images as constantly moving rather than as a series of still frames or image scans. If the images are moving quickly, this retinal "frame rate" causes them to blur. This is why a propeller spinning at high speed begins to resemble a disk.

The stop-motion animation used in classic films like King Kong is an excellent example of how movement looks without motion blur. No matter how skilled the animators, the photography of the models gave a series of still pictures. There was no realistic blur to indicate actual motion. The finished product, while impressive for the time, still looked wrong.

3D models without motion blur present a similar appearance. Adding motion blur to the graphics is a simple process that greatly improves the look and realism of the game.

Depth of Field. *Depth of field* is another photographic term. It refers to the distance between the nearest and farthest objects in the field of view that are in sharp focus. In photography this distance depends on the aperture opening on a camera. The depth of field becomes smaller as the aperture opening increases in size and larger as the aperture opening decreases.

Photographers and filmmakers often use a small depth of field to achieve a specific effect. If an object in the foreground is in sharp focus and the background is blurred, the focus is on the object. A rapid change in focus, often called a *rack focus,* is a cinematic effect that forces the viewer's eye to travel as the focal plane shifts. You will see this type of cinematic effects in a game's cut scenes.

Depth of field effects also appears in games. The recent console title Starfox Adventures: Dinosaur Planet, for example, used simulated depth of field effects in combination with depth cueing to simulate large environments.

Lens Flares. A third type of optical convention is the *lens flare.* When a camera lens is directed at a bright light, that light is often refracted like a prism, forming a sort of halo effect. This flare of light appears as a circular ring with reddish tinges at the periphery and violet near the center. Sometimes camera lenses create secondary, hexagonal flares by refracting light internally. As motion blur has come to represent dynamic motion, lens flares are associated with extremely intense sources of light.

Game designers often add lens flares to simulate the bright light of a sun or an enemy searchlight. The hero of the survival horror game Silent Hill 2 wielded a flashlight through much of the game that created realistic lens flares whenever it pointed at the game's "camera."

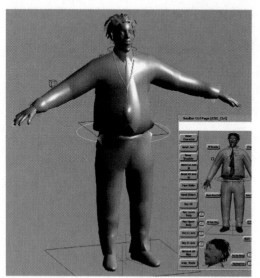

Image created by Joe Gardner for Entertainment Arts Research

Figure 4.7 3D Character Development.

Overview of Animation

Another important game design component is animation. The animation in a game is what breathes life into the creatures, characters, and landscapes of the game world. Most game animations fall into one of two categories: character animation and particle animation. Let's examine each of these in depth.

Character Animation. Character animation involves the creation of movements for all of the creatures and characters in a game. In a third-person game this will also include the player's avatar.

Traditional Character Animation Moves. Character animation consists of a series of short actions that combine to form a continuous string of believable movement. Separately rendered moves need to flow smoothly from one to the next. They also need to fit the needs of the game; a character in a basketball game, for example, would have no need for a death animation. However, many frequently used moves have become somewhat traditional. Some traditional moves include these:

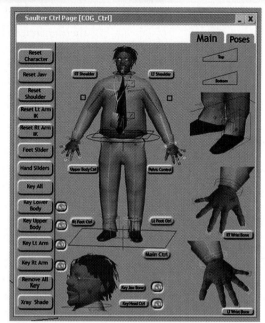

Image created by Joe Gardner
for Entertainment Arts Research

Figure 4.8 Animation choices.

- **Idle:** For a character or avatar to seem like a living, breathing entity, it must have some animated movements, even when at rest. Typical idle movements are yawning, glancing about, shifting weight from one foot to the other, and the like. In games today, players look for idle animations to be surprising and entertaining, in addition to being realistic.

- **Running:** In most action games, the default movement mode of the main character is running or jogging. This jog should seem natural and fitting for the character type because it is probably this animation that the player will see most frequently. The way characters or creatures move can reveal a lot about them. Do they strut, swagger, or slink? Do they have a limp? Are they male or female?

- **Walking:** When characters are not running, their walk is animated. This should be a logical variation of their running movement.

- **Sneaking:** Stealth games also require a sneaking animation. This has traditionally been a crouching walk, but recent stealth games like Splinter Cell have given the player contextual options for sneaking. For example, if players crouch with their backs to a wall, they can sneak sideways along the wall. If they leap up and hit the proper control while in a narrow corridor, they can do a special "split jump," pinning themselves against the walls of the corridor high above their enemies. These stealth options all require special animations.

- **Injury:** Characters must react in a realistic fashion to injury. This could involve any number of special animations, including shooting, stabbing, punching, and burning by fire.

- **Death:** In an action game, the character will likely die a number of times. Like the various types of injury reactions, there are death animations tailored to the various ways a character can meet an untimely demise. Death sequences do not cycle.

- **Attack:** There are many different types of attack animations, depending on the style of a game. Fighting games might require various punches, kicks, and flips, whereas shooters require aiming and firing animations. In a first-person game this might be as simple as showing the muzzle of the weapon of choice, but third-person games require much more complex animations.

- **Other actions:** Different types of games will require a variety of other custom animations. A fighting game might require "knock down" and "get back up" animations. Action adventure titles might require animations for ladder climbing, swimming, picking locks, driving cars, and so on. Almost all third-person games also use animations for jumping, crawling, climbing, talking, and adopting a defensive posture.

Animation Cycles. Some animated moves are cycles of motion. When a character is running, for example, the animation cycle will repeat to present the illusion of an extended run. A skillful character animator can synchronize the first and last frame of the move perfectly so that the cycle repeats smoothly and flawlessly.

The real difficulty comes in synchronizing the transition from one animated move to another of a completely different type. When a character is running and the player suddenly stops, crouches, and takes aim with a weapon, a number of moves begin in rapid succession. To make these types of transitions smoothly requires the animator to create shorter bridging motions; this is called blending.

The use of analog controls in the next generation consoles creates an additional challenge for character animators. For example, rather than activating a simple trigger switch from walking to running, sometimes the player can control character movement along a gradual range of motion. Therefore, designers add additional smooth animation states between walking and running.

Motion Capture. One popular and effective way to create realistic character animation is a process called motion capture. This involves placing motion capture sensors on various parts of an actor's body. These sensors allow a computer to capture information about the position of the actor's skeleton during a performed series of movements. This information can help a game designer precisely recreate those movements with a rendered character.

Motion capture has become popular in recent years; it can recreate fight choreography, dance moves, athletics, and even complex facial animations.

Particle Animation. Animating real-world effects like smoke, rain, fire, explosions, and the like are an extremely difficult matter using conventional methods of animation. Particle animation is a process that allows a vast number of virtual objects, or "particles," to move in accordance with a predefined set of rules. These particles can be very simple objects created with just a few polygons, or they can be much more complex. Thus a game can utilize particle animation to create effects as varied as a rainstorm or a swarming school of fish.

The predefined rules that affect the movement of the particles usually simulate the physical conditions of the real world. These rules incorporate factors that change the movement of the particles—gravity, wind, and surface texture—as well as properties of the particles themselves, such as mass and velocity.

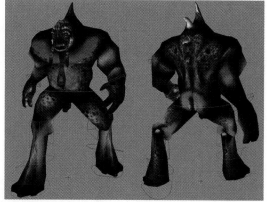

Image created by Joe Gardner
for Entertainment Arts Research

Figure 4.9 Animation choices at work.

Introduction to Modeling and Textures

3D modeling is the process of creating virtual objects that populate the game world using high-end imaging packages such as SoftImage, Maya, or 3D Studio Max. Modelers, working from concept art, use this software to create 3D wire meshes that define the size, shape, and properties of the objects. Sometimes modeling can also involve preparing an object for animation. Certain objects, like creatures or characters, can be fitted with skeletal framework that determines their kinetic movements.

After objects are modeled in wire mesh, they are fitted with "skins" that give them a more detailed appearance. This process is *texture mapping*. Texture artists create two-dimensional images that act as a sort of "wallpaper" that covers and/ or wraps around various objects in the game. Examples of commonly used textures for inanimate objects include metal, concrete, stone, brick, and wood grain. Organic textures, used for creatures and characters, include skin, scales, and fur. We will discuss the duties of the 3D modeler and texture artist at length at a later point in this book.

Game Cheats 4.1

Will video games look as real as real life?

Modeling and texture technologies with the latest generation game engines are pushing the envelope and providing images that are very close to reality. Normal maps and pixel and vertex shaders allow developers to create realistically detailed models that can run in real-time.

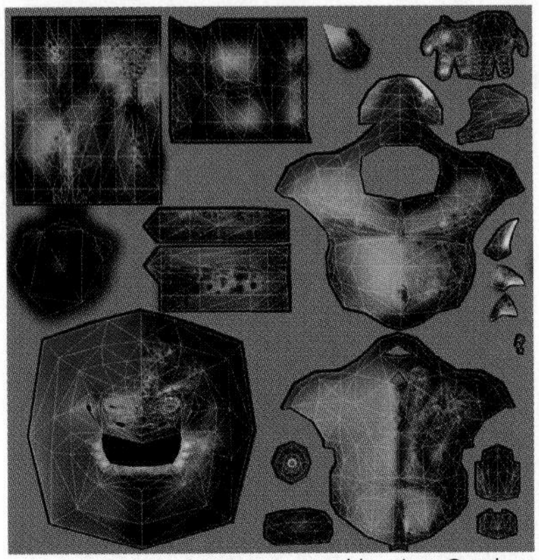

Introduction to Video

With the introduction of CD technology, game developers had the opportunity to add large amounts of audio and video elements to their games. Many early attempts to use video saw games that tried to be "interactive movies." Overall these games failed. Like the old Dragon's Lair arcade game, this type of gameplay sounds good but is ultimately too limiting. It quickly becomes dull and repetitious. However, video sequences have succeeded in another manner: as "cinematics" or "cut scenes."

Cut Scenes. Cut scenes are short, noninteractive sequences used to create atmosphere and forward the game's narrative. They can reward the player for completing a portion of the game or performing a certain task. They can also prepare the player for the next level of play by conveying important information.

Image created by Joe Gardner
for Entertainment Arts Research

Figure 4.10 Modeling.

Image created by Harshdeep Borah

Figure 4.11 Modeling and texturing.

The Command & Conquer and Wing Commander series of games are both excellent examples of games that made good use of live action cut scenes. Grim Fandango and Blade Runner are examples of games that used animated or "rendered" cut scenes in a satisfying way.

There is a danger in using cut scenes in a game. Say, for example, that the player sees an exciting introductory cut scene that features state-of-the-art graphics and special effects. This will almost certainly set up certain expectations in the mind of the player. If the look and feel of the actual game pales in comparison, the player will feel cheated and deceived.

Image created by 3D artist Harshdeep Borah

Figure 4.12 Mai – the Spider Killer.

Technological Components

"Any sufficiently advanced technology is indistinguishable from magic."[2]

Computer technology advances at such a rate that processing power doubles every 18 months. If we look at the rapid advances in game technology, this figure seems quite valid. It is certain that many of the concepts we have discussed will fall behind the state of the art. Such is the nature of technological advancements. However, without limiting ourselves too much, we can examine some general technological components involved in the science of game design.

Game Engines

The game and the *game engine* are two separate entities. The obvious analogy is that of an automobile and its engine. Without an engine, an automobile is useless. It cannot operate. However, there is more to an automobile than an engine. Different cars have different designs and features. They may have two or four doors. They may be sporty or utilitarian. The come in many different shapes, sizes, and colors. Their engines may work using the same principles, but the cars themselves can be very different.

---

[2] Clarke, A.C. (1961). *Profiles of the future*. Retrieved on September 26, 2005, from the Quotations Page Web site: http://www.quotationspage.com/quote/776.html.

Game Cheats 4.2

There are opinions, both pro and con, on the use of cut scenes in a game. Some feel that cut scenes add drama and can be a valuable addition to a game. For others, they distract the player from the essence of the game. For a discussion of opposing viewpoints on the use of cut scenes and cinematics see:

David Jaffe Hates Cut Scenes: http://www.1up.com/do/newsStory?cld=3147692

Opinion: Cinematics & Story *Do* Matter: http://biz.gamedaily.com/industry/feature/?id=11754

The same is true with games and game engines. Two games might use identical game engines but be completely different in appearance and gameplay. However, as with an automobile, the workings of the engine are vital to the game's performance. Let's examine some of the things that a game engine does.

- **Game lighting:** We have already discussed the use of light and shadows in games, but without an engine these components would not exist. The game engine determines how to display light and shadows and how objects within the game environment affect them.

- **Collision detection:** Collision detection is the basic physics of the game world and is a function of the game engine. Each time an object in the game moves, the game engine checks to see if that object is touching another object. If this check returns "true" (the object did collide with another object), the engine performs a specified action. That action might be to damage one or both of the objects, to cause one of the objects to explode, or to prevent a moving object from passing through a stationary object. Without collision detection, the game world would not contain any "solid" objects.

- **Editing:** To allow the game designer to create the game world, the game engine must have some sort of editing system. Editors usually allow modelers to import 3D objects created with other tools like SoftImage or 3D Studio Max. They also allow the designer to preview game levels, script events within the environment, and place "triggers" that will cause certain event scripts to run when the player enters a specific area.

- **Input control:** As we have discussed, game input determines how the player interacts with the game world. This is another function of the game engine. It must recognize commands from the game's input devices and allow a player's input to have an impact on the game world.

- **Rendering:** Most important, the game engine must take all the objects and textures of a game and render them as a complete environment. This is the primary function of the engine itself. It is what makes the game world come alive and makes the game itself playable.

Licensed Game Engines. Because games and game engines are unique and separate entities, many developers license game engines from other developers and use them to build and run their own games (see Table 4.2). This is a common practice in today's industry.

When developer 2015, Inc. created its best-selling game Medal of Honor: Allied Assault, the company licensed the Quake engine from Id Software. The gritty visuals of the World War II shooter could not have been more different from the surrealistic sci-fi worlds of Quake, but the versatile engine allowed 2015 to create an entirely different gameplay experience.

Other popular licensed game engines include the Unreal engine from Epic games, used for games like Deus Ex and Clive Barker's Undying, and the Lithtech engine from Monolith, used for No One Lives Forever and Aliens versus Predator 2. Another player in the game engine arena is Virtools. With its new productivity enhancement features, Virtools™ Dev 3.5 is poised to make the interactive 3D production process faster than ever and teamwork management smoother and more efficient.

TABLE 4.2	Examples of Current Game Engines	
Engine/Producer	**Technology**	**Sample Games**
Unreal 3 Epic Games, 2006	Advanced dynamic shadowing, physics, AI, normal mapping	Unreal Tournament 2007, Gears of War, Huxley
Source Engine Valve Software, 2005	Very scalable, lip synching, physics, AI	Half Life 2, CounterStrike: Source, Vampire The Masquerade - Bloodlines
Doom 3 id software, 2004	Dynamic lighting & shadows, displacement mapping, normal mapping	Doom 3, Quake 4
CryEngine CryTek, 2004	Very large terrains (2km), physics, DirectX 9 shader support, AI, "Polybump" normal mapping	Far Cry, Crysis
LithTech Jupiter, Monolith/Touchdown Entertainment, 2002	Physics, lip synching, particle effects, DirectX 9 support, AI	No One Lives Forever 2, Tron 2.0, F.E.A.R.
Virtools Virtools, 1999, 2005	Separates behaviors from objects, physics, supports PC, Mac and Xbox	Syberia, Syberia 2

Narrative Components

"Drama is life with the dull bits cut out."[3]

Traditional storytelling involves certain standard conventions like structure, setting, and character. If a designer is to add satisfying narrative elements to a game, it is important to understand these elements. It is equally important to understand how game narrative differs from traditional linear storytelling.

---

[3] Hitchcock, A. (n.d.). Retrieved on September 26, 2005, from the Quotations Page Web site: http://www.quotationspage.com/quote/268.html.

Narrative Structure

First let's look at classic dramatic structure and its application to games.

Traditional Three-Act Structure. The Greek philosopher Aristotle was the first to identify the basic three-act structure of narrative. Simply put, a story contains three distinct sections.

Act One. The first act of a story establishes the setting, the main character, and the primary conflict that will drive the story. There must be a reason why the story begins where it does. Act One will contain two important elements—an "inciting incident" and a "hook."

The "inciting incident" is an event that kicks off the events of the story. The "hook" is an event that draws the main character inexorably into those events. In the film *Star Wars* the inciting incident occurs when the two droids escape from the rebel ship with the secret plans to the Death Star. The hook occurs when Luke finds his aunt and uncle murdered and decides to leave Tatooine with Obi Wan Kenobi.

A well-written game will also contain these two elements. An excellent example is the recent game Max Payne. The inciting incident occurs when Max finds his family brutally murdered. The hook occurs when the same people who killed his family frame Max for the murder of a DEA agent. This forces him to enter the criminal underworld.

Act Two. When Luke leaves for Mos Eisley with Obi Wan Kenobi and when Max sets out to discover who destroyed his life, Acts Two of their stories begin. Act Two is by far the longest of the three acts. In film it is generally half of the running time or more. In games it can be even longer. During the second act the main character will overcome various obstacles, undergo numerous setbacks and reversals, and confront his or her inner and outer demons. Usually Act Two will contain a "dark moment" where things do not look good for the heroes. In *Star Wars* that moment is Obi Wan **Kenobi's** death. In Max Payne it occurs when Max's former colleague BB double-crosses him.

Act Two ends when the main character's final course of action becomes obvious. In *Star Wars,* when the rebels discover the flaw that will destroy the Death Star, Luke's duty is clear. In Max Payne, when Max discovers that Nicole Horne was the person responsible for the death of his family, he sets out to avenge them by killing her.

Act Three. In the third act everything comes to a head. The various plots and subplots come together, and the main character solves the major dilemma of the story. Usually this is where the hero and the villain finally go head-to-head. Luke defeats Darth Vader and destroys the Death Star. Max kills Nicole Horne and avenges his family.

Game Structure versus Traditional Structure

Even though many games follow the classical three-act structure, there is still a major difference between games and more traditional forms of linear narrative. A game is interactive. The player's choices should have (or appear to have) an effect on the narrative. This presents a problem. How does a designer create a narrative story if players are free to do whatever they choose?

In most games this problem is solved by giving the player freedom (allowing for emergent gameplay) within the confines of each specific area of the game. A game like Max Payne uses geographically defined areas with set boundaries. The adventure game Gabriel Knight 3 used periods of time to define areas of the game.

Within these areas, players have a specific goal or set of goals to accomplish. They are free to reach these goals through any method they can devise, but ultimately the result will be that they "complete" the area and move on to the next. How these individual areas are linked together forms a linear progression that moves the story along.

Interactive games allow players to, in a sense, "become" their characters. This allows them to do something that no other form of entertainment allows—make a completely different set of choices than they might make in real life. They can play tough-as-nails heroes or blood-crazed, violent villains and react to situations with their characters' motivations in mind. This is one of the great powers of interactive storytelling.

Narrative Devices in Games. Many devices are used in games to move the story forward. Let's look at some of them.

Cut Scenes. We have already discussed the use of cut scenes as a visual element in games. A primary reason for using cut scenes is to advance the storyline of the game.

Scripted Event. As we discussed earlier, emergent gameplay happens as the game's AI forces the player to choose specific actions to navigate the game arena there in manipulating the action as game AI reacts to the player's actions. However, sometimes developers prescript important events in a game, which trigger automatically when the player enters a certain area. Scripted events always play out in the same way, regardless of the player's actions. They can be useful for advancing the storyline. They can also give the game a real "wow" factor. Cut scenes pull players out of a game and let them watch a mini-movie. Scripted events are like cut scenes that happen all around the player. They are part of the action.

Many cite the Omaha Beach level from Medal of Honor: Allied Assault as one of the most effective game levels ever created. It recreates the beach landing portrayed in the film *Saving Private Ryan*. A big reason why this level is so effective is the use of scripted events.

The first, and probably the most effective, script occurs in the first few moments of the level. The player appears in a floating troop transport crammed with soldiers.

As the transport approaches the beach, artillery strikes another transport floating alongside and it explodes, sending bodies flying into the air. This scripted event sets the tone for the entire level. It instantly tells the players that they are in a fierce battle, and death could come at any moment.

Characters

Character development is another important component in game design and one that often receives short shrift. Although humor can certainly have its place and is often a welcome diversion, one-dimensional, cartoonlike characters do not allow the player to make any emotional investment. Let's look at the basic types of characters that are usually involved in a game's narrative.

Protagonist. The protagonist is the main character, or hero, of the game. In a first-person game players might never see the face of the hero. This can make it difficult to create empathy. Players gain information about first-person characters by observing how other characters react to them. Some first-person games have solved this problem by using third-person cut scenes, but this can be jarring because it constantly pulls players in and out of the character's point of view.

The protagonist should be someone that players root for. If they feel as though they have an emotional stake in the character they are playing, they will feel much more connected to the game. Certain types of heroes seem to lend themselves to empathy. Often this will give the character a "leg up" while trying to gain the empathy of the player. What are some common types of heroes?

Superhero. The superhero is a character with abilities far beyond those of the average person. This larger-than-life character will take chances and perform heroic deeds almost as a matter of course. These types of characters are fun to play from an escapist standpoint. After all, who can resist being a superhero? On the down side, superheroes seldom change. They usually have little or no "character arc." The character Arc is a dramatic term which reveals growth in the development of the main character in this case the super hero characteristics and development remain the same through out the game. Some examples of superheroes in games are Indiana Jones, Duke Nukem, and Lara Croft.

Everyman. The everyman is a character that everyone can identify with—a normal man or woman caught up in extraordinary circumstances. This type of character has a great potential for change during the game and can elicit a great amount of empathy from the player. Examples of the everyman in games include Gordon Freeman from Half-Life and Kate Walker from Syberia.

Underdog. Underdogs begin the game at a disadvantage. They can be down on their luck or something of a bumbler, but if they are inherently likable, players will almost certainly root for them. Overcoming great odds is even more rewarding for an underdog hero. Examples of underdog heroes in games include travel

Game Cheats 4.3

Character development is very important in a game because a character can become synonymous with the game. Examples include Mario (Super Mario Brothers), Sonic (Sonic the Hedgehog), Master Chief (Halo) or Samus Aran (Metroid).

agent Manny Calavera from Grim Fandango and Guybrush Threepwood from the Monkey Island series.

Antagonist. The antagonist is the villain of the game. Sometimes this will be a highly visible adversary; other times the antagonist's identity will be a mystery. Games often have multiple antagonists, but it is always important, from a storytelling perspective, to have a villain that is central to the plot. The player will often face increasingly powerful secondary villains at key points in the game. These are "boss" encounters. Bosses usually act as a gateway to some kind of advancement in the game. The player must defeat the boss to go to a new level, access a new room, or acquire a new weapon, power, or object.

Creating colorful and interesting villains can be both challenging and rewarding. Again, the player's emotional investment can depend heavily on how well the antagonists are developed. We will now discuss some techniques to create stronger villains.

Believable Motives and Goals. Players should always be aware of their goals. So too should the villain. The villain should also have goals and desires that are in direct conflict with the goals of the hero. The villain's worldview should be believable from his or her perspective, regardless of how twisted that perspective might be.

Keeping the game's overall goal in mind is a major design challenge because games play out over a much longer time than a two-hour movie. Players tend to concentrate almost solely on the immediate goal and can easily forget the main goal unless the designers keep reminding them. The overall goal needs to be extremely urgent and important, and the minor goals need to tie into and reinforce the main goal as much as possible.

Positive Attributes. An effective character-building tool is to give a villain some positive attributes that become obvious to the player. The added dimension also can make the villain a lot more convincing from a character perspective, and it is a lot more satisfying to overcome a "worthy" adversary.

Weaknesses. Every villain should have weaknesses to exploit. From a gameplay point of view, if the player identifies and exploits this Achilles heel, the final confrontation with the adversary will be that much more satisfying.

Secondary Characters. Secondary or nonplayer characters are often the mirror through which the player sees the character he is portraying. They define the player and his or her position in the game world. They also give depth and atmosphere to the game world and provide vital assistance and information to the player during the game.

Secondary characters should also have clear motivations, goals, strengths, and weaknesses. If the player develops an emotional tie to the nonplayer characters in a game, the world of the game can truly come alive.

This chapter has presented an overview of the visual design components, the nonvisual technical components, and the narrative components used in video games. These components, together with the components discussed in Chapter 3, provide the basis for an enjoyable gaming experience. Although these components do not make a good game in and of themselves, they are important to the success of a game.

The visual and technical components provide the "eye candy" that is a major factor in modern video games. The visuals of a game do not supersede the importance of good gameplay, but they do provide an important differentiating factor between games. Indirect lighting, realistic shadows, and fog and other weather effects using depth cueing effects can help make a game an immersive experience. Modeling and textures create real world objects and backgrounds using high-end imaging software like SoftImage, Maya and 3D Studio Max. The prerelease expectations for games such as Half-Life 2 and Doom 3 focused largely on the visual experience that these games would provide.

A game can use different types of lighting effects. Ambient and diffuse lighting is commonly used in game scenes, as are shadows which add realism and a sense of depth to an environment and can be used as part of gameplay, as in Doom 3. Motion blur, depth of field and lens flares are optical effects that can be used to improve the realism of a game, while particle animation effects can simulate smoke, rain, fire or explosions. Animation in a game is a science unto itself relying on kinematics (motion of a body) and kinesthetic (position and weight). Game animation falls into many categories including character animation and particle animation. Several games also uses motion capture, which involves capturing motion via sensors placed on an actor's body and can be used to simulate realistic movement. Motion capture can speed up the production process for a game. Examples of games that have used motion capture include: MBA Life 2004, Tiger Wood PGA Tour 2004, Ghost Recon: Desert Siege and Grand Theft Auto: Vice City.

However, visuals are only part of the effects provided by the latest generation of game engines. A game engine provides game lighting, collision detection, editing tools, input control and rendering. Current game engines also support realistic physics, surround sound, realistic character animation, and the ability of users to create their own content for a game. For example, the Unreal 3 engine provides advanced dynamic shadowing, visual physics modeling, multi-level AI (artificial intelligence) and a system for creating in-game cinematics (cut scenes). These all increase and help maintain the playability of a game. Game developers often license, or reuse, a successful game engine technology rather than invent an engine for each game. For example, Quake 4 uses a modified version of the Doom 3 engine.

Courtesy of *Into the Pixel*: Chinatown Level Study

Artist:
Rich Mahon, Jon Gwyn, Chandana Ekanayake

Story and character development are also important components in modern video games. Whereas early first-person shooters relied on the player running around shooting everything that moved, the current generation of games has, for the most part, moved into the realm of interactive storytelling. When compared to traditional dramatic structure, game structure differs in that games are interactive, giving the player a choice of actions. Providing background information, having "sympathetic" villains, and making heroes with their own flaws and weaknesses are all factors in current games. Examples of games that rely on an underlying story are Half Life and Half Life 2 on the PC and Halo and Halo 2 on the Xbox.

Visual Components: Lighting and Special Effects

Bill, D. (2001). *The world of 3-D graphics.* Retrieved September 17, 2005, from the GameDev.net Web site: http://www.gamedev.net/reference/articles/article1432.asp.

Möller, T., & Haines, E. (2000). *Real-time rendering.* Chapter 6: Special effects. Retrieved September 17, 2005, from the GameDev.net Web site: http://www.gamedev.net/reference/articles/article940.asp.

Tremblay, T. (1999). *3D basics,* Retrieved September 17, 2005, from the GameDev.net Web site: http://www.gamedev.net/reference/articles/article673.asp.

Yu, J. & Hsu, T. (1999). *Filtering and lighting.* Retrieved September 17, 2005, from the Firing Squad Web site: http://firingsquad.gamers.com/guides/videolightfilter/default.asp.

Visual Components: Animation

Anderson, E. F. (2001). *Real-time character animation for computer games.* National Center for Computer Animation, Bournemouth University. [Electronic copy.] Retrieved September 17, 2005, from http://ncca.bournemouth.ac.uk/newhome/alumni/docs/CharacterAnimation.pdf.

Grumet, T. (2001, November). Motion sickness: Motion capture technology makes digital people human. *Popular Mechanics.* Retrieved on September 22, 2005, from http://www.popularmechanics.com/technology/computers/1278801.html.

Maestri, G. (2001, August). *Animation for games.* Retrieved on September 22, 2005, from: http://www.informit.com/isapi/product_id~%7BB67BA41F-1093-405C-A0BE-6F65C22CE7EC%7D/content/index.asp.

Orbaz Technology. (1999–2005). *Gallery.* Retrieved on September 22, 2005, from http://www.orbaz.com/gallery.html.

Seyfarth, R. (2004). *Particle animation basics*. Retrieved on September 22, 2005, from http://orca.st.usm.edu/~seyfarth/animp/particle_basics.html.

Waggoner, B., & York, H. (1999, February). *Video in games: The state of the industry*. Retrieved on September 22, 2005, from the Gamasutra Web site: http://www.gamasutra.com/features/19990226/video_01.htm.

Technological Components: Game Engines

Isakovic, K. (1997). *Commercial 3D graphic game engines*. Retrieved on September 22, 2005, from http://cg.cs.tu-berlin.de/~ki/game_eng.html.

Simpson, J. (2002, April). *Game engine anatomy 101*. Retrieved on September 22, 2005, from the ExtremeTech Web site: http://www.extremetech.com/article2/0,3973,594,00.asp.

Narrative Structure

Cannell, S. J. (1998). *What is three-act structure?* Retrieved on September 22, 2005, from http://www.writerswrite.com/screenwriting/lecture4.htm.

Freeman, D. (2002, July). *Four ways to use symbols to add emotional depth to games*. Retrieved on September 22, 2005, from the Gamasutra Web site: http://www.gamasutra.com/features/20020724/freeman_01.htm.

Littlejohn, R. (2001, September). *Adapting the tools of drama to interactive storytelling*. Retrieved on September 22, 2005, from the Gamasutra Web site: http://www.gamasutra.com/features/20010914/littlejohn_01.htm.

CHAPTER ASSESSMENT

Practice Questions

What is the difference between ambient and diffuse lighting?

What is depth cueing, and what kinds of effects is it used for in a game?

What is an animation cycle, and what is its function in game animation?

How are 3D objects in a game given lifelike textures and surface detail?

How does the structure of a game differ from traditional three-act dramatic structure?

Lab Exercise

When designing a game, a designer must understand the importance of the game's visual components. The goal in performing this lab exercise is to analyze the visual components of a popular game.

Courtesy of *Into the Pixel*: Yellow Room

Artist: Stephan Martiniere

Each student computer should have the following free demos installed:

- Zork 1 (available at http://www.csd.uwo.ca/Infocom/Download/zork1.zip).

- Neverwinter Nights (available at http://nwn.bioware.com/downloads/demo.html).

    Choose one of the games included with the course materials.

1. As you play the demo level, note the different types of visual components that you encounter.

2. List as many examples as you can of visual components from the following categories: lighting effects, special effects, animation, video, textures, models. Specific individual models and textures should not be included. Rather, list broader categories such as character models, creature models, weapons models, city architecture, sewer textures, and so forth.

3. Describe the purpose of each of these components within the context of the game. For example, are the effects used for atmosphere? Are the effects an important part of the gameplay mechanics?

Written Assignment

Write an essay (750–1000 words) that describes your experience with the lab exercise. Your report should include a description of the different types of visual components used in the game demo such as lighting effects, special effects, animation, video, textures, and models. Describe the purpose of each of these components within the context of the game. Were the effects used properly? How would you change these effects to create a more exciting game?

Anderson, E. F. (2001). *Real-time character animation for computer games.* National Center for Computer Animation, Bournemouth University. [Electronic copy.] Retrieved September 17, 2005, from http://ncca.bournemouth.ac.uk/newhome/alumni/docs/CharacterAnimation.pdf.

Bates, B. (2001). *Game design: The art and business of creating games.* Prima Publishing.

Bill, D. (2001). *The world of 3-D graphics.* Retrieved September 17, 2005, from the GameDev.net Web site: http://www.gamedev.net/reference/articles/article1432.asp.

Cannell, S. J. (1998). *What is three-act structure?* Retrieved on September 22, 2005, from http://www.writerswrite.com/screenwriting/lecture4.htm.

Clarke, A.C. (1961). *Profiles of the future*. Retrieved on September 26, 2005, from the Quotations Page Web site: http://www.quotationspage.com/quote/776.html.

Eames, C. (n.d.). Retrieved on September 26, 2005, from the ThinkExist Web site: http://en.thinkexist.com/quotation/the-details-are-not-the-details-they-make-the/371679.html.

Egri, L. (1972). *The art of dramatic writing*. Touchstone Books.

Fernandez, A. L. (February, 2006), **Opinion: Cinematics & Story *Do* Matter,** Retrieved February 5, 2006 from GameDailyBiz Web site, http://biz.gamedaily.com/industry/feature/?id=11754

Freeman, D. (July, 2002). *Four ways to use symbols to add emotional depth to games*. Retrieved on September 22, 2005, from the Gamasutra Web site: http://www.gamasutra.com/features/20020724/freeman_01.htm.

Giambruno, M. (2003). *3D modeling basics*. Retrieved on September 22, 2005, from http://www.informit.com/isapi/product_id~%7B97EE91D3-9693-4C2D-AE4E-3BD3CBCADDC5%7D/content/index.asp.

Grumet, T. (2001, November). Motion sickness: Motion capture technology makes digital people human. *Popular Mechanics*. Retrieved on September 22, 2005, from http://www.popularmechanics.com/technology/computers/1278801.html.

Hallford N., & Hallford, J. (2001). *Swords and circuitry: A designer's guide to role-playing games*. Prima Publishing.

Hitchcock, A. (n.d.). Retrieved on September 26, 2005, from the Quotations Page Web site: http://www.quotationspage.com/quote/268.html.

Isakovic, K. (1997). *Commercial 3D graphic game engines*. Retrieved on September 22, 2005, from http://cg.cs.tu-berlin.de/~ki/game_eng.html.

Klepk, P. (February, 2006), David Jaffe Hates Cut Scenes, God of War creator avoiding Hollywood for PSP game, Retrieved from 1up.com Web site February 5, 2006, from http://www.1up.com/do/newsStory?cId=3147692

Littlejohn, R. (2001, September). *Adapting the tools of drama to interactive storytelling*. Retrieved on September 22, 2005, from the Gamasutra Web site: http://www.gamasutra.com/features/20010914/littlejohn_01.htm.

Maestri, G. (2001, August). *Animation for games*. Retrieved on September 22, 2005, from http://www.informit.com/isapi/product_id~%7BB67BA41F-1093-405C-A0BE-6F65C22CE7EC%7D/content/index.asp.

Möller, T., & Haines, E. (2000). *Real-time rendering*. Chapter 6: Special effects. Retrieved September 17, 2005, from the GameDev.net Web site: http://www.gamedev.net/reference/articles/article940.asp.

Orbaz Technology. (1999–2005). *Gallery*. Retrieved on September 22, 2005, from http://www.orbaz.com/gallery.html.

Courtesy of *Into the Pixel*: Enzo in Florence

Artists: Ben O'Sullivan, Gren Atherton, Mark Sharratt, Matt Watts

Rollings, A., & Adams, E. (2003). *Andrew Rollings and Ernest Adams on game design.* New Riders Press.

Segal, N. (1998). *3D animation workshop: Texture mapping basics,* Retrieved on September 22, 2005, from the WebReference Web site: http://webreference.com/3d/lesson54/part2.html.

Segar, L. (1990). *Creating unforgettable characters.* Henry Holt.

Seyfarth, R. (2004). *Particle animation basics.* Retrieved on September 22, 2005, from http://orca.st.usm.edu/~seyfarth/animp/particle_basics.html.

Simpson, J. (2002, April). *Game engine anatomy 101.* Retrieved on September 22, 2005, from the ExtremeTech Web site: http://www.extremetech.com/article2/0,3973,594,00.asp.

Tremblay, T. (1999). *3D basics.* Retrieved September 17, 2005, from the GameDev.net Web site: http://www.gamedev.net/reference/articles/article673.asp.

Vogler, C. (1998). *The writer's journey: Mythic structure for writers.* Michael Wiese Productions.

Waggoner, B., & York, H. (1999, February). *Video in games: The state of the industry.* Retrieved on September 22, 2005, from the Gamasutra Web site: http://www.gamasutra.com/features/19990226/video_01.htm.

Yu. J., & Hsu, T. (1999). *Filtering and lighting.* Retrieved September 17, 2005, from the Firing Squad Web site: http://firingsquad.gamers.com/guides/videolightfilter/default.asp.

Official Selection of the 2005 *Into the Pixel* art exhibition: Navy Shipyard ■ Artist: Tyler West

Company: EA ■ Game Title: GodFather

CHAPTER 5

Serious Games

The goal of this chapter is to provide an overview of the fast-growing and increasingly important serious game sector of the industry. Although games can be entertaining, their primary goal is to educate or enlighten the user. This is usually achieved by allowing the player to experience something that he or she could not normally experience or could experience only at great cost in resources. In either case, serious games make the impractical practical. For example, some serious games used by the armed forces allow them to stage battle simulations between far flung units that, under normal circumstances, would have required the units to travel to a common location and expend stocks of fuel, ammunition, and equipment – obviously, very expensive. Conversely, an anatomical simulation can be created to allow a surgeon to practice a procedure numerous times before trying it on an actual patient. The simulation could even allow the surgeon to travel into a body and witness a replay of her procedure from an organ-eye view to see where improvements can be made.

Serious games have generated an economical fervor for commercial and educational game developers. We are moving into a new era in educational games – one in which games constructively support learning on the cognitive and behavioral realm of knowledge. Most of today's games already teach you how to play without having to use the manual. Why can't a properly-designed game teach you how to perform your job without a manual? This is a broad arena with many opportunities for developers.

In this chapter we will look at serious games and what they mean to the growing gaming industry.

After completing this chapter, you will be able to:

- Describe the serious game sector of the industry
- Describe the challenges and opportunities in the serious game sector
- Describe the major players in this sector of the industry
- Describe new serious games
- Describe the strategic educational movement in serious games

Pro Tips 5.1   **Urban Video Game Academy**

The mission of the Urban Video Game Academy (UVGA) is to better prepare students in disadvantaged areas for postsecondary education and technology careers by teaching them the fundamentals of video game design and development. Our mission has three basic components: to *expose* disadvantaged students to career opportunities in video game design and development, to *educate* them in how to create games, and to *enhance* learning in academic subjects, such as math and writing, that are important in the video game development process.

The academy uses video game design and development to accomplish the following objectives:

1. Better prepare disadvantaged youth for college-level study in video game design and related fields such as computer science, digital art, and engineering.

2. Excite and inform disadvantaged youth about career alternatives in the video game design industry and related fields such as computer science, digital art, and engineering.

3. Instill in disadvantaged youth a positive self-image and teach them teamwork, leadership skills, positive social interaction, and good communication skills.

4. Provide after-school and weekend activities that will keep disadvantaged youth engaged in productive activities.

5. Encourage related businesses and public organizations to support these efforts.

UVGA Co-founders: Rodrick Woodruff, Mario Armstrong, and Joseph Saulter.

The Serious Game Movement

"A challenge for designers of educational games is to find ways to fuse educational content with the gameplay, so that students are solving authentic problems, engaging in meaningful scientific, mathematic, or engineering practices, thinking creatively within these domains, and communicating their ideas expressively."[1]

Serious Games (SGs) are a category of video and computer games. Serious Games can be of any genre but the main goal of a serious game is not to entertain, though they must also do this. A Serious Game is usually a simulation which has the look and feel of a game but is actually a simulation of real-world events or processes. The main goal of a Serious Game is usually to train or educate users (though it may have

---

[1] "Games to Teach Vision." Educationarcade. Retrieved November 7, 2005, from http://www.educationarcade.org/gtt/.

other purposes, such as marketing) while giving them an enjoyable experience.[2]

Based on the two previous statements, we can see that to be successful, Serious Games need to be so engaging as to hold the player's attention long enough for him or her to experience a paradigm shift. Whereas classic textbooks and training manuals simply place the information in front of the readers and leave it up to the readers to *absorb* it, Serious Games allow the players to *live* the same information and internalize it in each person's own best way. At the same time, these products count on the reliable techniques used in the most popular commercial games to keep the player engrossed in the activity until the information is proven to be internalized by the fact that the player wins the game.

Figure 5.1 Serious Gamers.

The Serious Game sector is a diverse collaboration between academia, business, and the commercial world of game design and development. It is a world where training, advertising, simulation, and education intersect to breed a hybrid collection of games for the purpose of educating students, training employees, attracting consumers, or developing the skillsets required to achieve specialized goals. Serious Games can be simulations that teach airline pilots how to fly or train scientists to navigate robots on extraterrestrial worlds. As mentioned previously, Serious Games allow soldiers to train and retrain for specific circumstances without risk of injury or consuming resources. The U.S. Army is a leading force in the serious game movement. As far back as World War II, the army has developed simulations to train soldiers how to perform their duties better, including: pilots who fly simulations to improve their real time capabilities and officers who plan statistical war game strategies utilizing the latest technological game simulators. For example, America's Army (a first-person shooter whose development was funded solely by the U.S. Army) has attracted over 5 million registered members and as many as 10,000 players have been online playing the game at any given time. That does not touch the 100,000-plus that have been recorded playing HalfLife but for a non-commercial game, America's Army is considered very successful.

What Games are Serious Games?

Marc Prensky has been involved with Serious Games since 1985 when he developed a training game for Scandinavian Air entitled Where in the World is Carmen Sandiego's Luggage? Five years later, he wrote *Digital Game-Based Learning,* in which he explored the 50 learning games he was able to identify on the market. When he updated the list

---

[2] wikipedia. Retrieved November 7, 2005, from http://en.wikipedia.org/wiki/Serious_game.

in 2004, there were over 500. By studying his compilations, it has become clear that there are three sources of Serious Games: COTS, mods, and custom.

COTS, or **C**ommercial **O**ff **T**he **S**helf, games are the ones you can buy in the store or online, are produced by mainstream publishers for retail, and were not designed specifically for educational or training purposes. These are games that just happen to teach you things if you play them enough. The classical examples of COTS games used in the Serious Games arena are the Civilization series, the Age of Empires series, and the Sim City series. Each of these titles were produced for their entertainment value but were later discovered to have rich educational value. High schools began using Civilization and Age of Empires in the classroom to demonstrate international dynamics, diplomacy, resource management, the causes of conflict, etc. Civil engineers and city planners began using *Sim City* to run models and simulations for training.

Mods, or modifications, are versions of COTS games that were changed to better fit a specific need. A history teacher might create a specific map of Crete to use in a game of Civilization but that would not be considered a mod. Mods involve altering the original assets and rules of a game in order to repurpose it. The U.S. Marines modified an early version of *DOOM* in order to teach better teamwork and squad coordination. They then modified the game Close Combat to create their own Marine Close Combat. Interestingly enough, a recent trend has seen projects specifically built for the military modified by the developers and repackaged for civilian retail sale. Games of this nature include Full Spectrum Warrior and Real War.

Custom games are games that were designed and developed from the beginning to be Serious Games. America's Army: Operations is probably the most widely known of this type. From its inception, it was created to provide the player with the experience of being part of the United States Army, with the intention that it would create enough interest to aid in recruiting (which by all reports it has).

The America's Army Case Study Development

Let's look more closely at the America's Army game development. The entire account here was posted at http://aaotracker.4players.de/thread.php?threadid=94097&sid=881b4e676c08e027fc8a69e05e9c749f&threadview=0&hilight=&hilightuser=&page=1.

In 1999, when the U.S. Army recruiting numbers hit their lowest point in 30 years, and after two straight years of missed recruiting targets, Congress decided to carry out "aggressive, innovative experiments" with regard to the number of recruitments.[3] The Department of Defense raised its spending for recruitment to more than $15 million, which paid not only for the Army Game Project but for

---

[3] http://www.cnn.com/US/9909/30/army.recruitment/#1.

an entire promotional campaign to polish the U.S. Army's image. For instance, the army wrote a new slogan and purchased a title sponsorship of a team taking part in NASCAR races while placing the America's Army logo there as well.

Lieutenant Colonel E. Casey Wardynski, director of the Office of Economic and Manpower Analysis (OEMA) and the head of the Army Game Project, persuaded the deputy chief of staff for personnel, as well as the deputy assistant secretary of the army for military manpower, that the idea of an online computer game designed and distributed by the army was a good one. He convinced them of the project's cost effectiveness, and from then on he has collaborated with Professor M. Zyda, mentioned later in this chapter.

In 2001 the French Canadian software company Ubisoft gave the Department of Defense permission to use Tom Clancy's Rainbow Six: Rogue Speara license to use its game for training military personnel.

On July 4, 2002, the first version of America's Army, named Recon, was released after three years of development and was made available free as either a download or on CD. Its production cost $7.5 million, and it quickly became one of the 10 most often played online first-person shooters—due mainly to the gameplay's similarity to Counter-Strike, the game's easy availability, the new Unreal Engine, and the large number of free servers sponsored by the army. The army is spending $3 million a year to develop future versions of the game and $1.5 million annually to support them. The army uses Ubisoft's Tom Clancy's Rainbow Six 3 and Raven Shield, 2003, for testing soldiers' skills.

America's Army: Soldiers, a role-playing game that was to elucidate career paths in the army, failed during development. However, the release on November 6, 2003, of version 2.0 of America's Army, with the full title of America's Army: Special Forces, was successful. The developers gave no reasons why the game used the U.S. Special forces in this and the following versions, and only a navy-produced booklet found by investigative journalist Gary Webb explained this shift. It stated, "The Department of Defense want[ed] to double the number of Special Forces soldiers, so essential [had they proven] in Afghanistan and northern Iraq; consequently, orders [had] trickled down the chain of command and found application in the release of [this version of America's Army]."[4]

Army deputy chief of personnel Timothy Maude testified before the Senate Armed Services Committee that America's Army was considered by the army to be a "cost-effective recruitment tool," aimed at becoming part of youth culture's "consideration set."[5]

[4] http://aaotracker.4players.de/thread.php?threadid=94097&sid=881b4e676c08e027fc8a69e0 5e9c749f&threadview=0&hilight=&hilightuser=&page=1.
[5] http://www.thenation.com/doc.mhtml?i=200...s=hodes20020823.

America's Army is the first game to make recruitment an explicit goal and the first well-known overt use of computer gaming for political aims. The game also extends the military entertainment complex (so-called militainment), further blurring the line between entertainment and war.[6] Military proponents state that this will help close the cleft between military and civilian life; opponents argue that it contributes to a militarization of society.[7]

Research papers from four different universities that have analyzed America's Army all confirm that the game is propaganda; one says, "Video game propaganda, whether morally right or wrong, is here to stay. It is not a passing phase, but an effective way that the U.S. government has discovered to recruit soldiers and something other nations are now beginning to experiment with as well." The paper predicts that "video game propaganda will prove to be most effective."[8]

After information about "Video Game Propaganda" research papers had been released, a poll by I for I Research said that 30 percent of young people who had a positive view of the military said that they had developed that view by playing the game. The game was influential in the military's meeting of enlistment quotas for two years after its release. At the U.S. Military Academy, 19 percent of the 2003 freshman class stated they had played the game.[9]

Director of the MOVES Institute Professor M. Zyda, while presenting the AA: Special Forces to public affairs officer M. Paul Boyce, was quoted as saying, "it would never be possible to find out what difference the game has made to recruitment numbers." He then said that he hoped no one used the game in enlistment decisions because America's Army does not attempt to help answer "hard questions" about the army, such as "Is it right for me, is it right for my family, and is it right for my country?"[10] In fact, America's Army focuses on the technological aspect of war rather than the moral one. "How We Fight," another name for the game, alludes to the U.S. government's series of films called "Why We Fight," which supported the World War II effort.[11]

In an interview with American journalist Gary Webb, Professor Zyda said, "We thought we'd have a lot more problems. But the country is in this mood where anything the military does is great... 9/11 sort of assured the success of this game. I'm not sure what kind of reception it would have received otherwise."[12]

---

[6] http://www.tomdispatch.com/index.mhtml?emx=x&pid=1012.

[7] http://www.gamasutra.com/education/these...5/ZLITHESIS.pdf.

[8] http://www-ugs.csusb.edu/honors/02/ResTravis.htm.

[9] http://www.notinourname.net/resources_li...game-7nov03.htm.

[10] http://www.detnews.com/2004/technology/0412/01/A01-20800.htm.

[11] http://www.mediaed.org/news/articles/militarism.

[12] http://www.newsreview.com/issues/sacto/2004-10-14/cover.asp.

You can download the America's Army in some 17 download mirrors, including AmericasArmy.com, Gamespot, and Worthplaying.

Figure 5.2 Game Developers Conference 2005

Serious Games as Social Triggers

Very few Serious Game developers have access to the resources and funds to the degree that the U.S. Army does. Nonetheless, there are a great many custom built SG's that are quite effective despite the smaller budgets. Dr. Ian Bogost is a professor at the Georgia Institute of Technology and is the founder of Persuasive Games, a studio that designs, builds, and distributes games for persuasion, instruction, and activism. Some of Persuasive Games' recent titles include Airport Insecurity, Activism: The Public Policy Game, and Take Back Illinois. According to Persuasive Games, these projects are:

> "... built from the ground up as rhetorical devices whose sole purpose is to influence behavior. Games are an experiential medium; players immerse themselves in an experience, make active decisions that affect the outcome of that experience, and think critically about the decisions they make. Our games are highly focused experiences that take advantage of gameplay to incite specific, real world action, like requesting a catalog, submitting information, making a contribution, or casting a vote."

Another developer who works along these lines is Gonzalo Frasca. He is the lead designer and producer at Powerful Robot, a game studio in Uruguay. His studio produces both commercial entertainment games like Ho Ho Ho Mojo Jojo for Cartoon Network and socially reflective games like September 12th, which was created for Newsgaming.com. Additionally, Persuasive Games and Powerful Robot teamed up to create videogaming history when they developed the first videogame ever commissioned for a U.S. election – The Dean for Iowa Game. Whereas The Dean for Iowa Game was used to attract and train the grassroots volunteers who were helping in Howard Dean's run for the Democratic nomination for the presidency, September 12th is a simple simulation that allows the player to experience some of the conflicting issues involved in the war on terror. The simulation cannot be won or lost but it does force the player to see the results of his actions or inactions. Powerful Robot followed up September 12th with Madrid, which focused on the terrorist attacks in Madrid, Spain.

Serious Games are also not limited by hardware. America's Army runs on PCs. The games developed by Persuasive Games and Powerful Robot are played through a Web browser. But Glucoboy is a blood glucose meter developed for a Nintendo GameBoy. The cartridge plugs into the handheld game device like any other game cartridge, but can be used to analyze the child's periodic blood samples. As a reward for maintaining the proper glucose levels, good test results unlock playable games for the child.

Blurring the Line Between Entertainment and Education

There was a time when a developer either made entertaining games or made educational games and it was blatantly obvious which type it was making. But recently, the industry has seen the growth of studios that develop products that can fit in either category and studios that develop specifically for both categories.

Muzzy Lane is a developer that exemplifies the first type. Their flagship product is Making History. The core engine is designed "to accommodate a variety of content packs that cover a broad range of subjects" according to their Web site. The game initially ships with "The Calm Before the Storm" which deals with the causes and consequences of World War II. Players act as the heads of state for the various nations and try to achieve prescribed goals for their nations while hindering the progress of other nations (even if that means going to war). The goals and consequences are based on historical data but the players are free to "rewrite history" if they think they can do better.

Left there, that description could fit any number of existing World War II simulations and strategy games. But the developers took production a few steps further by including tools and reports that would aid a teacher in adopting this software for curriculum use. Teachers can observe and play back portions of the game for the class to review. Report generators can produce printouts of in-game statistics to allow the class to discuss the progress of the game. And design tools allow teachers to modify existing games or create new ones depending on the needs of the class. By making the game controllable, recordable, and customizable, the developer makes the game attractive for any learning environment and easier to promote within an organization so as to get it approved for use.

The next type of developer is best exemplified by BreakAway Games. This developer, led by Doug Whatley, markets itself in two ways: BreakAway Games and BreakAway Federal Systems. Each aims at a specific market with specific requirements but the combined company benefits from the experiences learned by both halves. While the commercial game half focuses on titles like Emperor: Rise of the Middle Kingdom and Austerlitz: Napoleon's Greatest Victory, the serious game side develops commissioned work like Incident Commander, which was recently shipped to the Justice Department. They, in turn, plan to distribute the game for free to 40,000 police chiefs, fire companies, EMS departments, and school administrators. The game allows the players to participate as the on-scene manager of a number of simulated catastrophes. The decisions and reactions of the player are scored based on the procedures developed for the National Incident Management System. The game is flexible enough to allow local maps to be loaded into the game so as to make the tests more immediate and personal. In fact, shortly after the flooding of New Orleans, the Justice Department was in touch with BreakAway and arranged for flood scenarios to be added to future versions on the game.

Academic Leaders Join the Fray

Another model is one of cooperation between the industry and education. The Games-to-Teach Project is a partnership between the Massachusetts Institute of Technology and Microsoft. Its mission is to "develop conceptual prototypes for the next generation of interactive educational entertainment." One of the leaders of the program is Dr. Henry Jenkins, the director of MIT's Comparative Media Studies and one of the earliest researchers into the effects of audience participation in media culture.

Henry Jenkins

(born June 4, 1958, in Atlanta, Georgia) American Scholar, currently Ann Fetter Friedlaender Professor of Humanities and Director of MIT Comparative Media Studies. Professor of literature and author of *Textual Poachers: Television Fans and Participatory Culture* and *What Made Pistachio Nuts?: Early Sound Comedy and the Vaudeville Aesthetic.*

Jenkins was one of the first scholars to study the effects of audience participation in media culture and its effects. He is recognized as an expert in the influence of digital popular culture on behavior, including political behavior in a participatory media age.

Jenkins's most famous argument is that the boundary between text and reader has broken down, not merely in the way the reader "constructs" the text but also in the growth of fan cultures. These could be seen by how "fan genres grew out of openings or excesses within the text that were built on and stretched, and that it was not as if fans and texts were autonomous from each another; fans created their own, new texts, but elements within the originating text defined, to some degree, what they could do." He has also written extensively about the effects of interactivity, particularly computer games and "games for learning," and in this capacity was called to testify before Congress in 1999. Most recently he was featured in *Electronic Gaming Monthly* discussing the effects of violence in video games.[13]

 Jenkins seemed much more passive than Jack Thompson. In 1999 Thompson filed a $33 million federal products liability class action lawsuit against a number of entertainment companies, including Time Warner Inc., Polygram Film Entertainment Distribution Inc., Palm Pictures, Island Pictures, New Line Cinema, Atari Corp., Nintendo of America, Sega of America Inc., and Sony Computer Entertainment, on behalf of the parents of victims of the 1997 Paducah schoolhouse shootings, in which 14-year-old Michael Carneal shot at a group of fellow students as they were leaving a preschool prayer group in the school's lobby, killing three and wounding five. He was sentenced to life in prison. In 2002 the Sixth Circuit Court of Appeals upheld a federal judge's dismissal of the lawsuit in 2000, citing Kentucky tort law and absolving the companies of responsibility for Carneal's actions.[14] In 2003 the U.S. Supreme Court refused to review the case because it was not dismissed on First Amendment grounds.[15] The violence in video games argument continues and the outcome will affect all gamers.

Figure 5.3 Professor James Paul Gee, author of "What Video Games Have to Teach us About Learning and Literacy."

Another noteworthy and influential academic is Dr. James Paul Gee, a professor at the University of Wisconsin-Madison. He has brought his long experience with linguistics and education to the study of games as an environment for learning. His book *What Video Games Have to Teach Us About Learning and Literacy* lists 36 reasons why good video games can be better learning environments than most of today's schools. He also continued his research in *Situated Language and Learning*

[13] Farlex. (n.d.). *Henry Jenkins*. Retrieved December 08, 2005, from Henry Jenkins Web site: http://encyclopedia.thefreedictionary.com/Henry+Jenkins.

[14] Winipinia. *Video game controversy.* Jack Thompson. Winipinia. Retrieved December 9, 2005.

[15] Wikipedia. *Jack Thompson.* Jack Thompson. Wikipedia, the free encyclopedia. Retrieved December 8, 2005, from http://en.wikipedia.org/wiki/Jack_Thompson_%28attorney%29.

and *Why Video Games Are Good for Your Soul.* He is a regular and popular speaker at the annual Game Developers Conference.

The National Center for Education Statistics (NCES), which collects, analyzes, and makes available data related to education in the United States and other nations, says 83 percent of high school students are not proficient in mathematics at grade level.

Dr. Gee states, "In my opinion, schooling as it currently exists is profoundly out of date and out of touch with the contemporary world. Most students fully realize this at least by high school, and high school tends now to be the least popular level of our educational system."[16]

Dr. Gee is dedicated to developing a new arena for education. His abilities to play as well as digest the learning components of games have made him a star in the serious game movement. At the last 2005 Game Developers' Conference he skillfully demonstrated the science of cognitive learning, behavior modification, and critical thinking components that a child learns during extensive play using the Xbox and Ninja. The cognitive and behavioral learning model was extremely compelling considering that Dr. Gee demonstrated his Xbox skills in front of a room full of industry leaders hanging on his words. The constructive environment created by video games engages players while holding them accountable to critically analyze data, modify their decisions, play, and adjust viewpoints in a situational arena. Players thus develop and adapt their skills to the requirements of the game. These adjustments are recognizable learning components that adhere to a scientific paradigm for educational learning. Gameplay also allows the acquisition of hand–eye motor skills. Dr. Gee is a pioneer in the serious game movement, and his book *What Video Games Have to Teach Us about Learning and Literacy* is important for anyone moving into the serious game arena.

Serious Games in Action

Games-to-Teach:

> Replicate
>
> Biohazard
>
> Virtual U

CMU: Entertainment Technology Center:

> HazMat Hotzone

---

16 Gee, J. *What can education learn from the video game industry?* Institute for the Advancement of Emerging Technologies in Education. Retrieved November 7, 2005, from http://www.iaete.org/soapbox/transcript.cfm?&tid=What3080#9.

Serious Game Challenges and Opportunities

"A child born today will watch 20,000 hours of television, see 400,000 commercials, and spend 10,000 hours on video games before age 21. That's a total of 416 days."

attributed to Marc Prensky by Ntiedo Etuk, CEO of Tabula Digita Inc[17]

One difficulty for serious games is the contradiction inherent in the term. How can a game be serious? The connotation has considerable challenges with social implications. The culture of the game community reveals young men playing violent games that some fear might cause a social movement that will take over the world if not curtailed by authority. The popular culture of the hardcore game community has encroached on the lifestyle of the United States and international communities. But these challenges have created opportunities for a new culture of educational games, according to their developers and researchers. Video games that foster learning in a new school environment challenge students through constructive methods and engage students interactively in science, math, history, and the creative arts. School systems are adapting curricula to embrace the new generation of gamers who demand a new paradigm for instructional education. This dedicated field has educators, researchers, and developers focused on the many possibilities that game design and development hold for the educational arena.

Games-to-Teach/Educational Arenas of Serious Games

The Games-to-Teach Project is a partnership between MIT and Microsoft to develop conceptual prototypes for the next generation of interactive educational entertainment. In its first year, the program developed conceptual frameworks of games for math, science, and engineering education. It is now developing prototypes of two of these titles for testing and developing five more conceptual frameworks of games in the humanities and social sciences. Directed by MIT's program in Comparative Media Studies, Games-to-Teach is funded as a part of Microsoft iCampus and supported by the Learning Sciences and Technologies Lab at Microsoft Research.

---

[17] Etuk, N. *Perspectives on Serious Games Summit 2005*. Black Engineer.com. blackengineer. Retrieved November 7, 2005, from http://www.blackengineer.com/artman/publish/article_457.shtml.

NESTA Futurelab is helping to transform the way people learn. Using new and emerging technologies to create rich learning resources that are involving, interactive and imaginative.

The UK has a wealth of expertise in the education, technology and creative sectors that could contribute to improvements in the quality and use of digital learning resources. NESTA Futurelab mobilizes collaboration between these groups and provides an environment that stimulates new approaches to learning with technologies. Futurelab is all about educational innovation: offering the space for critical and creative thinking. Programs and practical experimentation acts as a catalyst for innovation and provides the mechanisms to nurture, resource and support new ideas. Conferences, Web site, and publications offer insights into the latest thinking and practice in educational ICT. Whether you are a software developer, a teacher, an educational researcher, or in a government agency, you are invited to help us to accelerate educational innovation.

An initiative of NESTA (the National Endowment for Science Technology and the Arts) and sharing its philosophy of supporting risk-taking and creativity, NESTA Futurelab is about enabling everyone to become active, engaged, inspired learners throughout their lives.[18]

The Educational Arena of Serious Games

Continuing the research in the serious game field are instructional technology educational researchers like Kurt Squire, who is pioneering the area of scientific learning and cognitive evolution in game development. His research includes design and simulations, pedagogical learning through educational game development, and a host of initiatives that lead researchers to develop educational theories that challenge and stimulate thought in academia as well as the commercial world.

It is apparent that collaboration between academia, commercial developers, and governmental institutions would move the serious game initiative closer to economic and institutional change. But right now the trust factor, as well as the corporative initiatives necessary for advancement of the serious game movement, is fragmented. Compartmentalized movements are evident but an outright collective

Figure 5.4 Education Arcade Conference 2005.

[18] Electronic Arts, NESTA FutureLab. "http://blogoehlert.typepad.com/eclippings/gaming_learning/index.html." *What is Teaching with Games?*. 23 Dec 2005. NESTA FutureLab. 19 Feb. 2006

assault on the challenges and opportunities would move the initiative faster in time and space. An example of this is the mobile game industry, which is bursting at the seams internationally. For instance, in Sweden, 95 percent of the country has mobile phones, and more than half of the country participates in mobile gaming. Industries work together cooperatively in research and development of projects for the gaming, government, corporate, and scientific learning communities. Kurt Squire wrote in Joystick 101.org. about his trip to Sweden, where he played "a new type of location-based game, called 'backseat gaming,' from the Interactive Institute in Sweden." Squire continues,

> The idea is to create digital games that bring the real world into the game. If you have ever taken a family trip, you know how boring a 15-hour drive is in the family minivan. Remember counting license plates or making games out of surrounding cars and drivers? Well, backseat games leverage this natural inclination to layer a game on top of the real world, but they use GPS, compass, and wireless Internet technologies to bring action, role-playing, and story into the backseat gaming experience. …

> This particular car game is Half Life played in the real world. You transport into a parallel universe populated by space creatures, where your mission is to help a scientist by capturing creatures and collecting information. Real-world locations are the focus of all the action. As you pass checkpoints, you trigger an interactive session, and you have a small window of time to complete the objective via an action game on the Pocket PC. In maybe the game's most unique feature, it uses compassing software to sense the exact position of the Pocket PC, so in order to catch the creatures you need to physically move the Pocket PC in space. …

> While this game is just a prototype, one can easily imagine other games built on the same model. Imagine other tourist games along Route 66 or Highway 101 in California. It is not certain what platform a game like this will eventually come on—my guess is cell phones. I believe that it is only a matter of time before games like this hit the market, probably driven by advertising dollars from businesses that want to be on your route. …

> The offering of Backseat Driver in Sweden is just one of about a dozen mobile games available. When most people think of "mobile games" they think of Tetris on a cell phone. A number of Swedish game designers, researchers, and government IT types are creating a radically different future for mobile gaming. Already Swedes are building and playing games where you battle giant robots over cell phones, hunt for trolls in national parks, play bomber man across PCs, consoles, and cell phones. The projects being developed in Sweden are staggering, especially when you

consider their diversity and depth. Mobile gaming is hot (see the GDC conference), and Sweden is in a position to be an international leader. How is it that a country of only 9 million people, about the size of the Chicago area, got such a jump on the market? …

Sweden is a large, spread-out country, so it basically has to solve two problems over and over again: Transportation and communications. Ericsson and now Sony Ericsson are based in Sweden. The Swedes have 98 percent cell phone adoption. …

Swedes are also gamers. For example, Swedes also play Counterstrike–a lot of Counterstrike. There are 30,000 clans in Sweden, and roughly 300,000–400,000 players active in Counterstrike leagues. Remember, this is a country of only 9 million people. In fact, Counterstrike is the third most popular sport in Sweden, right behind soccer and ice hockey. In Sweden, Counterstrike has naturally slid right into the club structure that characterizes European sports, In America, most youth sports are through schools, but in Europe, there are independent clubs. …

The future of mobile gaming has already arrived in Sweden. Its Alive launched its first game, Botfighter, about two years ago and has about 30,000 players in Europe. Using cell phones, players control robots that battle through SMS. Your bot is online 24/7 and is tied to your real-world location. Players track one another over the Web or scan for each other through their cell phones, and then battle through cell phones using text messages. The gameplay works like this: One person sends out a message on a cell phone to "ping" the area for other bots. He or she gets a message back detailing who is in the area and where they are. The other players also get a text message with the first player's location. From there, they begin exchanging missiles, also using text messaging. The missiles, robots shoot accurately within about 400 meters, and it takes about six to seven shots to kill someone. A good player can "launch" a round of shots in about 15 seconds. So the gameplay, among good players, becomes, ping, fire, fire, fire, fire, and run. Not surprisingly, most players check the game when they are on the move–on the subway, in the car, or on the road. It turns out that like in many games, the quality of the Botfighter experience depends on the community. …

In addition, that is where the team is going with Botfighters 2. You will be able to design a character that controls multiple bots–think Pokemon trainers. They are adding more graphics, although, interestingly, hardcore players eschewed such stuff as eye candy that interfered with the experience. Bots will be more differentiated–think of different classes in D&D.

In short, they hope to create and support more collaborative play by building a robust community around clan warfare and solving quests. … Second, hardcore and casual gamers exist in the game in very different ways. Casual players play on the way to work, or school, whereas hardcore players play all the time.[19]

Tom Soderlund, a lead designer, explained, "Casual players adjust the game to match their lifestyles, whereas hardcore gamers adjust their lifestyle to fit the game. We have not figured out how immersive realities are perceived yet. We're just starting to explore this."[20] In many ways persistent game developers are bumping into the same issues facing Massively Multiplayer Online Role-Playing Game developers. Both developers struggle with issues such as "Where does the magic circle of gaming begin and end?" and "How dedicated are we willing to be to our games?" says Squire. Part of what makes pervasive games so interesting is that they allow developers to play with these design issues in lower-overhead environments. It's Alive has only five to six developers on board and can crank out a game in just a few months. The team realizes that it is exploring virgin territory that could be the next Chop Suey Kung Fu or the next Majestic. "We still think Majestic was a great game." Soderlund says. "It was too big development-wise. The timing was bad and the market was not ready, but Majestic was a big role model for our games when we started."[21]

As the games industry grows up, and the development community struggles with the increased pressures that accompany these transformations, it is imperative that the games industry find avenues and mechanisms for experimentation. Academic contexts allow developers opportunities to explore ideas, prototypes, and questions free from market pressures. Some developers, such as Will Wright, already see the value in this and keep a finger on the pulse of various academic communities. At the core, the problem of collaboration in the United States is an issue of attitudes: Many developers, academics, and government agencies mistrust one another. They see only the differences and note that by working together on tough problems they could make a difference in the world.[22]

---

[19] Squire, K. (n.d.). *The future is Sweden—Kurt Squire*. Retrieved December 8, 2005, from The future is Sweden—Kurt Squire Web site: http://www.joystick101.org/story/2005/2/6/ 22938/72327.

[20] Squire, K. (n.d.). *The future is Sweden—Kurt Squire*. Retrieved December 8, 2005, from The future is Sweden—Kurt Squire Web site: http://www.joystick101.org/story/2005/2/6/ 22938/72327.

[21] Squire, K. (n.d.). *The future is Sweden—Kurt Squire*. Retrieved December 8, 2005, from The future is Sweden—Kurt Squire Web site: http://www.joystick101.org/story/2005/2/6/ 22938/72327.

[22] Squire, K. (n.d.). *The future is Sweden—Kurt Squire*. Retrieved Dec. 08, 2005, from The future is Sweden—Kurt Squire Web site: http://www.joystick101.org/story/2005/2/6/22938/72327.

We have looked at the Serious Game opportunities and challenges and have analyzed the scientific learning components that are currently being researched throughout the United States as well as the international community. We also discussed the leaders in the educational arena and simulated game development, namely the America's Army. We discovered that in Sweden the world of mobile gaming is enjoying collaboration between game developers and government and commercial entities.

The Serious Game movement will continue to flourish, and the opportunities for new game developers are unlimited. Students of game design and development programs should further investigate the serious game movement while it is in its infancy. Students and gamers should address the research community as well as the companies who need their expertise; gamers and students have a powerful voice as the developers of the future. The Serious Game arena will embrace developers who are dedicated to perfection and will offer new opportunities financially. Traditional education is on the brink of a paradigm shift: Serious Games are about to change the lives of future generations. Game design and development have affected the financial complexion across the United States and internationally and will soon be classified as an art medium equal to film.

Aldrich, C. (2003). *Simulations and the future of learning : An innovative (and perhaps revolutionary) approach to e-learning*. Pfeiffer.

Gee, J. P. (2003). *What video games have to teach us about learning and literacy*. New York: Palgrave Macmillan.

Kafai, Y. B. (2001). *The educational potential of electronic games: from games-to-teach to games-to-learn*.

Koster, R. (2004). *A theory of fun for game design*. Paraglyph.

Loftus, G. R., & Loftus, E. F. (1983). *Mind at play: The psychology of video games*. New York: Basic Books.

Reiber, L. P., Luke, N., & Smith, J. (1998). Project KID DESIGNER: Constructivism at work through play. Meridian: Middle School Computer *Technology Journal*.

Salen, K., & Zimmerman, E. (2004). *Rules of play: Game design fundamentals*. Cambridge, MA: MIT Press.

Courtesy of *Into the Pixel*: Chinatown Level Study

Artist:
Rich Mahon, Jon Gwyn Chandana Ekanayake

Practice Questions

1. What are the characteristics of a Serious Game?

2. How are Serious Games used in education and training? Please give some examples.

3. Create a list of the major innovators in Serious Game design. What are some of the challenges these designers faced?

4. How will the use of new technologies (e.g. mobile) affect the use of Serious Games in education and training?

Lab Exercise

This is a group project. Each member of your group will research an area of opportunities in the Serious Game movement. You will pick a project leader and put together an educational game concept. Serious Games are games that educate and teach. Your team game will introduce the student to components of learning in math, science, or the creative arts.

Oral Presentation

As a group, present your game idea to the class. We recommend presenting your ideas using PowerPoint or any other presentation tool to give your game visual communications.

MANUSCRIPT REFERENCES

America's Army—*Discussion*. ArmyOps—Tracker. America's Army Forums. Retrieved November 7, 2005, from http://aaotracker.4players.de/thread.php?threadid= 94097&sid=881b4e676c08e027fc8a69e05e9c749f&threadview=0&hilight= &hilightuser=&page=1.

Electronic Arts, NESTA FutureLab. "http://blogoehlert.typepad.com/eclippings/ gaming_learning/index.html." <u>What is Teaching with Games?</u>. 23 Dec 2005. NESTA FutureLab. 19 Feb. 2006 <http://www.nestafuturelab.org/research/teachingwithgames .htm>.

Etuk, N. (2005). *Perspectives on Serious Games Summit 2005*. Black Engineer.com. blackengineer. Retrieved November 7, 2005, from http://www.blackengineer.com/ artman/publish/article_457.shtml.

Engelhardt, Tom. "Guestdispatch: Zap, zap, you're dead." TomDispatch.com. 16 Nov 2003. Tom Dispatch. 19 Feb. 2006 <http://www.tomdispatch.com/index .mhtml?emx=x&pid=1012>.

Farlex. (n.d.). *Henry Jenkins*. Retrieved December 8, 2005, from Henry Jenkins Web site: http://encyclopedia.thefreedictionary.com/Henry+Jenkins.

David, Michael, Sande,Chen. "Proof of Learning: Assessment in Serious Games." 10 2005. Gamasutra. 19 Feb. 2006 <http://www.gamasutra.com/features/20051019/ chen_01.shtml>.

Games to teach vision. Educationarcade. Retrieved November 7, 2005, from http://www.educationarcade.org/gtt/. *Wikipedia*. Retrieved November 7, 2005, from en.wikipedia.org/wiki/Serious_game.

Squire, K. (n.d.). *The future is Sweden—Kurt Squire*. Retrieved December 8, 2005, from The future is Sweden—Kurt Squire Web site: http://www.joystick101.org/story/2005/2/6/22938/72327.

Webb, Gary. "The killing game." <u>News and Features</u>. 14 October 2004. SN&R News Review. 19 Feb. 2006 <http://www.newsreview.com/sacramento/Content?oid=oid%3A31755>.

Woodside, Travis. "Video Game Propaganda." <u>Research</u>. 2003. Cal State, San Bernardino. 19 Feb. 2006 <http://www-ugs.csusb.edu/honors/02/ResTravis.htm>.

Courtesy of *Into the Pixel*: Enzo in Florence

Artists: Ben O'Sullivan, Gren Atherton, Mark Sharratt, Matt Watts

CHAPTER 6

The Game Development Team

To understand the process of developing a game, it is first necessary to be able to identify the various members of a development team and the functions and responsibilities of each member. As you examine the game development team, keep this in mind: There are no industry-wide definitive descriptions for the responsibilities of those on a game development team because the industry is still young. This chapter examines the development team and identifies the key members of those teams and their functions.

We provide a brief overview of the usual team members, but it is important to remember that these descriptions will not work for every company or project. Different positions can overlap or blur; one company's associate producer may be another's director of development. Terms like *project, creative,* and *lead* are often paired with terms like *manager, director,* and *designer* to create somewhat nebulous job titles without clear definitions.

There are many different types of games, and each may have different types of teams. In addition, the creation of smaller, low-budget, and independent games will typically require fewer team members who will need to wear a number of hats and take on many different tasks.

After completing this chapter, you will be able to:

- Describe the functions and responsibilities of a producer, associate producer, and external producer.

- Compare the roles of a lead designer and level designer.

- Describe the skills required for a writer or content designer.

- Describe the functions and responsibilities of the software engineering team.

- Describe the tools used by modelers and texture artists.

- Describe the functions and responsibilities of the quality assurance team.

- State the areas of game development often handled by outside contractors.

Managing the Development Process

"You do not lead by hitting people over the head—that's assault, not leadership."[1]

Various roles and tasks are associated with the software development life cycle of computer and video games. Although each game development project requires artists, programmers, and managers, individual development companies often look at these roles in different ways and assign their responsibilities and tasks accordingly. Let's begin at the top by looking at the leaders of the team.

Producer

At the top of the team hierarchy are the producers; they hire team members and manage the entire production process, and much of their work is administrative. Producers are responsible for the development schedule and budget. They coordinate with the various department leads to make sure the project stays on track. They also serve as a liaison between the development team, the publisher, the marketing department, and quality assurance.

From a certain standpoint it would appear that the producer is in a position of power with regard to the rest of the team. On a well-structured team, however, this is not the case. Every team member works as part of the unit toward a common goal. Producers, like the department leads, simply have more responsibility than the others on the team. Part of their job is to make sure that the team is well oiled and happy. If personality conflicts or "power trips" arise, it is the producer's job to settle things for the good of the project.

The promotion to producer usually occurs from within a game development company. Some come from a technical background and begin as software engineers or designers, but another common way for a producer to get industry experience is as a quality assurance tester. Producers can also sometimes come from backgrounds in theater, television, or film.

Experience is critical. Without a good understanding of the game industry and an insider's understanding of the development process, it is virtually impossible to perform the required duties effectively. People need the right training to gain a foothold in the game design industry, and the best way to get that foundation is through a college education.

---

[1] Eisenhower, D. D. (n.d.). Retrieved September 27, 2005, from The Quote Garden Web site: http://www.quotegarden.com/presidents-by.html.

Strong creativity, design, computer, and problem-solving skills are essential, and college programs in game design stress these skills. Important courses include game technology, design process, animation, level design, and writing supporting documentation for 2D and 3D games as well as general education coursework. The educational objective of any college offering such degrees is to prepare people for employment in the field of game design.

Producer's Responsibilities. The main responsibilities of a producer include hiring development staff, scheduling and tracking project deliverables, maintaining the project budgeting, and serving as team liaison. Let's look at these functions in detail.

Hiring. The producer's first order of business is putting a team together, as shown in Figure 6.1.

Figure 6.1 The producer's first order of business is putting a team together.

The producer should sit down with the lead designer, the art lead, and the technical lead to determine their needs for the game. Adjusting the design may be necessary if staffing needs are more than company resources will allow. The team should base their estimations only on a standard workweek of 40 hours, and not consider overtime. When problems arise (which they will), this will allow some room for damage control; allowances should also be made for training, vacations, and sick days.

In Chapter 4 we described the types of skills and knowledge of animation and video techniques that are necessary in designing and developing a game. Finding the right team members can be difficult. Often the search may be nationwide or international, and relocation expenses become a major factor with out-of-town hires. Sometimes recruiters can be valuable, especially for smaller developers without human resources departments, but they can also be expensive, charging a percentage of the new hire's annual salary. This fee is usually several thousand dollars, which, when added to relocation expenses, can be prohibitive for many developers.

Finally, a producer should never underestimate the value of networking. Game developers tend to know other people in the same field. Recommendations from trusted team members and friends in the industry may help in locating the perfect candidate for any given position.

Scheduling. Producers are also responsible for scheduling. Creating a game development schedule involves identifying a series of development milestones—"safety checks" for both the developer and the publisher. Milestones usually consist of some kind of deliverable product like a playable demo or game level; the completion of each milestone signifies that another developmental phase is finished. The milestones in the schedule should occur regularly throughout the development process. Later in this book, we will discuss milestones in describing the production schedule.

When creating the schedule, the producer should identify and take into account specific risk factors. The producer will consider these factors and create a risk list so that the schedule reflects the extra time these may require. Items on this list are the elements that will probably consume the most time during development. The schedule should allow contingency plans; the implementation of an innovative game feature that looks great on paper may not actually work, and an outside contractor hired to create certain assets may not deliver on time or as promised.

Budgeting. In the preproduction phase of a project (described in detail later in this book), the producer creates a preliminary estimate of the budget. After the team is finalized a detailed budget is prepared. This budget considers all the development costs, including salaries, equipment costs, and external resources. This is a critical point in the development process. The detailed budget gives the team a realistic idea of what it can do. If the implementation of certain features does not fall within the budget and the schedule, then those features need either a different approach or to be eliminated. This can be painful, but it is necessary. The focus must shift to making the most of what is possible.

Team Liaison. The producer must represent the project to the various members of the team as well as to the publisher and any other external parties involved in its development. This means that the producer must be an excellent communicator and diplomat. The producer will be the main contact when the time comes to ask the publisher for a budget increase or a change in scheduling and will represent the project to the quality control testers, marketing, and public relations. The producer will also interface with the publisher to implement the publisher's wishes for the product.

As with many of the other functions, it is the producer's job to take care of the business and administrative side of things so that the team can concentrate on its task: creating a quality game.

Producer's Tools. Because so much of the producer's work is administrative, the primary tools used in managing a development project are word processing programs, scheduling and project management programs, and database applications for tracking and reporting (see Figure 6.2). The use of popular desktop software is a good practice because it allows team members to use software that is available and does not require additional training. The following are sample applications that a producer may use to administer a project:

Figure 6.2 Using common software is a good practice to follow in development.

- **Microsoft Word:** Microsoft Word is the most popular word processing software available. It is an essential tool for creating design documents, memos, correspondence, and the like.

- **Microsoft Project:** Microsoft Project is probably the most important organizational tool. It allows the producer to create a task list (for example, creating a budget, hiring department leads, establishing milestones, scheduling meetings with the publisher) on a grid that resembles a spreadsheet. Tabs like "Next Steps" and "Related Activities" allow these tasks to be addressed in an efficient and organized manner. The program also allows file sharing with other members of the team.

- **Microsoft Excel:** Microsoft Excel is a powerful database program that is useful for any number of tasks. Excel organizes data in rows and columns, allowing the producer to sort and calculate data. This is a valuable tool for creating and tracking the production budget. Graphs and charts allow the producer to quickly visualize projections. Templates developed for one project can be adapted for another.

- **Budgeting Software:** Some producers will use budgeting and scheduling software designed for feature films and television production. These can be especially useful for scheduling the production of live-action cut scenes, motion-capture sequences, and audio recording. Examples of this type of software include Movie Magic, Cinergy 2000, and Easy Budget.

Other Types of Producers. Though this varies from company to company, there are sometimes other types of producers on a given project. The two most common types are associate producers and external producers. Table 6.1 describes the roles and responsibilities for the producer, associate producer, and external producer.

TABLE 6.1	Producer, associate producer, and external producer roles and responsibilities.
Production Team Members	**Responsibilities and Desired Skills**
Producer	Has a good understanding of the game industry and an insider's understanding of the development process. Develops schedule and budget. Liaison between the development team, the publisher, the marketing department, and quality assurance. Excellent communicator and diplomat.
Associate producer	Assists the producer by managing various aspects of production and taking on administrative and support duties.
External producer	Works for a game publisher instead of a developer. Serves as the publisher's liaison to the developer and generally works with the game's internal producer. External producers will often work with several publishers simultaneously.

Design Team

"A designer knows that he has achieved perfection not when there is nothing left to add, but when there is nothing left to take away."[2]

The design team is the creative force behind the development of a game. Generally the design team consists of a lead designer, a number of level designers, and sometimes one or more writers as shown in Table 6.2.

Lead Designer. As a rule, the lead designer is the person with the vision of what the game will be like. A good lead designer has a real passion for the project and, in many cases, is the person who created the idea and the game's vision. Some of

---
[2] de St-Exupery, A. (n.d.). Retrieved November 12, 2005, from the BrainyQuotes Web site: http://www.brainyquote.com/quotes/quotes/a/antoinedes121910.html.

TABLE 6.2   Examples of design team functions and skills.

Design Team Members	Responsibilities and Desired Skills
Lead designer	Manages the design team. Creates the "vision" for the game. Creates and maintains the design document.
Level designer	Creates game levels. Creates game play and scripted events. Works with world editor or modeling package.
Writer or content developer	Creates detailed "bible" for game. Creates NPC dialogue and voice-overs. Writes in a nonlinear fashion. Writes for the ear, not just the eye. Presents strong writing samples.

the lead designer's responsibilities include creating the design document and story elements as well as managing the design team.

While producers manage the project as a whole, lead designers oversee the design team. They must keep the team on track by motivating them and focusing their energy on the project. The lead designer's enthusiasm should be a driving force that inspires the team.

Pro Tips 6.1

Bill Blakesley

SoftImage Master Class Developer

So you've decided to get into the game market. It is a lot of fun and it is always a lot of work. I will do my best to pass along things I have learned from my experience that you may find helpful.

The most important thing to strive for in a creative environment is to be a team player. You may be the next Einstein of 3D modeling, but if your colleagues cannot stand you it's going to be a long road. As artists, we are all trying hard to get better and better. Do not let self-achievement get in the way of the product goal.

If you are in an environment where roles are well defined, focus on an area that you enjoy and are proficient in. Again, your contribution to the team is important. It is a good idea to learn other areas of content creation because it makes you more marketable. Just make sure that if you are a texture artist on the project you strive to be the best texture artist on the planet.

Try to keep up-to-date on the latest technology. This involves checking key Web sites daily, reading the latest magazine releases, and keeping track of relevant forums. There is always a new tool or upgrade coming out, and it is important to evaluate these new advances and see if they can help speed up your production pipeline.

It is a rapidly changing industry, so try to be open to different or evolving workflows. Sometimes it seems like you have finally got your technique rock solid, and then a new tool or program comes out and makes it obsolete. This can be frustrating. Gone are the days of the craftsman who perfects his skills using the same tools through his entire career, but that's also the reason this industry is so challenging and exciting.

Finally, try to learn several applications that are key to your area of expertise. Most of the software we use has similar functionality, but it can differ widely in approach. One software package may have a much better workflow for achieving a certain effect than another. Get to know the strengths and weaknesses of relevant applications.

Content creation in the gaming market is an exciting way to make a living. It's challenging and fast-paced. For those of you up to the challenge, it's going to be a fun ride!

The lead designer creates the all-important design document and maintains it during the entire development process. The design document contains all the technical specifications for the game. It covers every aspect of the game, including story, gameplay, interface, and structure. In short, it is a map that gives the team all the information they need to create a complete and playable game. Discussion of the structure of the design document will occur at length in later chapters.

The lead designer supervises the creation of the introduction, cut scenes (or "extro"), and end movie that a game may require (see Figure 6.3). If a lead designer has writing ability, she may actually script these herself; if not she will hire a writer to do so. Later she will work with a storyboard artist to create a visual blueprint for these sequences.

Ultimately the lead designer's job is to make a great game. Toward that end, the lead designer is charged with making sure that the various aspects of the game, including gameplay, level design, art, storyline, and characters, fit the "vision" for the game. Every aspect should contribute to the atmosphere, playability, and fun factor of the game as a whole. To accomplish this, the lead designer must communicate with every department lead regularly. The lead designer conducts the design

Figure 6.3 Lead designers oversee the team.

team and inspires creativity in the development team. Together the lead designer, writers, artists, and software engineers compose a symphony through game design and development, and as all the applications come together they create a compelling game that stimulates and inspires the player.

Level Designer. Level designer is a relatively new position that has come into being only in recent years. As 3D games increased in popularity, so too did the number of amateur *modders* creating their own levels for existing games. Developers immediately recognized the talent of these modders and began hiring them to create game levels commercially.

A level designer is responsible for creating game levels—developing the environment in which the players become immersed. Each level stimulates players to continue their quest to win the game. The level designer creates a playing field that allows the player to discover challenges that make the game compelling. The court for the basketball player, the course for the golfer, the track for the car driver, the ring for the fighter, or the arena for the gladiator all give the player the opportunity to experience a realistic physical 3D world.

The job of the level designer is to use the assets created by the modelers and software engineers to create an area of the game world through which the player can move and interact with the environment. This can involve features like event triggers, monsters, nonplayer characters (NPCs), traps, and puzzles. Level designers are often responsible for creating the gameplay and scripted events in the levels they design. They do this by using a scripting language created by software engineers. A scripting language empowers nonprogrammers to create gameplay, enemy artificial intelligence (AI) logic, and game events. Level designers tend to work in open areas where they can freely share ideas and communicate with one another.

The primary tool of the level designer is either a world editor—a critical part of a proprietary or licensed game engine—or a modeling package like Maya or 3D Studio Max (see Figure 6.4). Level designers use many other programs as well because their job affects many different development aspects including administration, programming, and art.

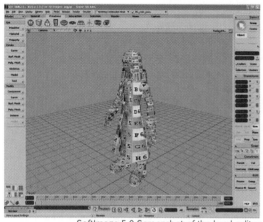

SoftImage 5.0 Screenshot of the level editor
Model the King by 3D Model artist John Walker

Figure 6.4 The level designer's primary tool is a level editor or modeling package.

The growing number of available editing tools can give an amateur designer enough experience to get an entry-level design position, but these people may find themselves unable to progress to more advanced positions without a college degree. As with most technical careers, an education can be extremely valuable. As gaming technology grows more complex with each passing year, any courses that examine different aspects of game development can help a would-be designer. Many early designers were self-taught, however. Of course, game designers must love games themselves; the value of playing games, knowing the game market, and learning what makes those games tick is immeasurable.

Writer. A writer (sometimes called a story or content designer) develops the story lines in a game. Traditionally on-staff writers have been rare in the game industry. In most cases freelance writers are hired on a contract basis. At other times designers and other members of the staff take on the writing chores themselves, but this can be a mistake. Writing compelling dialogue is not as easy as it appears. Another common mistake made by developers is hiring a writer late in the process, after the vast majority of the game is finished. This can lead to badly structured, weak story lines.

As the game industry matures, these trends are starting to change. Developers are beginning to understand the wisdom of having a writer from the beginning. Some of the most compelling games have a storyline creatively woven through the fabric of the design; as the industry matures, we are witnessing the multimedia collision of games, movies, music, and culture. Writers are especially critical for ongoing massively multiplayer online games with evolving storylines. Having a staff of creative writers can really bring an online game to life and make it more than just a "leveling treadmill." Online gaming and the ability of the player to get emotionally involved in the game through a communicator gives the player a power unlike any other entertainment vehicle.

A good game writer, under the best of circumstances, will work with the lead designer from the beginning. The writer will develop a detailed "bible" for the game containing the history of the game's world and the backstory that sets the plot in motion, as well as background information about the major characters. Incorporating this information into the game's design document is at the lead designer's discretion. The writer is also responsible for creating all of the NPC dialogue and voice-overs. Writers also write, edit, and polish any on-screen text or introductory information contained in the game's manual.

Game dialogue must be brief and to the point, yet it must convey character and move the story forward. The nature of games frequently sees the player repeating sections of a game several times. Long verbose dialogue that may sound good at the outset can become excruciatingly dull with repetition. Game writers must write for the ear, not just for the eye. Dialogue that reads well is not always dialogue that sounds good. Writing for the ear requires a distinct talent.

The writer's primary tool is a word processing program like Microsoft Word. For writing cut scenes in screenplay format, a writer may also use specialized scriptwriting software like Movie Magic Screenwriter, Final Draft, or ScriptThing. Sometimes writers will script shorter snippets of in-game dialogue that are triggered by certain events or game AI. Writing this type of dialogue is usually done in spreadsheet form using a program like Excel. This allows the sound designers to create a database of sound cues that can easily integrate into the game.

A well-rounded education and life experience are essential for writers. If they are to create believable, three-dimensional characters, they must have a wealth of knowledge to bring to those characters. Writers should also have an excellent understanding of and appreciation for the game industry, and they should certainly be avid gamers themselves.

Experience writing for other media can be valuable, but writers must realize that writing for games is an art in itself. Often developers will spend a large portion of their budget to hire a Hollywood screenwriter with no game industry experience and be extremely disappointed with the results. There is also a danger in hiring a writer who is a frustrated linear storyteller. This type of writer is generally more interested in telling stories than in facilitating good gameplay.

The interactive nature of games and game dialogue also forces the game writer to think and write in a nonlinear fashion. The writing of a conversation between a player and an NPC is not like writing a scene in a movie. The player has choices, and the dialogue branches out to cover a wide range of conversational topics.

Learning to write this kind of dialogue is a unique experience for most writers. In many ways they must learn to think like a software engineer. That is not to say that conventional screenwriting techniques do not come into play. The writing of cut scenes is like writing a traditional screenplay form. When using cut scenes, the writer must have a full understanding of screenwriting conventions.

Finally, if game writers wish to be hired, they must have strong writing samples that reflect their ability. No developer will hire a writer based on a degree or a list of credits; credible proof of talent is necessary.

Software Engineering Team

"A novice asked the master: 'What is the true meaning of programming?' The master replied, 'Eat when you are hungry, sleep when you are fatigued, program when the moment is right.'"[3]

Nothing in a game would work were it not for the hard work of the software engineering team. The code this team produces affects every aspect of gameplay, including game physics, AI, special effects, the game interface, the integration of art assets, and much more. Table 6.3 summarizes the roles and responsibilities of the key players on the software engineering team.

Technical Lead. The technical (tech) lead is on the project from the start. A big part of the job, early on, is to keep the producer, lead designer, and art lead aware

TABLE 6.3	Examples of software team functions and skills.
Software Engineering Team	**Responsibilities and Desired Skills**
Technical lead	Advises development team of the possibilities and limitations of the game platform and technology.
	Manages the software engineering team.
	Creates and maintains the technical design document.
	Has a strong background in math and physics, as well as programming languages.
Software engineer	Can specialize in several areas of game programming such as rendering engine, game physics, or the game interface.
	Has a strong background in math and physics.
	May be required to understand low-level CPU architecture and assembly languages.

---

[3] James, G. (1996). *The tao of programming*. InfoBooks.

of the possibilities and limitations of the game platform and technology. Often the tech lead will contribute greatly to the game's design and have a great deal of input regarding the game's final feature set. Some of the tech lead's responsibilities include creating the technical design document and the game architecture and managing the software engineering team.

The technical lead will almost certainly have started out as a game programmer and have a good background in math and physics, as well as programming and assembly languages. The technical lead will also need to have leadership, management, and communication skills in addition to technical skills. He or she builds, equips, and manages a team of programmers and keeps the team on track, motivated, and focused (see Figure 6.5). This rare combination of abilities makes the tech lead an extremely valuable member of the development team.

Figure 6.5 The technical lead is responsible for building, equipping, and managing a team of programmers.

The technical lead is responsible for creating and maintaining the project's technical design document. This document lists all the required programming tasks for the game for which programmers are responsible and target dates for their completion. He or she also takes the lead designer's vision and creates a workable architecture that plays to the strengths and compensates for the weaknesses of the target platform. If a particular feature or gameplay element is not working or is impractical given the budget and development schedule, the tech lead will make this case to the producer and lead designer and recommend reworking it or eliminating it. A large part of the job is to keep the technical risks at a minimum.

Software Engineer. Software engineers make the designer's vision a reality. The code they write affects every aspect of the game. Managed by the technical lead, most software engineers, especially in smaller teams, will work on several different areas of the game, but often they will specialize in a particular type of programming. Areas of specialization can include the rendering engine, game physics, tools, AI, the game interface, and many others.

Software engineers use many different tools, including text editors for writing code, compilers for compiling code, and debugging tools for testing code. Microsoft Visual C++ is commonly used, as are many custom and proprietary programs created in-house. Software engineers specializing in tools can also play a key role in scheduling. Because they provide the tools that the designers use, they can make a huge difference in a project's staying on schedule or falling behind.

Software engineers require more education than any other position on the development team. A good software engineer will have a strong background in math and physics. Subjects like linear algebra and vector mathematics are especially important for rendering and game physics. All software engineers should be fluent in several languages. For example, knowledge of the C/C++ programming language is important because they are efficient languages that help in maintaining and upgrading games, and they are the most popular languages used in game development. It can also help to understand low-level CPU architecture and assembly languages because these help in coding the game more efficiently.

Art Team

"An artist is paid not for his labor but for his vision."[4]

As graphics technology advances, the "look" of a game has become increasingly important. A captivating screenshot viewed in a magazine or on the Web will often convince a gamer to buy a particular title based on the look alone. A solid team of artists can truly make or break a title. This large team usually consists of an art lead, conceptual artist, modeler, texture artist, and animator. Table 6.4 summarizes the roles and desired skills of the members of the art team.

Art Lead. The art lead is responsible for a game's "look." The art lead works with the lead designer to develop a consistent visual style for the game world and for the objects and creatures that inhabit it. Early in the development process, the art lead and the lead designer will establish a style for designing the art assets and visual elements of the game. This look should be consistent and should appear in the user interface, character designs, menu options, and game environments. Next an "art bible" is created to guide style during development. This guide will include concept art, character sketches, equipment design, and so on. The art team will refer to the art bible and add to it throughout development as they create new art assets for the game.

The charge of the art lead is to deliver art assets on time. These assets affect every part of the game development process and can include character models, backgrounds, animations, and tile sets. He or she also hires, manages, and equips the team of artists. As with the other team leads, the art lead must keep the art team on track, motivated, and focused. The art lead's energy and enthusiasm should be a driving force that inspires them.

---

[4] Whistler, J. M. (n.d.). Retrieved November 12, 2005, from the Painter's Keys Resource Web site: http://www.painterskeys.com/getquotes.asp?fname=sw&ID=324.

TABLE 6.4   Examples of art team functions and skills.

Art Team Members	Responsibilities and Desired Skills
Art lead	Responsible for the game's look.
	Hires and manages the art team.
	Has a background in physical art such as drawing, graphic design, painting, or architecture.
Conceptual artist	Creates character, creature, environmental designs, props, and vehicles.
	Creates "model sheets" of various characters.
	Sketches out all assets in a game for modelers and texture artists.
Modeler	Develops the elements that make up the game environment and character.
	Uses 3D modeling packages such as SoftImage XSi, Maya, and 3D Studio Max.
Texture artist	Creates detailed surface textures for the environments, structures, creatures, and objects in a game.
	Uses packages such as Maya and 3D Studio Max.
Animator	Understands human anatomy, character expression, and locomotion.
	Uses packages such as Maya and 3D Studio Max.

Art leads should be artists in their own right. They must have a background in physical art such as drawing, graphic design, painting, and perhaps even architecture. They also need to understand lighting, animation, and especially 3D rendering. As with any lead position, art leads also need strong management and administration skills.

Conceptual Artist. Conceptual artists work with the art lead and lead designer to create the initial sketches and artwork that make up the art bible and define the visual look of the game. They are visionaries and the creative image creators. Conceptual artists create the landscape characters and creatures in the 2D world on canvas and sketchpads. They create the vision for the storyboard artist, and often they take on this role as well. The conceptual artist lays the foundation for the design elements of the game. Concept art organizations across the country are stimulating an underground art movement in the art world as well creating an exciting arena for young artists to develop creative concepts as they develop their artistic skills.

Conceptual artists' main areas of responsibility include character design, creature design, environmental design, props, and vehicles. For example, their creature designs are a stimulus for the modelers and animators. They decide, "Is the creature slimy, is it aquatic, or does it walk on all fours? Is the creature a combination of a human and an insect?"

Conceptual artists also create "model sheets" of the various characters in a game; these sheets are included in the art bible. These sketches show multiple views of the characters and serve as a blueprint for the modelers and animators who will bring them to life. As technology fuels creativity, character design becomes more detailed. The characters created must stimulate the modelers who give 2D character designs their 3D lifelike qualities.

Figure 6.6 Modeling a 3D character.

The conceptual artist must sketch every weapon, spacecraft, and gadget used in the game before the modelers and texture artists render them for inclusion in the game. Sometimes the conceptual artist will create storyboards of the cut scenes and scripted sequences that will be included in a game. A storyboard is a series of sketches, shot by shot, that shows how a sequence will play out.

Modeler. Modelers use 3D modeling packages like SoftImage XSi, Maya, and 3D Studio Max to create the models that represent objects, characters, and scenery in the game environment. As technological applications continue to fuel creativity, the 3D modeler must construct the world that the gamer plays in. New consoles and new technology give the 3D modeler new arenas. Game engines that once could only handle low-polygon characters are now handling high polygon counts, allowing the modeler to handle creations that are more detailed. In the game world, the modeler develops the universal elements that make up the environment and characters that the player manipulates. The modeler plays an essential role in the look and feel of a well-developed game (see Figure 6.6).

Using the conceptual artist's sketches as a blueprint, the modeler creates objects using 3D wire mesh; adding texture to the mesh gives the objects the appearance of solidity, as shown in Figure 6.6. These models are "art assets" that will be used by the level designers and animators to create the game world itself. New technology and the next generation of game consoles are giving 3D game modelers the tools necessary to develop artistic skills that will enhance the game industry's ability to create interactive entertainment. The responsibility of the game modeler is to manipulate the tools to enhance the details of the characters and environment for the player. The more detailed the 3D world, the more stimulating it is for players. A good balance between gameplay and 3D world content make a game that looks and plays well.

Texture Artist. This important member of the art team creates everything from the surface of a brick wall to the beard stubble on the face of the hero. Once the modeler has created a wire mesh 3D object, it is up to the texture artist to make it look real. The texture artist's primary tools are Adobe Photoshop, various painting programs, and a 3D package like Soft Image XSi, Maya, or 3D Studio Max.

The texture artist creates detailed surface textures for the environments, structures, creatures, and objects in a game. The addition of surface texture to objects is possible thanks to the creation of 2D textured "skins" that wrap around the wire frame models. These skins are "image maps" or "texture maps." Many different techniques are used to create textures. Table 6.5 provides an overview of some of the common techniques used in creating textures.

TABLE 6.5 Examples of techniques used to create textures.
Example Techniques
Photo manipulation: A common technique used to create texture maps is to photograph real surfaces, scan them, and touch them up with photo manipulation software (such as Photoshop).
Hand painting: For some high-end close-up work, the texture artist may use a significant amount of hand painting to add detail to a texture map.
Procedural texturing: Using the process of procedural texturing (sometimes also called *algorithmic texturing*), the texture artist can alter the appearance of an object without using a texture map. This process uses mathematical computer algorithms to change the appearance of a surface. Fractal noise is one example of procedural texturing.
Bump mapping: The process of bump mapping is a way to add detail to an image map without increasing the polygon count. This is a clever way to add texture without decreasing the speed of the game. Bump mapping does not actually change the surface of an object, but uses light reflection calculations to create the appearance of small bumps.

Animator. The final member of the design team is the animator, who adds life and movement to the characters and creatures that populate the gaming world. The lead designer will give the animator a list of all the activities that each creature will perform within the game. The animator then creates a series of animation movements that allow the creature to perform those actions in a realistic and believable way. The animator also creates the animation "cycles"–that is, character's actions that are complete and that always loop back to the starting position.

The primary tool of the animator is a 3D modeling package like Maya or 3D Studio Max. Like other artists, animators may also employ paint programs and hand-drawn sketches to develop the animation moves and cycles. Animators must have an excellent sense of human anatomy, character expression, and locomotion. There is also a lot of character development revealed through animation. How characters move can reveal a lot about what they are like. The study of traditional 2D animation is responsible for acquisition of these skills. Most game animators study traditional animation at a university or art school first. Once they have learned the basics of traditional animation, they can move more easily into computer graphics animation.

Quality Assurance

"The significant problems we face cannot be solved by the same level of thinking that created them."[5]

Quality assurance (QA) is the department that tests games. QA's role in the development process is a vital one. The writing of the first code signals the beginning of testing, which continues until the product ships. The QA team in the development of a game generally consists of a test lead and game testers. In this section and in Table 6.6, we describe their roles and the different types of testing that are vital to the success of a game.

Test Lead. The test lead is responsible for overseeing the QA team and making sure that when the game ships, it will be as bug-free and as polished as possible. His or her responsibilities include developing a test plan, conducting preliminary testing and feedback, and leading alpha and beta testing.

The test lead begins development with a small team, whose job at this point is to provide feedback as the software engineers begin to implement code.

[5] Einstein, A. (n.d.). Retrieved November 12, 2005, from the Jef's Web Files Web site: http://www.jefallbright.net/node/2398.

TABLE 6.6   Examples of QA functions and skills.

Quality Assurance Team	Responsibilities and Desired Skills
Test lead	Manages the QA team. Creates the test plan document. Directs alpha and beta testing.
Game tester	Tests games for months. Documents all game errors. Does not require previous game industry experience.

The feedback is critical at this time because the early mechanics of gameplay and game features are still in the planning stages. The game testers play portions of the game, and their feedback helps the software engineers develop the game elements.

The test lead begins to create a test plan document as the project reaches the alpha stage. This document mirrors the schedule of the design document and details the team's bug reporting system and tracking process. The test plan acts as a rubric for the testers to follow as they test the game.

Upon the completion of the alpha version of the game, alpha testing begins. The alpha version is usually playable from beginning to end, though it may have gaps or incomplete features. At the alpha stage, the test lead brings on a complete team of game testers to evaluate the game and its playability.

The next testing phase begins when a beta version of the game is completed. The beta release should have all features complete and be close to the final version of the game. Bug fixes and balancing issues are now of primary importance because most of the game features are locked. The process of tracking down and repairing every bug occurs in this vital, nit-picking stage. The testing team is at its largest during this phase and sometimes will even include volunteer testers from the gaming community; this is especially common with online multiplayer games.

At the end of the process, the test lead decides whether the game is ready to ship. Many developers will not allow a title to ship without the approval of the test lead.

Game Tester. Testers are notoriously underpaid and overworked and are certainly at the bottom of the development team hierarchy. Ironically, these unsung heroes perform one of the most vital tasks in the entire process. Many people incorrectly assume that game testing is a "fun" job. Who would not want to play games all day long? Paying game testers for playing a game makes the position sound ideal, but an understanding of the testing process reveals the position to be anything but fun. However, a tester's role is vital to the success of a game.

Testers work on the same game for months on end, routinely replaying the same levels dozens of times to locate and repeat certain bugs. They must create accurate and specific bug reports. It is not enough to say that something is not working properly. They must describe the bug and provide as much information as possible about the circumstances that triggered it. Were there any error messages when the bug occurred? Is the bug repeatable? What was the exact location in the game where the bug occurred?

Testing is one of the few jobs that do not require a lot of previous game industry experience. A love of games and a desire to work hard and create accurate reports are enough. For this reason, game tester is often an entry-level position. Test leads, producers, and even lead designers have gotten their start in QA. However, advancement in the industry usually requires a college degree in gaming or a related field.

Outside Contractors

"The world is full of willing people, some willing to work, the rest willing to let them."[6]

So far we have described the common titles and terms you will encounter in the development team for a typical big-budget, 3D action-oriented title from a major publisher. However, a game development company frequently will not have the resources to create every asset for a game. Sometimes a company must turn to outside contractors (see Table 6.7) to create specialized assets like voice acting, music, and sound effects.

Voice Acting. Table 6.7 shows examples of the roles and responsibilities of the game development artists who participate as outside contractors in the development of assets for many games. For example, most games require some kind of audio voice-over recordings (voice-overs), but few developers have the facilities or resources to do such sound recording.

---

[6] Frost, R. (n.d.) Retrieved November 14, 2005, from the Thinkexist Web site: http://en.thinkexist.com/quotes/robert_frost/2.html.

TABLE 6.7	Examples of roles and function of outside contractors in game development.

Functions Performed by Outside Contractors
Provides voices for characters (actors, voice-over artists).
Performs casting and directing of voice talent (voice director).
Composes and manages all music for the game (music supervisor, composer).
Manages sounds used in a game (sound designer, audio director).
Handles all technical aspects of sound recording (sound engineer).

Professional actors who fill this role are generally members of the American Federation of Television and Radio Artists (AFTRA). Utilizing them will require certain minimum pay scales and official paperwork, but it will almost certainly be worth the time and expense to have professional, knowledgeable, and reliable performers. It is important to use trained actors whose voices can withstand hours of grueling recording and who know how to do natural-sounding cold readings. Generally there is little or no rehearsal time in a recording session.

Voice directors cast the various roles required and direct the audio recording sessions. Often the lead designer and producer attend the session to help the actors understand the context of their lines as they pertain to the storyline of the game. A sound engineer handles the technical aspects of the recording. Voice processing consists of cleaning up and editing the recorded lines for quality, then processing them so they sound right in the 3D game environment—using voice audio "raw" is seldom possible. Because many games contain thousands of lines of dialogue, voice editing and processing can be a huge task.

Music. Music is another critical game component that usually relies on outside contractors. Music can set the tone of a game by heightening tension and adding atmosphere. Like a good film score, a game's music can make a tremendous difference in the game's overall feel. A music supervisor is responsible for all of the music in a game. In some circumstances the music supervisor may also be a composer or may hire a composer to create original music. The music supervisor may also license the rights to use existing music. The recent title Grand Theft Auto 3: Vice City licensed a number of hit songs from the 1980s for use on the game's soundtrack. This is an attractive idea, but it can be expensive.

Game Cheats 6.2

Game music is entertainment in its own right. Video Games Live (http://www.videogameslive.com/index.php?s=info) is the first video game music tour featuring the music from games such as Mario, Tomb Raider, and Halo. The 2005 tour features a full orchestra and choir and a specially designed laser and light show.

Composing music for games is an art form. Like film composers, game composers will often create themes for specific characters or areas in a game. They must also create atmospheric music for certain areas and actions. There can be specific musical pieces to create tension, lighten the mood, or give a sequence a romantic feel.

Game scores have unique problems that come about because the games are interactive, and the various pieces of music must blend into each other seamlessly when the player makes certain choices. Creating "modular" pieces of music that allow for easy transitions will help in this regard, but there is a danger here as well. If the modular pieces are too short, they will quickly become repetitive and annoying to the player.

Sound Effects. Outside contractors often handle the sound elements for a game. Well-designed sound effects will immerse the player in the game world and provide important feedback during the game. The uses of sounds in a game are the responsibility of the sound designer. Theses sound effects can come from a number of sources, including sound libraries, synthesized sounds, and Foley artists.

Pro Tips 6.2   **Nathan Smith**

Sound Designer/Audio Director for NL3 Audio in Los Angeles CA. NL3 Audio (http://www.nl3audio.com) is a leader in sound design for major video games and films.

Whether one works in a linear media such as film or in a nonlinear media such as gaming, the sound designer's goal remains the same: telling a compelling story. Each project brings its own challenges, but success is defined by a sound designer's ability to assemble sonic elements that deepen the listener's immersion in the project.

There are many steps involved in achieving effective sound design, but the process varies by medium. Video games, because of memory limitations, consist mainly of hard sound effects. Thus a single sound designer has an incredibly important role to play in the game's final sound.

A video game sound designer is responsible for managing most audio assets all the way to a game's ship date. Thus it is important to have a strong knowledge of recording raw sonic materials, commercial recordings for those sounds you can't record yourself, as well as careful records of the thousands of sounds you create.

Recording in the field is terrific for getting sounds in the context of their environments, but sometimes you want sounds that are clean, clear, noise-free, and devoid of ambience. For those situations, studio recording is the way to go.

Recently I recorded some particularly loud sounds for some video games: a big rig air horn, a jet engine, and a spray paint flame. Such sounds require some experimentation when setting up microphone placement. The first thing to consider is where you will be placing the sound in the game. In the case of the air horn, I was looking for a blaring truck horn to use while a character in The Incredibles (Pixar/Disney) runs through congested traffic. Because I wanted the sound of the horn without the truck, I chose to record this in the studio. Being the passionate sound designer I am, I happen to have a big rig air horn in the studio Foley closet. In the case of the jet engine, I was able to find an exposed jet engine that was not attached to a plane. This is obviously not something one could bring into a studio, but finding an engine that is not attached to the jet and not at an airport eliminated many recording problems.

To record the sound of a flaming paint can (do not try this at home) for an Atari game trailer, I used a Sony shotgun microphone and tried to get as close to the ignition point as possible. Recording fire or flames renders different results as you get closer to the combustion point. To avoid any potential problems with the can exploding you can use a plastic straw that comes with some spray can products. This way the straw will melt before the can explodes in your hand. I take safety very seriously and never recommend trying anything that can endanger you or anyone else. Always have an extinguisher handy when working with fire.

Some sound effects are easy to find and record. Others require more creativity. But with careful attention to the needs of the game, proper microphone placement, and an in-depth knowledge of recording equipment, a sound designer can greatly enhance the acoustic quality of a product.

The purchasing of stock sound effects from sound libraries (companies that sell prerecorded sound effects along with the right to use them) is common. They are usually available in CD format or as a download from the company's Web site. There are many such companies, and the quality of their sound effects can vary; but professionally produced sound libraries can be very good. A synthesizer or audio software can create sound effects so that these effects are inexpensive and clean, without recording problems like background noise.

Foley artists use props to create specific custom sound effects in the recording studio—for example, boots crunching on gravel or glass shattering. This can be valuable because such sound effects can be tailor-made and fitted to specific actions in the game or cut scene, which can be much more effective than importing clips from sound libraries and trying to make them fit.

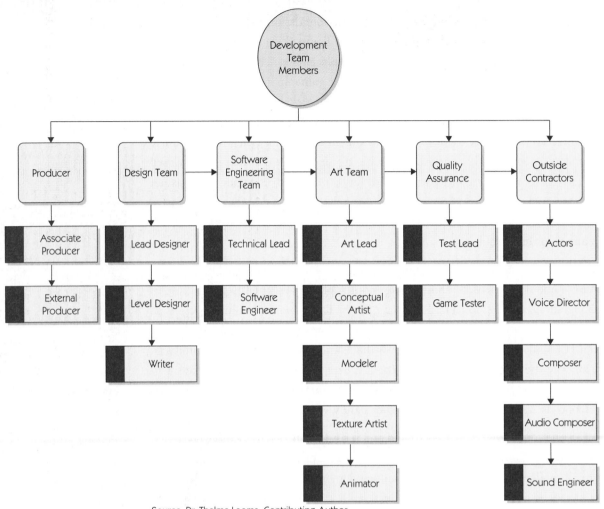

Source: Dr. Thelma Looms, Contributing Author

Figure 6.7 Development team members.

SUMMARY

This chapter provided an overview of the different roles you will encounter in the development team for a typical 3D action-oriented title from a major publisher, as shown in Figure 6.7. Although titles in the game design industry are still fluid, as are the responsibilities assigned to each position, the basic terminology used here is such that you should have a firm grasp of the essentials.

The producer is responsible for hiring, scheduling, budgeting, and serving as the team's liaison with the publisher. The producer is the administrative person who is ultimately responsible for getting everything done in a timely fashion, which means that he or she needs to be an excellent communicator and diplomat. In addition, without a good understanding of the development process, it is virtually impossible to effectively perform these duties.

The design team is the creative force behind the project. Led by the lead designer, the team, which usually consists of level designers and writers, strives to fulfill the vision for the game. The lead designer is responsible for creating and maintaining the design document that covers every aspect of the game. The lead designer makes sure that the various aspects of the game, including gameplay, level design, art, storyline, and characters, fit the vision for the game because every aspect contributes to the success of the game.

The level designers are responsible for developing the environment in which the players are immersed. Each level must create the challenging stimuli that cause the players to continue the game. The job of the level designer is to create gameplay that involves the players by allowing them to interact with the game environment. Others involved with the design team include the writers and the technical lead and his or her software engineering team. The technical lead, like the lead designer, creates, motivates, and manages a team. These software engineers make the game design real by writing the necessary code. Software engineers, who often specialize in a particular area such as AI or game physics, will usually work on numerous areas of the game.

As graphics have become more sophisticated, players come to expect more realistic and intriguing screens for their games. The art team, under the direction of the art lead, is responsible for the appearance of the world and characters within the games. The art lead works closely with the lead designer as he or she develops the art bible, which becomes a style guide for the visual aspects of the game.

Another important member of the art team is the conceptual artist, who is responsible for character and environmental design. The modeler uses those designs to create actual models using 3D wire that will be used by the level designers and animators to create the game. Once the modeler has finished, the texture artist creates the details that add reality by using photo manipulation, painting by hand, procedural texturing, and bump mapping. Members of the art team need to understand lighting, animation, and 3D rendering. Skills in packages such as SoftImage XSi, Maya, and 3D Studio Max are essential in performing these roles and functions.

Once work starts on the game, the quality assurance team begins testing for bugs. The test lead is ultimately responsible for ensuring that the game is bug-free and that the final product has a polished appearance. A test plan document is prepared that directs the testers and details the team's progress. Outside contractors—actors, voice-over talent, sound engineers, musicians, and sound effect experts—also have a part in creating a game. The successful creation of a game requires the skills and cooperation of many people.

Managing the Development Team

Crosby, O. (October, 2005). *Jobs in video game development*. Retrieved November 12, 2005, from the GIGnews.com Web site: http://www.gignews.com/crosby1.htm.

Doyle, M. (August, 2000). *Structuring a game development team*. Retrieved November 12, 2005, from the TechZone.com Web site: http://www.thetechzone.com/articles/how_to/game_making/index.shtml.

Hendrick, A. (February, 1998). *Hiring game designers, game developers*. Retrieved November 12, 2005, from the Gamasutra.com Web site: http://www.gamasutra.com/features/19980320/hiring_designers_01.htm.

Ryan, T. (February, 2003). *Risk management with development schedules*. Retrieved November 12, 2005, from the Gamasutra.com Web site: http://www.gamasutra.com/features/20030206/ryan_01.shtml.

Sloper, T. (n.d.). *Game biz advice*. Retrieved November 12, 2005, from the Sloperama.com Web site: http://www.sloperama.com/advice.html.

Design Team

Chen, S., & Brown, D. (July, 2001). *The architecture of level design*. Retrieved November 12, 2005, from the Gamasutra.com Web site: http://www.gamasutra.com/resource_guide/20010716/chen_01.htm.

Freeman, D. (July, 2002). *Four ways to use symbols to add emotional depth to games*. Retrieved November 12, 2005, from the Gamasutra.com Web site: http://www.gamasutra.com/features/20020724/freeman_01.htm.

Hancock, H. (April, 2004). *Better game design through cut scenes*. Retrieved November 12, 2005, from the Gamasutra.com Web site: http://www.gamasutra.com/features/20020401/hancock_01.htm.

Pagan, T. (July, 2001). *Where's the design in level design?*. Retrieved November 12, 2005, from the Gamasutra Web site: http://www.gamasutra.com/resource_guide/20010716/pagan_01.htm.

Saltzmann, M. (March, 2002). *Game design: Secrets of the sages—creating characters, storyboarding, and design documents*. Retrieved November 12, 2005, from the Gamasutra.com Web site: http://www.gamasutra.com/features/20020308/saltzman_01.htm.

Software Engineering Team

GameProgrammer.com. (n.d.). Retrieved November 12, 2005, from http://www.gameprogrammer.com/.

Patel, A. J. (2005). *Game programming information*. Retrieved November 12, 2005, from Amit's game programming information Web site: http://www-cs-students.stanford.edu/~amitp/gameprog.html.

Courtesy of *Into the Pixel*: Yellow Room

Artist: Stephan Martiniere

Art Team

Ahern, L. (December, 2001). *Creating base textures*. Retrieved November 12, 2005, from the Animation Artist Web site: http://www.animationartist.com/2001/12_dec/tutorials/ahearn12_24.htm.

Carmenisch, A. (2001). *The human head: A resource for 3D modelers*. Retrieved November 12, 2005, from the Mississippi State University Web site: http://coldfusion.art.msstate.edu/camenisch/theHumanHead. Dean, Z. Z. B. (n.d.). *Character animation: What it takes*. Retrieved November 12, 2005, from the 3D Ark Web site: http://www.3dark.com/archives/animation/ca_what_it_takes.html.

Keith, D. (October, 2001). *3D character animation: Posing and staging*. Retrieved November 12, 2005, from the G4TV.com Web site: http://www.g4tv.com/techvvault/features/34140/3D_Character_Animation_Posing_and_Staging.html.

Quality Assurance Team

Forsey, D. (n.d.). *Game testing primer*. Retrieved November 12, 2005, from University of British Columbia Computer Science department Web site: http://www.cs.ubc.ca/spider/forsey/448/Primers/09_GameTestingPrimer.doc.

Outside Contractors

Borders, C., & Case, M. (March, 2003). *The seven secrets of voice-over production*. Retrieved November 12, 2005, from the Gamasutra.com Web site: http://www.gamasutra.com/gdc2003/features/20030307/borders_01.htm.

Harland, K. (February, 2000). *Conceptual problems of interactive game scores*. Retrieved November 12, 2005, from the Gamasutra.com Web site: http://www.gamasutra.com/features/20000217/harland_01.htm.

Price, B. (August, 1996). *Tricks and techniques for sound effects design*. Retrieved November 12, 2005, from the Gamasutra.com Web site: http://www.gamasutra.com/features/19960819/prince_01.htm.

Stevenson, R. (September, 2000). *The art of noise: Game studio recording and Foley*. Retrieved November 12, 2005, from the Gamasutra.com Web site: http://www.gamasutra.com/features/20000922/stevenson_01.htm.

Practice Questions

1. Describe the main responsibilities of a game producer.
2. What are the major differences between a concept document, a game proposal document, and a design document?
3. What is the primary tool of a level designer?

4. Is it necessary to have a well-rounded education to be a producer in the game industry?

5. What must a technical lead take into account when creating a game's architecture?

6. What document serves as a style guide during the development of a game?

7. What are the major phases of testing during game development?

Lab Exercises

The goal in performing this lab exercise is to participate in the development of a game concept to gain a better understanding of the process.

Partner with another student for the next few lab sessions.

1. Brainstorm and write down ideas for a new game concept. This concept can be based on any one of the following:

   - A licensed property (e.g., based on a film, TV show, book).
   - A new title for an existing game franchise.
   - An original idea in a popular current game genre.
   - A brilliant and inspired idea that creates an entirely new genre. (Be prepared to explain the feasibility of such an idea.)

2. With your partner, begin developing a concept document for your new game by detailing

   - A brief description of the game.
   - The game's genre.
   - The target platform(s).
   - Key game features.
   - An overview of gameplay mechanics.
   - A story summary.
   - Simple concept art.

Written Assignments

1. Meet and communicate with your partner via e-mail and telephone to continue developing a concept document for the idea you created. This two- to three-page document should detail

   - A brief description of the game.
   - The game's genre.
   - The target platform(s).
   - Key game features.

- An overview of gameplay mechanics.

- A story summary.

- Simple concept art.

2. Over the next few lab sessions, you will develop a fully formed idea, pitch the idea to the class, and create a series of game documents describing it. By actively participating in the creation of a game concept, you will gain a better understanding of the game development process.

Ahern, L. (December, 2001). *Creating base textures*. Retrieved November 12, 2005, from the Animation Artist Web site: http://www.animationartist.com/2001/12_dec/tutorials/ahearn12_24.htm.

Bates, B. (2001). *Game design: The art & business of creating games*. Roseville, CA: Prima Publishing.

Borders, C., & Case, M. (March, 2003). *The seven secrets of voice-over production*. Retrieved November 12, 2005, from the Gamasutra.com Web site: http://www.gamasutra.com/gdc2003/features/20030307/borders_01.htm.

Carmenisch, A. (2001). *The human head: A resource for 3D modelers*. Retrieved November 12, 2005, from the Mississippi State University Web site: http://coldfusion.art.msstate.edu/camenisch/theHumanHead.

Chen, S., & Brown, D. (July, 2001). *The architecture of level design*. Retrieved November 12, 2005, from the Gamasutra.com Web site: http://www.gamasutra.com/resource_guide/20010716/chen_01.htm.

Crosby, O. (October, 2005). *Jobs in video game development*. Retrieved November 12, 2005, from the GIGnews.com Web site: http://www.gignews.com/crosby1.htm.

de St-Exupery, A. (n.d.). Retrieved November 12, 2005, from the BrainyQuotes Web site: http://www.brainyquote.com/quotes/quotes/a/antoinedes121910.html.

Dean, Z. Z. B. (n.d.). *Character animation: What it takes*. Retrieved November 12, 2005, from the 3D Ark Web site: http://www.3dark.com/archives/animation/ca_what_it_takes.html.

Doyle, M. (August, 2000). *Structuring a game development team*. Retrieved November 12, 2005, from the TechZone.com Web site: http://www.thetechzone.com/articles/how_to/game_making/index.shtml.

Einstein, A. (n.d.). Retrieved November 12, 2005, from the Jef's Web Files Web site: http://www.jefallbright.net/node/2398.

Eisenhower, D.D. (n.d.): Retrieved Tuesday, September 27, 2005, from The Quote Garden Web site: http://www.quotegarden.com/presidents-by.html.

Forsey, D. (n.d.). *Game testing primer*. Retrieved November 12, 2005, from University of British Columbia Computer Science department Web site: http://www.cs.ubc.ca/spider/forsey/448/Primers/09_GameTestingPrimer.doc.

Freeman, D. (July, 2002). *Four ways to use symbols to add emotional depth to games*. Retrieved November 12, 2005, from the Gamasutra.com Web site: http://www.gamasutra.com/features/20020724/freeman_01.htm.

Frost, R. (n.d.) Retrieved November 14, 2005 from the Thinkexist Web site: http://en.thinkexist.com/quotes/robert_frost/2.html.

GameProgrammer.com. (n.d.). Retrieved November 12, 2005, from http://www.gameprogrammer.com/.

Hallford, N., & Hailford, J. (2001). *Swords & circuitry: A designer's guide to computer role-playing games*. Roseville, CA: Prima Publishing.

Hancock, H. (April, 2004). *Better game design through cut scenes*. Retrieved November 12, 2005, from the Gamasutra.com Web site: http://www.gamasutra.com/features/20020401/hancock_01.htm.

Harland, K. (February, 2000). *Conceptual problems of interactive game scores*. Retrieved November 12, 2005, from the Gamasutra.com Web site: http://www.gamasutra.com/features/20000217/harland_01.htm.

Hendrick, A. (February, 1998). *Hiring game designers and game developers*. Retrieved November 12, 2005, from the Gamasutra.com Web site: http://www.gamasutra.com/features/19980320/hiring_designers_01.htm.

James, G. (1996). *The tao of programming*. InfoBooks.

Keith, D. (October, 2001). *3D character animation: Posing and staging*. Retrieved November 12, 2005, from the G4TV.com Web site: http://www.g4tv.com/techtvvault/features/34140/3D_Character_Animation_Posing_and_Staging.html.

Menscher, M. (2002). *Get in the game: Careers in the game industry*. New Riders Press.

Oglesby, D. (March, 2003). *Art management for artists*. Retrieved November 12, 2005, from the Gamasutra.com Web site: http://www.gamasutra.com/gdc2003/features/20030306/oglesby_01.htm.

Pagan, T. (July, 2001). *Where's the design in level design?* Retrieved November 12, 2005, from the Gamasutra Web site: http://www.gamasutra.com/resource_guide/20010716/pagan_01.htm.

Patel, A. J. (2005). *Game programming information*. Retrieved November 12, 2005, from Amit's Game Programming Information Web site: http://www-cs-students.stanford.edu/~amitp/gameprog.html.

Price, B. (August, 1996). *Tricks and techniques for sound effects design*. Retrieved November 12, 2005, from the Gamasutra.com Web site: http://www.gamasutra.com/features/19960819/prince_01.htm.

Rollings, A., & Adams, E. (2003). *Andrew Rollings and Ernest Adams on game design.* New Riders Press.

Ryan, T. (February, 2003). *Risk management with development schedules.* Retrieved November 12, 2005, from the Gamasutra.com Web site: http://www.gamasutra.com/features/20030206/ryan_01.shtml.

Saltzmann, M. (March, 2002). *Game design: Secrets of the sages—creating characters, storyboarding, and design documents.* Retrieved November 12, 2005, from the Gamasutra.com Web site: http://www.gamasutra.com/features/20020308/saltzman_01.htm.

Sloper, T. (n.d.). *Game biz advice.* Retrieved November 12, 2005, from the Sloperama .com Web site: http://www.sloperama.com/advice.html.

Stevenson, R. (September, 2000). *The art of noise: Game studio recording and Foley.* Retrieved November 12, 2005, from the Gamasutra.com Web site: http://www.gamasutra.com/features/20000922/stevenson_01.htm.

Whistler, J.M. (n.d.). Retrieved November 12, 2005, from the Painter's Keys Resource Web site: http://www.painterskeys.com/getquotes.asp?fname=sw&ID=324.

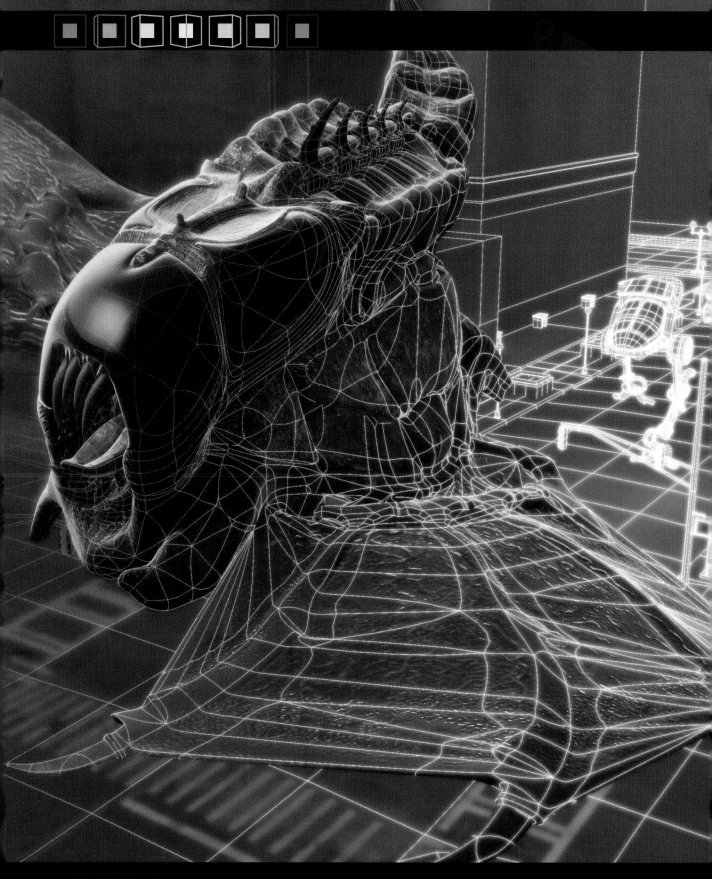

Courtesy of 3D artist Bill Blakesley

CHAPTER 7

Game Development Process Part One:
Concept and Preproduction

In the previous chapter we described the roles and tasks of the development teams in producing a game title. In this chapter we begin our examination of the processes and procedures in the software development lifecycle of video and computer games. The development of a video game passes through several phases, starting with the initial concept phase, followed by preproduction, production, release, and postrelease. We will start by looking at the initial concept and preproduction phases.

A game begins with an idea. The creation of the initial game concept is the first step in the concept phase. In this phase the development team analyzes the marketplace and investigates current gaming trends. The two major deliverables from this phase are the concept and proposal documents. The goal of the preproduction phase is to describe the roadmap for the production process. The major deliverables from this phase are the game's design and technical design documents.

A detailed and thorough knowledge of the process of creating the design document is essential because it is the single most important document in the development process. Here we need to consider its various features as well as the importance of the game's technical design document. Once these are in place it is time for the creation of a game prototype.

After completing this chapter, you will be able to:

- Describe the process of creating an initial game concept.
- Describe the sections in a game's concept document.
- Describe the process of creating a game's proposal document.
- Explain the process of creating and maintaining a game's design document.
- Describe the various features of a design document.

President and CEO of Stormfront Studios

Don Daglow's Law of Authorship: Game development teams that are really teams will, over time, always outperform groups built on the "one designer and many implementers" model. This doesn't mean there is not one design leader guiding the creative process—in fact, games designed by committee often suffer from a lack of clear vision and consistent fun. It does mean that lead designers who involve everyone in the team and look for creativity in every craft will produce far better games than dictators who micromanage every move. Of course, where does micro-management stop and establishing a clear vision for the team begin?

The next time you see a movie you really enjoyed, take a moment to watch the credits scroll by and watch how many names are there. Did the director tell each and every one of them exactly how to do their jobs?

Initial Concept Phase

"Don't worry about people stealing your ideas. If your ideas are any good you'll have to ram them down people's throats." [1]

Now that we have familiarized ourselves with the various members of the game development team, we will examine the development process itself. As with the positions on the development team, the steps outlined here are not set in stone. Though some standardization is starting to occur, many companies have different approaches to preproduction and production, which means that some steps may not occur, whereas others may occur at different times.

Rarely does the process occur in such a neat and orderly fashion. We will look at the most common development steps as they might occur on a big-budget action project by a major publisher. Whether a game is developed and produced in a matter of months or years, the process will pass through a specific series of generalized phases. Let's examine these phases in detail, along with the steps that might be included in each phase. We'll begin with the creation of the game concept.

Game Concept

A game begins with an idea. If a team exists at the outset, it will be small—generally just a lead designer, a technical lead, a producer, and perhaps a conceptual artist

---

[1] Atkins, H. (n.d.). Retrieved November 14, 2005, from the Thinkexist.com Web site: http://en.thinkexist.com/quotation/don-t_worry_about_people_stealing_your_ideas-if/11068.html.

if the lead designer is not taking on this job. These core team members will flesh out the idea, but where does the idea come from in the first place? Some common sources for game concepts include licensed properties, game franchises, and current gaming trends, which lead to marketplace demands and of course inspiration.

Licensed Properties. Licensed properties are an extremely popular source for game concepts. In this case the publisher must acquire the rights to make a game based on a popular movie, television show, sports figure, or personality. This can be an expensive proposition, but in the end it can be worth it. In many cases a licensed game will have a pre-sold audience. This is a safer bet for the publisher; even if the game is mediocre, it can still turn a healthy profit.

Acquiring the license of an untested property, on the other hand, can be risky. If someone had spent a lot of money developing a game based on a box office disaster like *Battlefield Earth* or *Cutthroat Island,* the game would have likely been a flop even if the design was excellent. Some examples of games based on licensed properties include The Lord of the Rings: Battle for Middle Earth, Harry Potter and the Chamber of Secrets, Britney's Dance Beat, Star Wars Galaxies, Enter the Matrix, Tiger Woods PGA Tour 2005, and Who Wants to Be a Millionaire.

Game Franchises. Existing game franchises are another popular source of ideas. If a game turns out to be a runaway hit, sequels, spin-offs, and expansion packs are inevitable. Often a publisher will hire a developer to create a sequel to a game even if that publisher did not create the original. Some examples of popular game franchises include Splinter Cell, Half-Life2, The Sims, Command & Conquer, Metal Gear Solid 3: Snake Eater, Might & Magic, Medal of Honor, and Warcraft.

Current Gaming Trends. When a particular game is a hit, an inevitable slew of copycat games follow. This has been true since the early days of Pong. Witness the endless Tycoon simulation games that followed the popular game Sid Meier's Rollercoaster Tycoon. Although the name Sid Meier is a franchise in itself, there was no way to copyright the single word *tycoon.* The game documentation site Mobygames.com lists no fewer than 42 games with the word *tycoon* in their titles. Some of the games on that list include such unlikely titles as Trailer Park Tycoon, Rock Band Tycoon, and even Moon Tycoon.

Again, this source is not without risk. After the incredible success of Sony's Everquest, dozens of developers announced their own MMOG (massively multiplayer online game) titles. A flood of these games oversaturated the market, and none has come close to being as popular as Everquest. Even the highly anticipated The Sims Online, based on the most successful computer game in history, had a disappointing launch. The introduction of the urban game genre by Rock Star the GTA series has created a new environment, and the copycats are finding shelf space—L.A. Rush, 25 to Life, and Urban Reign just to mention a few.

Marketplace Demands. A publisher might decide to develop a game based on a recommendation from its marketing department. If analysis of current marketplace trends shows that a particular type of game is underrepresented, the publisher might decide that a new title in that style or genre might do well. The development team with its sights on new trends in the underground movement will find creative lifestyles and content for game development. The marketplace often reflects youth movement.

Inspiration. Surprisingly, inspiration is the rarest source of new game ideas. Sometimes a designer, artist, or producer simply has an inspired idea so original and compelling that the company will decide to develop it on its own merit. The lack of originally inspired games does not come from a lack of original ideas: Game people tend to be creative. The lack is due to the fact that publishers are reluctant to take risks or try anything new, but this does occur.

Although this is a risky proposition, under the right circumstances it can be lucrative. Occasionally one of these inspired games is a huge hit, and if the developers were smart enough to maintain control of the intellectual property (IP) rights, they can literally make millions by licensing it to other media. Whereas plenty of games have been based on movies, recently popular games are also becoming the basis for movies. The owners of the IP can make millions selling the movie rights to Hollywood. Some examples of inspired game ideas that have become hugely popular include Doom, Mortal Combat, House of the Living Dead, Tomb Raider, Max Payne, and Deus Ex.

Concept Document

After a concept is accepted, it is time to flesh it out and commit it to paper. A lead designer, a technical lead, a producer, and perhaps a conceptual artist will probably be the only members of the initial development team, if one exists during this phase. Creating a concept document is the first goal of the team. This two- or three-page document will describe the game in brief and simple terms. In essence, this document will become the sales pitch used to get financing for the project. Typically the concept document contains the "high concept" description, the genre, the target platforms, key game features, an overview of gameplay mechanics, a story summary, and concept art. The following sections provide a brief description of each section of this document.

High Concept Description. The term *high concept* came from the movie industry. It is simply a one- or two-line description that describes the game in a simple, exciting way. The key here is to generate excitement for the project and to allow the reader to see the idea's potential immediately.

Consider this description of the recent Illusion Softworks game Mafia or Vivendi's Scarface: "Mafia is a third-person 3D action and driving game about organized crime in the 1930s. The player takes the role of a mob foot soldier and must complete various missions in order to work his way to the top of the organization."

This is an accurate description of the game, but it does little to reveal the "feel" of the game and does not generate any excitement. Figure 7.1 shows an example of a more effective "high concept" description of the game Mafia:

> **"Enter the sordid underworld of the 1930s and gain the respect of the Salieri family in a 3D action epic filled with car chases, mob hits, beautiful dames, and dangerous dons. Begin as a getaway driver and work your way to the top, eventually becoming a 'made man'. However, be careful whom you trust. Even your closest friends could betray you. Mafia. It's not personal. It's just business."**

Figure 7.1 Example of a high concept descript for Scarface, from Vivendi Universal.

This description is exciting. It reveals much more about the style and tone of the game, which it sells. Comparison with other popular games, movies, or TV titles is another tool that is part of the high concept description. By comparing the game to other familiar pop culture references, the reader can immediately see the commercial potential of a concept. Here are a few examples of recent games described in this manner.

- ☐ Mafia: The Godfather meets Grand Theft Auto 3.

- ☐ Metal of Honor: Allied Assault—Saving Private Ryan: the video game.

- ☐ Earth & Beyond: Everquest in space.

- ☐ No One Lives Forever: A female James Bond in the psychedelic 1960s.

These types of high concept lines should never replace an exciting description, but they are often effective at the end of the description to cement the idea in the reader's mind.

Genre. The next part of the concept document contains a brief description of the game's genre. It should first indicate which of the general, commonly identified genres best describes the game; then it might add a few descriptive words to specify the game's niche genre. The traditional genres include action, adventure, role-playing, real-time strategy, massively multiplayer, simulation, "god" game, first-person shooter, driving game, and so on. Niche genres include such categories as space opera, cyberpunk, postapocalyptic, medieval fantasy, or superheroes.

Target Platform(s). This area discusses the target platform or multiple platforms. It should also include descriptions of any possible online, network, or multiplayer support that will be provided. This section should describe the gaming platform(s) that will be supported (e.g., PC, PlayStation 2, Xbox, Nintendo DS) as well as any special features that will be supported if the game is played on handheld or wireless devices.

The target platform section should also list any special hardware required by the game. For example, many PC-based games list both their recommended and minimum hardware configurations. The hardware in the minimum requirements will allow a user to play the game, whereas the recommended list is what's needed for a good gameplay experience. The latest generation of game consoles (e.g., PlayStation 3, Xbox 360) have a number of optional components such as hard drives that make this type of information important in the console world as well.

Key Game Features. On the back of the box, most games have a bulleted list of key game features that might appeal to potential buyers. These features should be unique and make the game stand out, and a similar list of features should be included in the concept document. Here are some examples:

> Sprawling futuristic environments: Battle the enemy in a mind-boggling variety of environments, including lush jungles, barren wastelands, underground labyrinths, and stunning cityscapes!

> Multiplayer action: Internet or LAN multiplayer mode supporting up to 135 players!

Kaos character development - artist John Walker

Figure 7.2 Concept art for the Entertainment Arts Research game, Kaotic Foolz.

Overview of Gameplay. This is a brief but exciting description of what the player does during the game, covering all the different elements of gameplay. The writing of this section often occurs in second person and avoids the specifics of keystrokes or mouse clicks. For example,

> You move through the bombed-out ruins of a city battling renegade cyborgs with an array of deadly weapons.

Concept Art. Using concept art to help sell a project is common. A sketch of the main character, some interesting creatures, or an imaginative landscape can help readers visualize the game and convince them of its viability. Figure 7.2 shows concept art for the game Kaotic Foolz from Entertainment Arts Research.

Game Proposal Document

A publisher that expresses interest in a project will certainly require more information before committing to funding its development. The next step, therefore, is the creation of the game's proposal document. The proposal document is an expanded and more detailed version of the concept document. In addition to pitching the idea, this document will contain an analysis of the game's marketability, legal issues like licensing, and a technical evaluation (see Table 7.1).

TABLE 7.1	**Major sections in a game proposal document.**	
Section	**Focus**	**Responsibility**
Game concept, gameplay mechanics, and key game features	Expanded description from the initial concept document.	Technical lead and producer
Marketing analysis	Presents demographic information about targeted consumers.	Producer
Technical analysis	Outlines technical challenges and requirements.	Lead software engineer
Legal	Defines legal issues, including intellectual property, licensed technology, and copyright.	Legal department, producer
Profit and loss statement	Estimates the cost and projected revenue of the title.	Producer

Typically the proposal document will include the game concept, gameplay mechanics, and key game features along with a technical analysis. Usually a market analysis, the main selling points, and a profit and loss statement are included, as is a report on any legal issues that might arise. Concept art is also presented to help the producers get a better grasp of the game. The following sections provide an overview of the major sections of this document.

Game Concept, Gameplay Mechanics, and Key Game Features. These three categories will be revised and expanded versions of the descriptions in the initial concept document. The team members will arrive at any changes by evaluating the original concept. The tech lead will perform a technical evaluation, while the producer will evaluate the marketing and budgeting aspects of the game. The entire team will consider the evaluations. Although the initial concept might have been ambitious, the proposal document must begin to look at the project in a realistic way and determine what is doable given the available resources and budget. Any modification of the concept by changing or removing problematic game features takes place at this point, and then these changes are incorporated in the document.

Marketing Analysis. If the publisher has a marketing division, the producer might seek its help in compiling a marketing analysis. If not, the producer must compile this information. Accurate information is essential. There are many Internet resources for such information. The marketing analysis (see Table 7.2) should cover a number of specific areas including the game's target market, other similar titles in the market, and comparison of selling features.

Technical Analysis and Concept Art. The lead programmer usually writes the technical analysis section. The section outlines the technical challenges and requirements of the project. The overall outlook should be promising. If the analysis seems risky or pessimistic, game concept and features should be reconsidered. In the end, this will save a lot of time and money and give the project a far greater chance of success.

Game Cheats 7.1

Some marketing information resources on the Internet:

DFC Research Service: http://www.dfcint.com/research_services.html

Game Market Watch: http://www.gamemarketwatch.com

Game Stats: http://www.gamestats.com

Moby Games: http://www.mobygames.com

TABLE 7.2   Examples of market analysis in the development of a game proposal.

Market Analysis Areas
Game's target market: Who will be playing the game? What is the targeted age group? Gender? Player type?
Similar titles in the same market: An analysis of some successful titles in the same market. Present sales figures in terms of dollars and units shipped, as well as information about sequels, spin-offs, and other franchise opportunities that these titles might have generated.
Comparison of selling features: Analysis of the selling features of these other titles (broken down for comparison with the features of the proposed game). Make special note of any innovations that might make the title stand out in the marketplace.

A package of concept art is also important at this stage. Even if the concept document did not include artwork, the proposal should certainly have it. It will likely be the first thing the publisher looks at. If it does not impress, it might also be the last thing.

Profit and Loss Statement. The profit and loss statement is an important section in the proposal document. The profit and loss statement estimates the development cost and projected revenue of the title. The figures in the profit and loss statement should be promising to justify the risk of funding the game's development. This section outlines the budget, including projected equipment costs, salaries, overhead, license fees, estimated marketing costs, publishing costs, and so on.

The creation of a revenue projection depends on the market analysis. Arriving at the projected revenue and return on investment (ROI) figures comes after subtracting the cost of the project. This figure demonstrates to the publisher that it will be profitable to publish the game. If this figure is not impressive, the publisher will not be able to justify the risk of funding the game's development.

Preproduction Phase

"The general who wins the battle makes many calculations in his temple before the battle is fought. The general who loses makes but few calculations beforehand."[2]

With the initial game concept established and the game's proposal completed and signed off, the next phase in the development process is preproduction. The ultimate goal of this phase, often called the *proof of concept phase,* is twofold: first, to develop a road map for the production process, and second, to prove to the publisher that the game concept is viable and worth creating. The major deliverables from this phase are the design and technical design documents.

Design and Technical Design Documents

The design and technical design documents are, without a doubt, the most important documents created during the entire production process. These massive documents will exhaustively outline every functional and technical aspect of the game and will guide production. Updating these documents occurs constantly throughout development. Everyone on the team will refer and contribute to this document, but it is the lead designer's primary responsibility to see that it always reflects the most accurate and current information about the game.

The technical design document commonly lays out the design strategy in a detailed and highly technical way. It will describe in detail the tools used to create the game and whether they are proprietary or licensed from a third party. It will also set the standards for asset conversion, code design, the save game system, and the version control system. The technical design document is the technical lead's plan for realizing the vision set forth in the design document. Therefore, the focus of this section will be to examine the major sections of this document.

Although there is no template or standard layout for a design document for a computer or video game, this is a software development project with certain areas to stress. Figure 7.3 shows a summary of the elements found in the design document.

---

[2] Tzu, S. (n.d.). *The art of war*. Retrieved from the Wikipedia Web site: http:/en.wikipedia.org/wiki/en:The_Art_of_War.

These include the game overview, the game story, the development of characters and creatures, the way players advance, and the user interface. Other important areas include the level design requirements, the gameplay mechanics, the use of artificial intelligence, the music and audio effects, and the concept art. Let us look at these elements in detail.

Kaos takes his fighting stance.

Vic regains balance and gets back in fighting stance.

Kaos rushes Vic and begins punching.

Storyboard artist Haji Abdullah, Kaotic Foolz, Entertainment Arts Research

Figure 7.3 Sample Storyboard from Kaotic Foolz

Game Overview. The design document will start with a complete table of contents to allow team members to refer quickly to any section during development. This first section is a brief overview of the game. The game overview section of the design document will include information on key features, the target audience and platform, and the competitive genre titles (Table 7.3). It will also outline the story summary and cover the environments or areas. Also included are the risks of producing the game. These can be ambitious design plans, untested technologies, complex programming tasks, recruitment of team members, and reliance on external resources. This section should provide a contingency plan for each identified risk.

Many of these topics were in the proposal document, but proposals are inherently vague and are essentially detailed sales pitches. The design document approaches these topics in a realistic and specific way. As presented in the overview, these topics will be brief paragraphs that get directly to the point and are for quick reference. The detailed specifics will come later in the document.

Characters and Creatures. The next section of the design document describes the characters in the game and usually contains concept art or model sheets for each character. These may include the player character (PC), friendly nonplayer characters (NPCs), enemy NPCS or "mobs," boss NPCs, and any other important NPCs.

Game Cheats 7.2

"Mobs" are the designation given to enemy NPCs, which are often creatures. This is a shortened form of the term *mobile*, though some designers insist that it is an acronym for "monster or beast." "Bosses" are powerful enemy NPCs that the PC faces at certain points during the game. Boss encounters are usually at the end of a specific mission or level to act as a sort of climax for that portion of the game.

TABLE 7.3   Topic areas in a game overview section of a game's design document.

Topic Area	Description
Target area and platform(s)	Describe the game's market by its platform(s) and genre. This section also presents demographic information about the target consumer.
Key features	Consists of a bulleted list of key game features that will make the game different from and better than competing titles.
Story summary	Presented in one or two paragraphs, provides a brief summary of the game's storyline
Environments or areas	Outlines the number of environments, areas, locations, and/or levels that make up the game.
Competitive genre titles	Lists all known titles that will be in direct competition with the game, whether they are already on the market or currently in development.
Risk assessment	Assessment of the problems that might arise during development.

For example, role-playing games like X-Men Legends II: Rise of the Apocalypse and Dragon Quest VIII do not have specific player characters. These games allow the player to create a character based on a number of different choices. Outlining the player's character options will be necessary. What are the different classes? What are the special abilities of each class? Background information, descriptions, and concept art should be included for these as well.

Level Design Requirements. This section in the design document is a detailed description of each game level in order of play. Each level should have one or more clear objectives for the player. These objectives may change during the level, but the player should always be aware of the current objective. The following list outlines some elements the level design requirements should describe:

☐ **Character locations:** The location of all NPCs and mobs contained in the level, and any special NPC functions listed by location.

☐ **Special features:** The descriptions of special features, scripted events, puzzles, or secrets contained in the level.

☐ **Special equipment:** Listing of any special equipment, special abilities, or "power-ups" (Figure 7.4) that the player will need to complete the level, as well as their location and any other equipment or abilities from this level.

Player Advancement. This section describes how the player advances and gains abilities and other rewards through the game. Some of the topics covered here

Image created by Bill Blakesley

Figure 7.4 Boss NPCs are usually visually imposing to add a sense of drama to the culmination of a scene or level.

include difficulty settings, damage and healing, and scoring systems. Most games have numerous difficult settings to increase their appeal, including different types of players and skill levels. The section will also contain a description(s) of the components developed for the game's health system (Figure 7.5). For example, are there healing potions or first aid kits, or does the player simply rest in order to heal?

The design document should also describe the scoring system. For example, a player might see statistics about the number of kills made, items found, or medals earned at the conclusion of each level. In an RPG, the scoring system might consist

3D artist Harshdeep Borah

Figure 7.5 Soldier Character Development.

of "experience points" awarded during play. These points allow the character to increase abilities and personal attributes by "leveling up."

Gameplay Mechanics. We conclude our discussion of the design document with the section on game mechanics. This important, large section describes the mechanics of gameplay. It should describe the game genre (e.g., action, adventure, role-playing, real-time strategy, simulation, hybrid genre) and game perspective (e.g., first-person, third-person, side-scroller, top-down).

A brief description of the game world is included. This might include the period, the various environments, and perhaps some general backstory or history. In addition, this section will also describe the player controls and will probably include a map of the keyboard or, if the game is a console title, a sketch of the game pad controller. It should include the various moves the player might make and the proper controls to initiate those moves.

Any item in the game world that the player can interact with is a gameplay element. This can include doors, elevators, levers, traps, vehicles, and the like. Descriptions of these elements and their function in the game appear here in detail. If the game will support multiplayer modes, these must be detailed. The various types of multi-play (e.g., team-based, head-to-head, capture the flag) should be listed and described. This description should also detail the difference between multiplayer mode and the single-player game as reflected by the gameplay elements.

This section also lays out all of the game logic in each level, animation by animation. This is especially true in adventure or action/adventure games, where the puzzles can be complex and have many different possible states. Describing game logic means describing all of the possible states for each puzzle object and all of the ways these states affect character states and vice versa. This often takes the shape of IF, THEN, AND, and BUT statements. For example,

If the character steps on the pressure plate and is not wearing the magnetic shoes, then A occurs.

If the character steps on the pressure plate and is wearing the magnetic shoes but does not yet have the door key, then B occurs.

If the character steps on the pressure plate and is wearing the magnetic shoes and has the door key, then C occurs. Character says line ALI_035B.

If the character steps on the pressure plate and is wearing the magnetic shoes and has the door key but has not yet talked to the Wizard, then D occurs. Character says line ALI_035C.

This detailed sample of game logic includes all the recorded lines and under what conditions they are "called" by the game. It includes all player actions and animations and sounds that can occur in all possible situations; all inventory items, power-up moves, and weapons and how they behave in all situations; and so forth. Because this is such a complex task, the game logic section will often take up a large portion of the design document.

Also included in this section is a discussion of the game physics, which describes the physics of the game with regard to movement, combat, and collision detection. The technical lead and the software engineering team usually contribute this information. This team is also responsible for outlining the AI requirements of the game. Areas to be covered will include enemy path finding, collision handling, enemy spawning, and enemy damage systems.

TABLE 7.4   Summary of deliverables from the initial concept and preproduction phases.

Deliverable	Description
Concept document	Provides a brief overview of the target platforms, key game features, gameplay, and game mechanics.
Game proposal	Includes market analysis, profit and loss statement, and technical analysis.
Design document	Describes characters, level design requirements, gameplay mechanics, user interface, music, and audio effects.
Technical design document	Lays out the design strategy and tools used to create the game; sets the standards for asset conversion, code design, and the version control system.

SUMMARY

The development process for a video game passes through several phases. These include the initial concept phase, preproduction and production phases, and finally release and postrelease phases. A good rule of thumb is that more work should occur in the initial concept or analysis and design phases. What the development team accomplishes in these early phases in the process will dictate how smoothly the implementation of the game title proceeds during the production phase, as well as the quality of the game.

The development team creates several documents during the initial concept and preproduction phases that will be used as roadmaps in the implementation of the game title. These include initial concept, game proposal, design, and technical design documents (see Table 7.4). Contracting the services of a good technical writer, if one is not already on the development team, is important because these documents should present information in a technical as well as clear and concise manner. Maintaining these documents throughout the life-cycle of the project is also important.

A game begins with an idea. During the initial concept or analysis phase, the team analyzes current gaming trends and marketplace demand. The game concept can originate from a number of sources, including existing franchises or licensed properties. In addition, the team may have an original idea for a game; although this may be a risky way to develop a new title, the game may become a huge success. It is important in this case to keep control of the intellectual property rights for the game.

If the concept for a game is accepted, a team fleshes it out and documents their ideas in a concept document. This team generally includes a lead designer, technical lead, producer, and conceptual artist. This is a high-level document that contains brief descriptions of the game genre and target platform(s), as well as key game features and an overview of gameplay. The goal of this document is to sell the game idea to a publisher, so game descriptions should jump off the page and concept art should be imaginative and convincing.

The game proposal document expands on the concept document. It contains an analysis of the game's marketability, legal issues, and a profit and loss statement. The largest deliverable from the preproduction phase consists of the design and technical design documents. These documents provide the technical and artistic requirements for the game. Sections in the design document outline, in detail, the game mechanics, descriptions of character and creatures, and level design requirements

In previous chapters we described many elements that make up additional sections of the design document. These include the user interface (UI), game save and pause systems, game story, and music and sound effects. As with the other sections of the design document, these sections contain detailed descriptions so that implementation of components occurs quickly and reliably during the production phase. For example, the details of the UI should be specific enough to allow the software engineering team to create the interface and should include sketches and conceptual art. Specific areas this section covers include the main menu, options menu(s), heads-up display (HUD), design, and inventory management system.

The game story section should provide a listing and description of any cut scenes in the game. These should be laid out in chronological order and include any diverging plot elements or optional sequences. The HUD design describes information displayed as overlays or framing graphics during gameplay. Concept art is included, along with detailed descriptions of each output device and the information it will convey. The technical documentation should also include a complete list of all music cues and sound effects that occur before, during, and

after the game. Typical sound and music files for a game might include installation theme, title theme, character sound effects, or interface sound effects. Each individual audio file should be listed by name ("orc_attack3.wav") and include a description of the use of the sound or music within the game.

The technical design document is the plan for realizing the vision set forth in the design document. This document lists all the software engineering tasks the game will require. It assigns all tasks to members of the team and estimates how long they will take to complete each task. This allows the technical lead to estimate how much time the project will require and the size of the software engineering team.

The final product of the preproduction process is a prototype—a working software program that demonstrates the look and feel of the project. In many cases it won't even be a playable game level. The idea is to simulate the game. Even if the game engine or other necessary technology has not been implemented, the game's real-time appearance can be simulated using prerendered graphics. The purpose of the prototype is to demonstrate to the publisher why the game is unique. It presents the game vision in the best possible way by giving a glimpse of what the game will be like upon completion. It also shows the publisher what the development team can accomplish and demonstrates that the production path they have established is viable.

This is the critical proof of concept stage in the development process. It will almost certainly be when the publisher decides whether to fund the game's actual production. If so, then actual production can begin. We will examine the production phase in the next chapter.

Game Proposal

Ahearn, L. (2002, December). *The game proposal, part one: The basics.* Retrieved November 20, 2005. from the Gamasutra.com Web site: http://www.gamasutra.com/features/20021220/ahearn_01.htm.

Pirouz, D.M. (1998, February). *Writing a business plan for independent gaming ventures.* Retrieved November 20, 2005, from the Gamasutra.com Web site: http://www.gamasutra.com/features/business_and_legal/19980220/business_plan_intro.htm.

Ryan, T. (1999, October). *Documentation guidelines for the game concept and proposal.* Retrieved November 20, 2005, from the Gamasutra.com Web site: http://www.gamasutra.com/features/19991019/ryan_01.htm.

Sloper, T. (2001, December). *How the game development/production process works.* Retrieved November 20, 2005, from the Sloperama.com Web site: http://www.sloperama.com/advice/lesson10.html.

Preproduction

Freeman, T. (1997, August). Creating a great design document. *Game Developer Magazine*. Retrieved November 20, 2005, from the Gamasutra.com Web site: http://www.gamasutra.com/features/19970912/design_doc.htm.

Ryan, T. (1999, December). *The anatomy of a design document, part two: Documentation guidelines for the functional and technical specifications*. Retrieved November 20, 2005, from the Gamasutra.com Web site: http://www.gamasutra.com/features/19991217/ryan_01.htm.

Design Document

Cobb, L. (2001, October). *The technical design document for Radical Entertainment's Mirth*. Retrieved November 20, 2005, from the University of Calgary Web site: http://www.cpsc.ucalgary.ca/Research/vision/Games/MonstersInc_FEDesign.pdf.

Saltzman, M. (2003, March). *Game design: Secrets of the sages: Creating characters, storyboarding, and design documents*. Retrieved on November 20, 2005, from the Gamasutra.com Web site: http://www.gamasutra.com/features/20020308/saltzman_05.htm.

Practice Questions

1. What are the major differences between a game concept document and a game proposal document?
2. What is the reason for including a profit and loss statement in the proposal document?
3. What are the primary areas covered by a design document?
4. What is the purpose of a technical design document?
5. What piece of software is the end result of the preproduction phase?

Lab Exercise

The objective of this lab exercise is to actively participate in the development of a game concept so that you will continue to gain a better understanding of the process.

During the lab, you should have the following games installed on the system: Zork 1 and Neverwinter Nights.

Activity

1. Using the information provided in this chapter, you will begin to document the game concept from the last lab in Chapter 6 by creating a concept document. Sections in the document should include

   - A high concept description.
   - The game's genre.

- The target platform(s).
- Key game features.
- An overview of gameplay mechanics.
- A story summary.
- Concept art.

2. Now expand your shorter concept document into a more detailed proposal document that will include

- The game concept.
- Gameplay mechanics.
- Key game features.
- Market analysis.
- Selling points.
- Technical analysis (see note).
- Legal issues (see note).
- Profit and loss statement (see note).
- Concept art.

Note: Precise technical information and/or financial estimates are not necessary for these categories. Simply describe your vision for the game with regard to these areas and indicate the kind of information that you would include.

Preparation for Next Week's Assignment

This week you will prepare a concept document and proposal document; you will submit them next week. Be prepared to pitch the game as part of an oral presentation in next week's lab. Good luck!

Courtesy of *Into the Pixel*: Ryu Hayabusa

Artist: Tomonobu Itagaki, Hiroaki Matsui

MANUSCRIPT REFERENCES

Ahearn, L. (2002, December). *The game proposal, part one: The basics.* Retrieved November 20, 2005, from the Gamasutra.com Web site: http://www.gamasutra.com/features/20021220/ahearn_01.htm.

Atkins, H. (n.d.) Retrieved November 14, 2005, from The Thinkexist.com Web site: http://en.thinkexist.com/quotation/don-t_worry_about_people_stealing_your_ideas-if/11068.html.

Bates, B. (2001). *Game design: The art and business of creating games.* Prima Publishing.

Cobb, L. (2001, October). *The technical design document for Radical Entertainment's Mirth.* Retrieved November 20, 2005, from the University of Calgary Web site: http://www.cpsc.ucalgary.ca/Research/vision/Games/MonstersInc_FEDesign.pdf.

Davies, D. (2000, December). *Common methodologies for lead artists.* Retrieved November 20, 2005, from the Gamasutra.com Web site: http://www.gamasutra.com/features/20001204/davies_01.htm.

DFC Research Service. (n.d.). *DFC intelligence: Research services.* Retrieved November 20, 2005, from http://www.dfcint.com/research_services.html.

Freeman, T. (1997, August). Creating a great design document. *Game Developer Magazine.* Retrieved November 20, 2005, from the Gamasutra.com Web site: http://www.gamasutra.com/features/19970912/design_doc.htm.

Gamasutra. (n.d.). *Gamasutra: The art and science of making games.* Retrieved November 20, 2005, from http://www.gamasutra.com.

GameStats. (n.d.). *GameStats: Cheats, movies, screenshots, previews and reviews.* Retrieved November 20, 2005, from http://www.gamestats.com.

Hallford, N., & Hallford, J. (2001). *Swords and circuitry: A designer's guide to role-playing games.* Prima Publishing.

Moby Games. (n.d.). *MobyGames: A game documentation and review project.* Retrieved November 20, 2005, from http://www.mobygames.com.

Pirouz, D. M. (1998, February). *Writing a business plan for independent gaming ventures.* Retrieved November 20, 2005, from the Gamasutra.com Web site: http://www.gamasutra.com/features/business_and_legal/19980220/business_plan_intro.htm.

Rollings, A., & Adams, E. (2003). *Andrew Rollings and Ernest Adams on game design.* New Riders Press.

Ryan, T. (1999, October). *Documentation guidelines for the game concept and proposal.* Retrieved November 20, 2005, from the Gamasutra.com Web site: http://www.gamasutra.com/features/19991019/ryan_01.htm.

Ryan, T. (1999, December). *The anatomy of a design document, part two: Documentation guidelines for the functional and technical specifications.* Retrieved November 20, 2005, from the Gamasutra.com Web site: http://www.gamasutra.com/features/19991217/ryan_01.htm.

Saltzman, M. (2003, March). *Game design: Secrets of the sages: Creating characters, storyboarding, and design documents.* Retrieved on November 20, 2005, from the Gamasutra.com Web site: http://www.gamasutra.com/features/20020308/saltzman_05.htm.

Sloper, T. (2001, December). *How the game development/production process works.* Retrieved November 20, 2005, from the Sloperama.com Web site: http://www.sloperama.com/advice/lesson10.htm

Tzu, S. *The art of war.* Retrieved November 14, 2005, from the Wikipedia Web site: http://en.wikipedia.org/wiki/en:The_Art_of_War.

Courtesy of *Into the Pixel*: Enzo in Florence

Artist: Ben O'Sullivan, Gren Atherton, Mark Sharratt, Matt Watts

Courtesy of 3D artist Bill Blakesley

CHAPTER 8

Game Development Process Part Two:
Production and Postrelease

This chapter provides an overview of the challenges and issues related to producing and releasing a game. The production phase of a game's development can last anywhere from six months to two years. Some games have taken even longer to produce, but a game that takes over two years to complete is running a high risk. Because gaming technology continues to advance at a rapid pace, the game might seem obsolete when compared to titles developed quickly, using the latest tools and innovations.

We continue our examination of the game development process and discuss factors important to developing and marketing a game, including the production schedule and postrelease and marketing strategies. Whereas the creation of a detailed design document was an important component of the preproduction phase, creating and maintaining the production schedule is crucial during the production process.

In this chapter we identify threats to keeping a project on track and the tools used to ensure that development is on time and within the allocated budget. We also examine the different stages of production and the additional challenges associated with the postrelease phase, including coordinating support and selling and marketing strategies.

After completing this chapter, you will be able to:

- Describe the components for tracking a production schedule.
- Describe the challenges of creating and meeting a production schedule.
- Describe several challenges in meeting a production schedule.
- Describe the critical phases of the production process, from alpha to gold release.
- Describe several strategies for marketing and selling a game.

Production Phase

"One of the most difficult tasks men can perform, however much others may despise it, is the invention of good games. And it cannot be done by men out of touch with their instinctive values."[1]

The production phase is the major part of the development process for a game. It can also be the most expensive. Therefore, it is essential to begin with a realistic production schedule. We begin our discussion of the production phase of game development with an examination of the production schedule.

Production Schedule

As with all development efforts, the production schedule for a video game is not a static document. The schedule must be refined and altered during the process because the feature set can change. New tasks will arise, and others will become unnecessary. Some tasks will take less time than planned, while others will take far longer than estimated. Because of these factors, the schedule will require regular maintenance.

Tracking Progress. Because the production process can be long and complex, it becomes necessary to break it into small, manageable chunks with specific goals. By carefully tracking these specific segments of production, the team will be able to track the progress of production and gain some idea of whether they remain on schedule. Two different tools are usually used to track the progress of a project during production–checkpoints and milestones.

Checkpoints. *Checkpoints* are internal checks for the developers themselves. When the team reaches these important points in the production process, they can look back at the tasks they have completed to ensure they are on track with the production schedule. Checkpoints also give the team a chance to look for incomplete tasks, flaws, or other production problems before continuing. If there are any problems, the team should address them immediately and make sure that the production schedule incorporates any changes.

Checkpoints should be evenly spaced throughout production. There should not be so many that they create undue stress, but they should not be spaced too far apart. The functions of a checkpoint include

---

[1] van der Post, L. (1975). *Jung and the story of our time*. New York: Pantheon Books. [Electronic copy]. Retrieved August 12, 2005, from the HipBone Games Web site: http://home.earthlink.net/~hipbone/IDTWeb/WhyGame.html.

☐ Allowing the developer to determine whether production is on schedule.

☐ Giving the team a chance to identify flaws, incomplete tasks, and other problems and correct them before proceeding.

☐ Keeping the pace of production on track and moving forward.

Milestones. *Milestones* are checkpoints for the publisher and can relate to the contractual delivery of payments and other resources to the developer. Milestones are, therefore, vitally important points in the production process. The functions of a milestone include

☐ Giving the publisher the tangible means to track the progress of the project.

☐ Providing the developer with specific goals during the course of production.

☐ Identifying potential problems and correcting them before they threaten production.

☐ Providing a logical and efficient payment schedule based on actual progress by the developer.

Milestones are not as common as checkpoints and normally occur every few months. Figure 8.1 shows an example of a project schedule with associated milestones. Each milestone should include the latest build of the game, which should be as playable as possible given its current state. The publisher will expect a tangible, deliverable sample of the progress made since the last milestone.

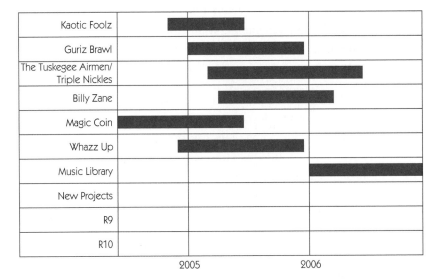

Figure 8.1 Entertainment Arts Research Sample project schedule with milestones.

Production Challenges

During the production phase, certain challenges will inevitably arise that might make the project fall behind schedule. Some common problems include

- Unrealistic expectations.

- "Feature creep."

- Emergent features.

- Multiple platforms.

- External pressures.

- Internal pressures.

Unrealistic Expectations. At the beginning of the production process, the development team will be full of ideas and energy. Often the initial excitement of getting the "green light" from the publisher, combined with the ambition and pride of the team members, can create dangerous overconfidence and unrealistic expectations.

This can cause problems that will follow the developer throughout the production process if not addressed early on. Most commonly such problems involve poor planning and scheduling. Developers may overlook important and fail to address potentially risky tasks early in the development schedule. Later, as they emerge, these tasks can affect production and create enormous delays.

When developer Gas Powered Games created the RPG Dungeon Siege, the overly ambitious team created an enormous volume of problems for themselves in just this manner. The team had never created a role-playing/action title before, and they set out to make one that pushed gaming technology to the limit. Their overly optimistic plans called for the team to develop the feature-laden game in two years, but it took them nearly four years to release the game.

Feature Creep. Feature creep is a well-known phenomenon in game development. Almost invariably members of the development team fall prey to the "Wouldn't it be cool if…?" school of brainstorming. This can result in truly innovative ideas when these ideas are carefully considered. However, there will always be a need to abandon some ideas with a seemingly irresistible "coolness" factor.

As more ideas are added, the development schedule grows longer. Any padding placed in the schedule as part of risk management may disappear quickly. When problems arise, the game can fall months, or even years, behind schedule.

How can developers keep feature creep under control? First, it is important to remove any features that do not have a direct impact on gameplay. They will simply waste time and hog resources. The development team should rank new feature requests according to their importance. Some of the things to consider when reviewing new features are these:

- Does the feature involve any new or unproven technology?

- If so, how much time will it take to create and test that new technology?

- How often will players use the feature?

- How will the feature affect gameplay?

When the design team gets excited about adding a new feature, it is the producer's responsibility to ask these questions because he or she is responsible for budgeting and scheduling. The producer must explain any cost overruns to the publisher. If the cost outweighs the benefit, the producer must step in and nix the idea for the good of the project.

For example, "feature creep" plagued the development of Westwood Studios' Command & Conquer: Tiberian Sun. When Westwood Studios developed Command & Conquer: Tiberian Sun, the follow-up to their best-selling RTS game Command & Conquer: Red Alert, the temptation to add new features was irresistible. Not only did the team have inspired ideas, but the huge Command & Conquer fan base was quite vocal about things they would like to see in the game. Westwood did its best to please them by adding features. This ultimately proved to be a big mistake. The team spent too much time focusing on these features and not enough on gameplay itself. The game was successful but was not nearly as much fun to play as previous Command & Conquer titles.

Emergent Features. "Is it a bug or a feature?" This is a common question during the development process. It illustrates how some features arise not as "cool ideas" but rather spontaneously out of gameplay. When an "emergent" feature suddenly manifests itself, the team must decide whether to keep it or remove it.

This can be problematic. What if removing the emergent feature disables another feature that is critical to gameplay? Changing the gameplay to correct the problem can affect other parts of the game and may result in additional emergent features. When unplanned features emerge, the lead designer and producer must consider them carefully. Only if they are useful and do not interfere with gameplay mechanics or create other problems should they remain.

Multiple Platforms. Today it is common for the development of games on multiple platforms to occur simultaneously. This can be a daunting task. The game's code must be platform-independent, and the developers must create engine code for each platform at the same time. Milestones often call for the delivery of several platform-specific builds at the same time. These factors can lead to scheduling nightmares.

Also, because every platform has different graphics capabilities and memory requirements, decisions must be made in accordance with the capabilities and limitations of each platform. For example, when creating a game for the PC and the Xbox, the developer will need to use more detailed models for the PC version so that the

Figure 8.2 Screenshot of a new mobile game developed by Entertainment Arts Research.

Artist Kenneth Karr

game looks as good as possible on high-end machines. Less detailed models will be necessary for the Xbox version. This may require the team to create several different sets of assets at the same time. Blue Tongue Software's Jurassic Park: Operation Genesis is one of the many games developed simultaneously for the PC, PlayStation 2, and Xbox.

External Pressures. During production, complications can arise from a variety of external sources. The publisher might insist on releasing a game at a certain time, placing undue pressure on a developer. For example, there might be pressure to release a game before a similar competing title. Getting a title on the shelves in time for the holiday shopping season is a notoriously common external pressure.

Internal Pressures. Internal pressures with the design team itself can create problems and throw a project off schedule. Two common problems are team morale and employee turnover.

Team Morale. The morale of a development team is a critical factor. If the team becomes disillusioned or dissatisfied, it can spell disaster. Because of this, game producers, managers, and leads must foster enthusiasm and a sense of team spirit. Good work should be recognized and rewarded. The enthusiasm of the team leads should be infectious and spread throughout the company.

Regular company events will go a long way toward fostering team spirit. Taking a break to play a LAN game, sponsoring a company softball team, paintball tournament, or family picnic, or taking time off for an employee screening of the latest movie—all of these things can improve team morale and, in the end, influence the final project.

If apathy sets in, so will resentment. At times the team will simply be going through the motions. Innovation will cease to exist because the developers will avoid trying anything that might possibly extend the development schedule. If they grow to despise the game they are working on, it may already be too late.

Employee Turnover. The job market in the game industry is extremely competitive. People are constantly leaving one company and joining another. If a member of a development team is unhappy, there are always other opportunities available. Employee attrition can have a huge impact on the ability to complete a project on time and on budget, and because the workflow remains the same, the loss of key personnel can make life miserable for the employees that remain.

This can affect every level of the team. New hires might be at a tremendous disadvantage because the increased workload prevents senior staff members from giving them the proper training and supervision they deserve. When important milestones are looming, it is easy to overlook simple task list reviews and quality control procedures because time does not allow any pause in production. Again, the importance of team morale is critical here. Fostering loyalty and enthusiasm can make or break the entire project.

Production Phases

A project must generally pass through three critical stages. Each phase has a specific goal: the completion of a full version of the game in accordance with a specific set of criteria. The three versions to be completed are alpha, beta, and gold (release to manufacturer). Let's take a closer look at these critical stages of development.

Alpha. In the alpha stage the game is usually playable, even in a rough form, from start to finish. Most, if not all, of the code is in place, and the engine and user interface are completed. There may still be some gaps, and often certain elements like cut scenes, titles, music, and the like might not be fully incorporated or in their final form. There will almost certainly be issues of game balance to address and numerous bugs to track down and fix. This stage is also the last chance to examine all the game features and decide what changes to make, if any, to remain on budget and on schedule.

When the alpha version of a project is submitted to the publisher, it will go through a rigorous examination because a large advance payment is usually due once it is accepted. The publisher will generally present the developer with a list of any major bugs and required changes. The development team must address these changes before the alpha version is complete.

When the publisher signs off on the alpha version of the project, a shift in focus will occur for the developer. The initial building process is now complete, and it is time for refining and polishing. Although testing has been constant throughout the pre-alpha portion of production, the serious and intense bug testing now begins. Quality assurance will increase the size of the testing team and ramp up its efforts.

Beta. A project reaches the beta stage when a complete version of the game, with all of the game's assets, is ready. At this point development has ended. The features are complete, and aside from minor text rewrites or art tweaks, the game is essentially finished. The beta phase is almost exclusively a testing phase. The QA testers will play and replay the game hundreds of times in an attempt to "break" it (find a major game-stopping bug.) They will also look for any minor bugs, annoyances, graphical glitches, typographical errors, and so on. As the team identifies bugs, they prepare detailed bug reports and pass them to the development team for repair.

This is, perhaps, the most difficult part of the entire development process. The game is complete, but the bug fixes can go on for weeks or even months. Repairing one bug might create several more. The team will often work long and difficult hours. All-nighters are not uncommon, and tempers are likely to flare. During all of this there is usually tremendous pressure from the publisher to ship the game on schedule.

As the beta phase nears its end, the project will reach "code freeze." At this point the project should be completed and all of the bugs fixed. Now is the time to create the candidate master disks. During the testing of these master disks the team will fix only major bugs (errors that crash the game).

Gold (Released to Manufacturing). Ultimately one of the candidate masters will pass its tests and be accepted. This will become the gold master. The name used for the process of releasing this version to manufacturing is "going gold."

Postrelease

"When the fun and games are over, the serious foolishness starts."[2]

Once a game has "gone gold" and hit store shelves, the developers can celebrate, and probably for the first time in many months get a good night's sleep. How the public receives the game is out of their hands. However, in many cases their job is not yet finished. Postrelease responsibilities still lie ahead. We now look at some of these tasks.

Postrelease Support

The game development process does not end with the game's release. The game developer needs to provide support to help users with problems (such as how to set up the game) and provide patches to fix errors and incompatibilities. It is also beneficial to provide support for the user community.

Postrelease Patches. PC games often require downloadable patches after their release. It is a common misconception that postrelease patches are the result of a rushed release or sloppy testing. Although this can sometimes occur, more often than not patch releases are due to unforeseeable hardware conflicts. With myriad computer manufacturers and a wide variety of operating systems, graphics cards, sound cards, drivers, and peripherals on the market, it is impossible to test a game with every possible configuration. When problems inevitably arise, it is the developer's responsibility to release a patch to address the problem.

---

[2] Smelser, J. (2004) *Re: Dual master configuration* (reply to discussion thread). Retrieved September 12, 2005, from the Neohapsis Archive Web site: http://archives.neohapsis.com/archives/mysql/2004-q2/3120.html.

Technical Support. Once a game goes on the market, buyers will inevitably have technical questions. Installation problems, hardware conflicts, game crashes, and the like are all common. To assist players there must be a knowledgeable customer service department supporting any major release. Customer service personnel provide support via telephone, e-mail, and often via online support forums.

Community Support. Another important type of support is for the gaming community. If a developer wants its game to be successful, developing an online community can be important. Often Web sites will be set up far in advance of a game's release to generate excitement.

For ongoing massively multiplayer online games (MMOG), or any titles with online modes of play, this can be especially important. An MMOG community will require a place for players to post messages, form guilds, share strategies, make suggestions, and the like. A loyal user community can be a tremendous asset for the developers because it gives them a pool of players who are often willing to participate in online beta testing, bug reporting, and so on.

Another popular method of boosting community support is for a developer to release "fan site kits" on the Web for download. These kits contain artwork, screenshots, backgrounds, icons, and the like and allow fans to create their own professional-looking Web sites dedicated to their favorite games.

Extending the Game

There are several ways to extend the lifespan of a game title in the market. These include migrating (or porting) the game to additional platforms, translating the game to additional languages, adding content to the game, and providing sequels to the original game. In this section we review some available techniques.

Localization. Localization is the practice of translating a game into multiple languages for distribution worldwide. This can be vital to a game's success: A game released in the United States can easily double its revenue via overseas distribution. It involves translating any dialogue and text in the game, as well as any documentation, marketing copy, and packaging that the title might require.

In a modern world of high-speed Internet connections, game reviews and word-of-mouth can spread around the globe quickly. Even a highly anticipated title will see sales drop off if reviews are negative, so the early days of distribution and sales are critical. As a result, more publishers are demanding a same-day release internationally. To accomplish this, localization must be part of the production process itself, not an afterthought.

If a developer waits until a game is virtually complete before considering localization issues, the process can be difficult and time-consuming. Some languages contain words that are much longer than their English counterparts and might not fit on the game menus and interface buttons. Lip-synching for cut scenes and in-game dialogue can be equally difficult. Most Asian languages require completely different alphabets. This can require each character of text in the game to be assigned two bytes rather than one. Another important localization issue is the game content itself. Some countries have strict rules regarding violence and sexuality. More than one developer has had to change the color of enemy blood from red to green to meet strict censorship codes.

Context is another important issue to consider. The English language has many words with multiple meanings depending on how they are used. For example, does the word *train* refer to a locomotive or the process of teaching someone a particular skill? Common idioms can also be problematic. If game developers provide literal translations of phrases, the meaning can be lost completely. "You have to go with the flow" could become "You must follow the rushing water." "She is very hard-headed" could translate as "Her head is very hard." Although these phrases are perfect translations from an objective standpoint, the meaning of the dialogue is changed.

Ports. When a game made for a particular platform is successful, the publisher will usually look into porting the title to a different platform to increase its marketability and extend its life. PC ports to consoles, console ports to PC, and ports between different types of consoles are all quite common, and ports for the Linux and Mac operating systems are becoming increasingly popular. Porting games makes good business sense: Many of the development concerns (story, gameplay, character design, and so on) are complete, and a port makes the game available to a wider audience.

Unfortunately, sometimes differences in the graphics capabilities between platforms can make a ported game seem like a pale imitation of the original. Recently developers have begun to look for interesting ways to compensate for these differences by creating additional content or adding features to ported games. For example, the PC port of the PlayStation 2 title Grand Theft Auto 3 featured higher-quality graphics and a number of added features, including the ability to import MP3 music files that would play on car radios during driving sequences. The PS2 version of the XBox title Resident Evil Code: Veronica X added additional cut scenes, and the PS2 port of the PC Game Splinter Cell featured an additional mission set in a Chinese embassy.

Live Teams. The recent popularity of massively multiplayer online games has created another postrelease demand. In addition to ongoing technical support, online "worlds" like Norrath (Everquest) and Dereth (Asheron's Call) require constant attention and updates. The developers of these types of games want to keep players coming back (and continuing to pay the monthly subscription fee), so they cannot let their worlds become static and dull.

Most MMOGs have "live teams." The ongoing job of these teams of writers, designers, and programmers is to update and expand these online worlds, adding new NPCs, locations, quests, storylines, and so forth. Much of this content is available at no additional charge to the players, but companies sell larger content packages as boxed "expansion packs."

Expansion Packs. Expansion packs come in many forms. Some add content for online games by allowing those who purchase them to visit new areas of the world or use special new game features. Others release packages of additional missions and scenarios for offline play.

Expansion packs are less expensive than a full-featured game, and rightly so. To play them, the gamer must already have the original game installed. The game engine and basic mechanics are the same. The expansion simply adds new assets that allow for additional gameplay. Some ambitious expansions truly feel like sequel games, and include additional cut scenes and added features.

Sequels. If a game is a success, sequels and spin-offs are almost inevitable. Franchise series like Command & Conquer, The Sims, or Tomb Raider are no-brainers for a publisher to finance because they already have a proven track record and a waiting audience. The developer of the original game may develop the sequel; but often a publisher that controls the rights will take a sequel to a new developer in the hope of getting a fresh perspective and innovative features.

Selling the Game

"Business is a good game—lots of competition and a minimum of rules. You keep score with money."[3]

The videogame market has become very competitive. The best game in the world will not succeed if the potential players do not know it exists, and the marketing of games has become an industry of its own. Industry trade shows, online demos, and free demo versions in magazines are part of the strategy to build player interest in new games. Let's look at how game developers and publishers sell and market their games.

Selling and Marketing Strategies

Creating games can be a risky business for publishers and developers alike. A few years ago there was not much competition for shelf space, so a game title had months to find an audience. With the explosive growth of the game industry, that has changed.

---

[3] Bushnell, N. (n.d.). Retrieved on September 26, 2005, from Rand Lindsly's quotation Web site: http://www.ashep.com/archive/loQtus/rand.html.

Pro Tips 8.1   **Nichol Bradford**

Global General Manager, Vivendi Games

Always respect the consumer. Video game consumers, core or casual, are smart. They know when they are being lied to or misled. If something is hidden in the game, expect them to find it. Always treat the gamers with respect. That does not mean they do not want to be marketed to…they do. What it does mean is that you cannot fool them for long…so do not try.

Retail Sales Realities. Today the average shelf life of a game is approximately one to six months. There are a few exceptions. The Sims continues to sell, as does Everquest and a few other MMOGs, but this probably would not be the case if their developers did not continue to support them with expansion packs and interesting new features. Typically a game will make most of its profits in the first three months. After that sales dwindle, and the title usually hits the bargain bin in about six months. The release of expansion packs often extends the life of the original game, and as sales of the expansion fall off, a third boost in sales sometimes occurs when the game and the expansion are bundled together and sold at a discounted price.

Some value-priced games seem to have a longer shelf life than full-priced releases. Publishers develop low-budget titles specifically as "value" titles and price them between $10 and $20. The profit margin on a single game is not as high, but these budget titles are much less expensive to market and distribute.

Pro Tips 8.2   **Don L. Daglow**

President and CEO of Stormfront Studios

Don Daglow's Law of Marketing: Sizzle sells software. Steak sells sequels. Marketers often discuss whether they sell the "sizzle" of products or the "steak." Sizzle is the imagery, the mood they create with TV commercials and glossy magazine ads. So when you see a supermodel wear La Boheme perfume to a Paris dinner party you want to rush out to buy it for yourself or your girlfriend. Steak is how well the product really works. Does the Tiger Woods golf club really hit the ball farther and straighter?

When we created The Lord of the Rings: The Two Towers for PS2 and Xbox, the popularity of Peter Jackson's movies helped sell millions of copies. That's sizzle. But if the game was not fun, the *next* game in the series would have lost that sales momentum—without the "steak" of a fun game the "sizzle" of a hot property does not carry you for long.

Fortunately, the game won major awards and received strong reviews. I should also add the corollary to this law. Last year's sizzle is this year's fizzle: Those who stand still are lost.

Shareware. Releasing a game as "shareware" is not as popular as it was in the age of Wolfenstein 3D and Doom, but some budget titles still go this route, particularly addictive puzzle-style games. Shareware titles are initially free and are available via download, on a gaming magazine's monthly demo disk, or as part of a CD shareware collection sold in stores. Usually these titles allow the game to be played for a limited amount of time, and then require the user to pay for a special "code" to unlock the game for unlimited play. Others simply have a portion of the game with certain features removed. Paying for the game unlocks these features. Bejeweled from Popcap Software is an example of a shareware game that has become incredibly popular in recent years.

Demos. To increase visibility, one of the most common ways to market a game is by releasing a game demo. Demos, like shareware games, are available via download or on promotional CDs that ship with most current gaming magazines. Game demos will typically offer an enticing game level or mission in the hopes that the gamer will play through it and then purchase the full version of the game.

Although most demos are simply the first level of game play, sometimes a publisher will create a special demo that stands apart from the full game. An excellent example of this is the LucasArts action game Jedi Knight II: Jedi Outcast. The demo for the game consisted of an exciting level of play that did not actually exist in the shipped game.

Figure 8.3 The Electronic Entertainment Expo in Los Angeles, 2005.

Trade Shows and Conferences. Trade shows and conferences can be a big part of marketing a game. Every publisher with an upcoming release will almost certainly have a presence at shows that feature exhibits, and conferences are great places to network and make industry connections. For the larger Trade Shows like E3, big publishers like Electronic Arts, Nintendo, and Sony will spend an exorbitant amount of money to set up flashy exhibits, give away free T-shirts and promotional items, and hire models and actors to staff their booths or dress up as characters from various games.

E3 (Electronic Entertainment Expo). The biggest of all the game industry trade shows is E3 (the Electronic Entertainment Expo). It takes place in May in Los Angeles (Figure 8.3), California, and it is quite an event. The booths and exhibits fill several large convention halls, and all sorts of conferences, lectures, and workshops are part of the festivities.

Most of the large game publishers wait until a week or two before E3 to announce their slate of upcoming titles for the year. There are always surprises; consequently, the event is highly anticipated. Attendance is limited to working members of related industries.

Figure 8.4 Spike TV Game Awards E3 Conference 2005.

TGS (Tokyo Game Show). TGS (Figure 8.4) is Japan's version of E3, and it is every bit as flashy. It usually takes place in September in Chiba City. Unlike E3 and GDC, the Tokyo show is open to the public. Admission to the show is also relatively inexpensive.

ECTS. ECTS is the European equivalent of E3 and TGS. This trade show takes place in London, usually in August.

GDC (Game Developers' Conference). The GDC started out as a small gathering of local developers in San Jose, California, but it has grown into another enormous annual event. Though not as commercial as E3, in recent years an exhibit hall has been added for booths and game demos. But the primary purpose of the GDC is for game developers to get together and attend and participate in all types of events including lectures, roundtables, workshops, and panel discussions.

D.I.C.E. (Design, Innovate, Communicate, Entertain Summit). The D.I.C.E. summit is sponsored by the AIAS (Academy of Interactive Arts and Sciences) and takes place in March, usually in Las Vegas. Like the GDC, the summit's primary focus is on creative discussion and workshops. The AIAS presents its annual interactive achievement awards here, as well.

Other Trade Shows. Some other trade shows that feature games or peripheral technologies include these:

- AMOA EXPO: This arcade game trade show is held annually in Chicago (http://www.amoa.com/).

- CES: The Consumer Electronics Show is a generalized Trade Show for all types of consumer electronics, including games (http://www.cesweb.org/).

- EUROGRAPHICS: The European graphics arts trade show (http://www.eg.org/).

- GDC EUROPE: The European Game Developer's Conference (http://www.gdc-europe.com).

- INTERNATIONAL GAME TECHNOLOGY CONFERENCE & IDEA EXPO: Another annual show, this time in Hong Kong (http://www.gametechnology.org).

- JAMMA: Japan's trade show for arcade games (http://www.jamma.or.jp/).

- MILIA: Another interactive trade show in Cannes, France (http://www.milia.com).

- SIGGRAPH: The largest trade show for graphic arts (http://www.siggraph.org/).

- THE TOY FAIR: The largest toy industry trade show takes place in New York City in February (http://www.toy-tma.org/AITF/).

- XTREME GAMES DEVELOPERS CONFERENCE (XGDC); This technical conference takes place in September in Santa Clara, California (http://www.xgames3d.com/xgdcmain.htm or http://www.xgdc.com).

SUMMARY

This chapter completes our discussion of the game development process. This process starts with the initial idea for a game and (it is hoped) concludes with an extremely successful game title. The entire process can take several years and involves production, development, and marketing teams. The software development lifecycle of a game starts with the initial concept and moves through the design, production, and release stages.

A video game can take several months to produce, and developers must monitor the production process to ensure that a game release occurs on schedule. The production schedule is constantly refined and altered during production. Checkpoints and milestones ensure that tasks are logically spaced throughout the production process. They also help both the developers and the publisher track the progress of the game's development.

Developers need to manage a number of challenges as they write, test, and release a game, especially if a game is intended for release on multiple platforms. These challenges include but are not limited to unrealistic expectations, "feature creep," and differences between target platforms. Developers must also deal with internal pressures, such as team turnover and poor morale, and external factors including market pressure from competing games and pressure from the publisher to meet a specified release date. They must address these challenges as the game moves from the development stage through alpha and beta testing and into release.

The alpha and beta versions of a game evolve from the early prototype developed in the preproduction phase. The alpha version is usually playable from start to finish, with most (if not all) of the code in place. The beta version is a complete version with all assets in place. The quality assurance team will play this version until they have identified all problems. All game features are locked at this time. The gold master is the final, polished game, and it is then that the game is ready for manufacturing and shipping.

Developers also need to be aware that the process does not end with the game's release. It will be necessary to develop program patches both to fix programs "bugs" and to resolve incompatibilities that can occur with graphic card device drivers or other programs. The developer, or publisher, must also provide technical support to users who encounter problems setting up or playing the game. Users may obtain this support via telephone or e-mail, or by accessing a Web site. It is also beneficial to support the user community as a whole by providing materials that allow fans to set up their own Web sites dedicated to the game. These community sites provide publicity for the game and allow users to help each other. They can also act as an important source of feedback for the developer about what is right and wrong with the game.

Extending the life of the game is as important as the initial release because the shelf life of a game is typically one to six months. A number of methods can extend a game's lifespan. Localization is the process of translating the text and dialogue in a game into other languages. This can greatly expand the markets for a game. However, localization involves more than literal, word-for-word translations. Depending on the target market, text and dialogue may need to change to reflect what is acceptable in the market's culture.

Another method for extending a game's lifespan is to port the game to other platforms. The porting of console games to personal computers, and vice versa, is commonplace. Halo, Doom 3, and Half-Life 2 are examples of games ported from one platform to another. Porting to another platform sometimes involves the addition of gameplay features and game content. Depending on the target platform, a game port can require almost as much effort as the initial development.

Expansion packs provide additional content for a game. This content can include forms of gameplay or additional levels and maps. Expansion packs usually require the full version of the game. In a similar manner, sequels for successful games have become common in the game industry. However, sequels are full versions of a game and are often created by a different development team than the original version.

Finally, the marketing of games has become a business. A number of trade shows and conferences are dedicated to the development and marketing of games. These include the Electronic Entertainment Expo (E3) and the Tokyo Game Show.

Production Schedule

Mullich, D. (1997). *Milestones and glass houses: Protecting your development schedule from shattering.* Presented at the Computer Game Developer Conference, April 1997. Retrieved September 12, 2005, from the Gamasutra.com Web Site: http://www.gamasutra.com/features/production/061997/milestones1.htm.

Production Challenges

Chan, K. (2003). *Postmortem: Blue Tongue Software's Jurassic Park: Operation Genesis.* Retrieved September 12, 2005, from the Gamasutra.com Web site: http://www.gamasutra.com/features/20030317/chan_01.shtml.

Crabtree, S. (2000, October). *Killing feature creep without ever saying no.,* Retrieved September 12, 2005, from the Gamasutra.com Web site: http://www.gamasutra.com/features/20001020/crabtree_01.htm.

McCusky, M. (2000). *Lone wolf killers part II: The development phase.* Retrieved from the GameDev.net Web site: http://www.gamedev.net/reference/articles/article943.asp.

Robinson, E. (1997, April). *Recovery mode: Taking control of an out-of-control project.* Presented at the Computer Game Developer Conference, April 1997. Retrieved September 12, 2005, from the Gamasutra.com Web site: http://www.gamasutra.com/features/production/061997/recovery_mode.htm.

Stojsavljevic, R. (2000, April). *Postmortem: Westwood Studios' Command & Conquer: Tiberian Sun.* Retrieved September 12, 2005, from Gamasutra Web site: http://www.gamasutra.com/features/20000404/tiberiansun_pfv.htm.

Production Phases

Omoruyi, O. (2001). *Managing digital assets in game development.* Retrieved September 12, 2005, from the GameDev.net Web site: http://www.gamedev.net/reference/articles/article1371.asp.

Sikora, D. (2001). *You got game! Part 4: The development.* Retrieved September 12, 2005, from the GameDev.net Web site: http://www.gamedev.net/reference/articles/article1343.asp.

Postrelease Phase

Allread, J. (1999, July). *Retail and internet strategies.* (Gamasutra.com). http://www.gamasutra.com/features/19990730/allread_01.htm.

Bennis, G. (2002). *Game localization.* Retrieved September 12, 2005, from g4tv.com.com Web site: http://www.g4tv.com/techtvvault/features/35361/Game_Localization.html.

Gordon, R. (2002, February). *The whys and hows of porting software.* Retrieved from the Pyrogon.com Web site: http://www.pyrogon.com/about/diary/2_26_2002.php.

Gruber, D. (1997). *The business of games: What if you wrote a game and nobody came?* (MakeGames.com). Retrieved September 16, 2005, from the fastgraph.com Web site: http://www.fastgraph.com/makegames/chapt4.html.

Kinderfield (2002, March). *Porting—the good and the bad.* Retrieved September 12, 2005, from the Into Liquid Sky Web site: http://www.intoliquidsky.net/site/articles/0302_ports.html.

Mandel, B. (2000). *Unraveling the mysteries of game localization.* Retrieved from the Adrenaline Vault Web site: http://www.avault.com/articles/getarticle.asp?name=local.

Mulligan, J., & Patrovsky, B. (2001, May). *Managing an online game post-launch.* Retrieved September 12, 2005, from the Gamuasutra.com Web site: http://www.gamasutra.com/features/20030521/mulligan_01.shtml.

Murdock, D., and Allen, M. (2000, August). *Successful multimedia localization.* Retrieved September 12, 2005, from the Simultrans.com Web site: http://www.simultrans.com/Seminardetail.cfm?PostingID=20.

Kramer, C. (1997, July). *On the edge: How current legal issues affect game development and marketing.* (Gamasutra.com). http://www.gamasutra.com.

Palumbo, P. (1998, January). *Online vs. retail game title economics.* (Gamasutra.com). Retrieved September 16, 2005, from the Gamasutra Web site: http://www.gamasutra.com/features/business_and_legal/19980109/online_retail.htm.

Parker, P. (2001, October). *Video game marketing mania.* (ChannelSeven.com). http://www.channelseven.com.

Puha, T. (2001). *Eurospeak: Localizing games for the European market.* Retrieved September 12, 2005, from the Gamasutra.com Web site: http://www.gamasutra.com/features/20010403/puha.htm.

Sloper, T. (2001). *Trade shows and conferences—Are they worthwhile?* (Sloperama.com). Retrieved September 16, 2005, from the Sloperama Web site: http://www.sloperama.com/advice/lesson6.html.

Trade Shows and Conferences

The Design, Innovate, Communicate, Entertain Summit http://64.49.205.17.

The Electronic Entertainment Expo, http://www.e3expo.com.

The Game Developers' Conference, http://www.gdconf.com.

Game Developers' Conference Europe (ECTS), http://www.ects.com.

The Tokyo Game Show, http://www.cesa.or.jp/tgs/.

Practice Questions

1. What is the difference between a checkpoint and a milestone?

2. What questions should be asked by the development team when they are considering adding a new game feature?

3. What are some of the challenges involved with developing a game for multiple platforms?

4. Why do most MMOGs have live teams?

5. What is the typical retail shelf life of a game?

Lab Exercise

The objective of this lab exercise is to be able to pitch game ideas using a concept document. Pretend that the class is a room full of game publishers looking for new projects to fund. Pitch your game concept in an exciting and appealing way. Discuss all the topics covered in the concept document and briefly talk about any relevant information contained in the proposal document. Use any visual aids or concept art that you believe might help convince the publishers that your game is viable and will be profitable.

Written Assignment

Write an essay (750–1000 words) that describes your experience with the lab exercise. Your report should explain why you included particular visual aids and other materials in your presentation. How did you show that the game would sell?

Allread, J. (1999, July). *Retail and Internet strategies*. (Gamasutra.com). Retrieved September 16, 2005, from http://www.gamasutra.com/features/19990730/allread_01.htm.

Bates, B. (2001). *Game design: The art and business of creating games*. Roseville, CA: Prima Publishing.

Bennis, G. (2002). *Game localization*. Retrieved September 12, 2005, from g4tv.com.com Web site: http://www.g4tv.com/techtvvault/features/35361/Game_Localization.html.

Bushnell, N. (n.d.). Retrieved on September 26, 2005, from Rand Lindsly's quotation Web site: http://www.ashep.com/archive/loQtus/rand.html.

Chan, K. (2003). *Postmortem: Blue Tongue Software's Jurassic Park: Operation Genesis.* Retrieved September 12, 2005, from the Gamasutra.com Web site: http://www.gamasutra.com/features/20030317/chan_01.shtml.

Crabtree, S. (2000, October). *Killing feature creep without ever saying no.* Retrieved September 12, 2005, from the Gamasutra.com Web site: http://www.gamasutra.com/features/20001020/crabtree_01.htm.

Gordon, R. (2002, February). *The whys and hows of porting software.* Retrieved from the Pyrogon.com Web site: http://www.pyrogon.com/about/diary/2_26_2002.php.

Gruber, D. (1997). *The business of games: What if you wrote a game and nobody came?* (MakeGames.com). Retrieved September 16, 2005, from the fastgraph.com Web site:: http://www.fastgraph.com/makegames/chapt4.html.

Hallford, N., & Hallford, J. (2001). *Swords and circuitry: A designer's guide to role-playing games.* Roseville, CA: Prima Publishing.

Kinderfield (2002, March). *Porting—the good and the bad.* Retrieved September 12, 2005, from the Into Liquid Sky Web site: http://www.intoliquidsky.net/site/articles/0302_ports.html.

Kramer, C. (1997, July). *On the edge: How current legal issues affect game development and marketing.* (Gamasutra.com). http://www.gamasutra.com.

Mandel, B. (2000). *Unraveling the mysteries of game localization.* Retrieved from The Adrenaline Vault Web site: http://www.avault.com/articles/getarticle.asp?name=local.

McCusky, M. (2000). *Lone wolf killers part II: The development phase.* Retrieved from the GameDev.net Web site: http://www.gamedev.net/reference/articles/article943.asp.

Mencher, M. (2002). *Get in the game: Careers in the game industry.* Berkeley, CA: New Riders Press.

Mullich, D. (1997, April). *Milestones and glass houses: Protecting your development schedule from shattering.* Computer Game Developer Conference. Retrieved September 12, 2005, from the Gamasutra.com Web Site: http://www.gamasutra.com/features/production/061997/milestones1.htm.

Mulligan, J., & Patrovsky, B. (2001, May). *Managing an online game post-launch.* Retrieved September 12, 2005, from the Gamuasutra.com Web site: http://www.gamasutra.com/features/20030521/mulligan_01.shtml.

Murdock, D., & Allen, M. (2000, August). *Successful multimedia localization.* Retrieved September 12, 2005, from the Simultrans.com Web site: http://www.simultrans.com/Seminardetail.cfm?PostingID=20.

Courtesy of *Into the Pixel*: Enzo in Florence

Artist: Ben O'Sullivan, Gren Atherton, Mark Sharratt, Matt Watts

Omoruyi, O. (2001). *Managing digital assets in game development.* Retrieved September 12, 2005, from the GameDev.net Web site: http://www.gamedev.net/reference/articles/article1371.asp.

Palumbo, P. (1998, January). *Online vs. retail game title economics.* (Gamasutra.com). Retrieved September 16, 2005, from the Gamasutra Web site: http://www.gamasutra.com/features/business_and_legal/19980109/online_retail.htm.

Parker, P. (2001, October). *Video game marketing mania.* (ChannelSeven.com). http://www.channelseven.com.

Puha, T. (2001). *Eurospeak: Localizing games for the European market.* Retrieved September 12, 2005, from the Gamasutra.com Web site: http://www.gamasutra.com/features/20010403/puha.htm.

Robinson, E. (1997, April). *Recovery mode: Taking control of an out-of-control project.* Presented at the Computer Game Developer Conference, April 1997. Retrieved September 12, 2005, from the Gamasutra.com Web site: http://www.gamasutra.com/features/production/061997/recovery_mode.htm.

Rollings, A., & Adams, E. (2003). *Andrew Rollings and Ernest Adams on game design.* Berkeley, CA: New Riders Press.

Sikora, D. (2001). *You got game! Part 4: The development.* Retrieved September 12, 2005, from the GameDev.net Web site: http://www.gamedev.net/reference/articles/article1343.asp.

Sloper, T. (2001). *Trade shows and conferences—Are they worthwhile?* (Sloperama.com). Retrieved September 16, 2005 from the Sloperama Web site: http://www.sloperama.com/advice/lesson6.html. Smelser, J. (2004) *Re: Dual master configuration* (reply to discussion thread). Retrieved September 12, 2005, from the Neohapsis ArchiveWeb site: http://archives.neohapsis.com/archives/mysql/2004-q2/3120.html.

Stojsavljevic, R. (2000, April). *Postmortem: Westwood Studios' Command & Conquer: Tiberian Sun.* Retrieved September 12, 2005 from Gamasutra Web site: http://www.gamasutra.com/features/20000404/tiberiansun_pfv.htm.

van der Post, L. (1975). *Jung and the story of our time.* New York: Pantheon Books. [Electronic copy]. Retrieved August 12, 2005, from the HipBone Games Web site: http://home.earthlink.net/~hipbone/IDTWeb/WhyGame.html.

Official Selection of the 2005 *Into the Pixel* art exhibition: Design & Construction ▪ Artists: John Kendrew, John Machin, Darren Douglas, Lee Carus

Company: Sony Computer Entertainment Europe - Studio Liverpool ▪ Game Title: Wipeout PSP

The Business of Game Development, Current Gaming Trends, and the Future of Game Development

Our examination of the game development process concludes with a brief examination of key business elements, a discussion regarding current gaming trends, and a look at how changes in gaming technology might affect the future of the industry. An exploration of these topics is an important part of any examination of the science of game development, and a look at the future is an excellent way to conclude our study.

After completing this chapter, you will be able to:

- Discuss the issues involving game industry contracts.
- Describe the different types of game development deals.
- Define the issues involved with developer payments and royalties.
- Discuss the importance of confidentiality and nondisclosure agreements.
- Discuss the use of completion bonds in game development.
- Describe the impact of player-created content on the game industry.
- Discuss the impact of online virtual worlds.
- Discuss the impact of controversial games and game censorship.
- Describe the ESRB rating system and its impact on the game industry.
- Discuss the impact of technological advances on the future of game development.

Senior Vice President, The Abernathy MacGregor Group

One of the most significant choices people make during their lifetime is what career they will pursue. People spend about half of their waking lives at work.

So stop for a moment and think. If you were offered the choice to spend half your life casting steel or producing movies, which would you choose? Building houses or creating music? Marketing soap or designing video games? Would you rather hang out with suits at a bank or the creative/production crew on a movie set? Would you rather write contracts for a law firm or for a radio company? Would you rather run financial statements for hospital or for a TV show?

The entertainment industry is the most dynamic and creative industry that exists. It is America's largest export product to the world. It has been one of the most lucrative industries on the U.S. stock market over the last decade. And, it is an incredibly fast moving industry currently experiencing rapid transformation due to technology and the Internet.

If watching a great movie inspires you, or if seeing a great TV ad makes you laugh, or if hearing a great song puts you in a good mood, the entertainment industry could be a good place for you to spend a lifetime.

The Business of Game Development

"Drive thy business or it will drive thee."[1]

Any thorough exploration of game development must include an examination of the business side of the industry. An important part of being a game developer is negotiating development deals with a publisher. Let's examine some issues involved with these negotiations.

Contract Issues

A carefully negotiated contract is important to any development deal. It ensures that the publisher is committed to the project and protects the development team if things go wrong. A lawyer should always review any contract, even if the developers

---

[1] Franklin, B. (n.d.). *Poor Richard's Almanac*. Retrieved on September 26, 2005, from http://www.answers.com/topic/poor-richard-s-almanac.

did the negotiating themselves. Some of the key issues involved with development contracts include

- Types of development deals.

- Payment schedules.

- Ancillary revenues.

- Proprietary technology.

- Confidentiality.

- Completion bonding.

Next we examine each of these issues.

Types of Development Deals. There are many different types of development deals. The most common types include

- Work-for-hire.

- Pick up.

- Pitched deal.

- Completion funding deal.

Let's look at each type of deal.

Work-for-Hire. With a "work-for-hire" deal the publisher will hire a developer to create a game based on a specific property that the publisher owns or has licensed. It might be a movie tie-in, a new title in an existing game franchise, or a new concept developed by the publisher.

Because the material is preexisting, a work-for-hire deal gives the developer minimal negotiating power. Obtaining a high royalty percentage is unlikely, but work-for-hire deals are a great way for new developers to create steady income and establish a presence in the industry.

Following the success of the 1999 title Medal of Honor, Electronic Arts hired the young developer 2015, Inc., to create a sequel. Medal of Honor: Allied Assault was even more successful than its predecessor was, which established 2015 as a major industry player.

Pick Up. In the case of a pick up deal, the developer will finance the game with its own money and shop the completed game to various publishers. Of all development deals, this type gives the developer the strongest position in negotiating a contract. By the time the publisher comes on board, the game will be approaching gold master and be nearly ready for release.

The publisher will be able to see the complete game as it will ship and judge it on that basis, eliminating much of the risk of conventional development. The developer will also be in a much stronger position to negotiate favorable intellectual property and ancillary rights for such a project. If the game is a hit, these rights can be worth millions of dollars.

Pitched Deal. This type of deal involves the most risk for the publisher. With a pitched deal the developer will present a concept to a publisher and seek financial backing based on that pitch. Because the concept originates with the developer, a pitched deal will offer a better negotiating position than a work-for-hire situation. However, because of the high risk to the publisher, the developer will probably need to have a history of developing popular titles on time and on budget.

Before the publisher backs a pitched deal, it will almost certainly require a detailed design document from the developer. The publisher might also require some sort of playable demo to prove that the technology is viable.

Completion Funding. This type of deal is similar to a pick up. The developer will begin financing and creating a game independently. Later, at some point in development, a publisher will step in and provide the financing to complete the game.

For the developer, this deal strikes a nice balance. The developer begins development with creative control and maintains autonomy for as long as finances will allow. Then the developer takes the latest build of the game to a publisher. Because development is further along, the publisher's risk is minimal. The developer will usually be able to show the publisher a working, playable demo that proves how marketable the game will be. As with the pick up deal, when the publisher's risk is minimal, the developer will be in a much better position to negotiate royalty percentages and ancillary rights.

Developer Peter Molyneux (Populus) and his Lionhead Studios began developing his latest game, The Movies, without a publisher attached. Recently Lionhead signed a deal with Activision to distribute the game worldwide.

Payment Schedules. When a development deal is completed, one of the most important deal points for the developer is the method of payment. Payments generally come in two forms: advances and royalties.

Advances. An advance is part of the royalty paid to the developer before the game releases; once it is paid, the publisher cannot reclaim it. In most cases a first advance comes after signing the contract, and subsequent advances come when milestones are completed.

Once sales reach the profit level covered by the advances, the developer will earn additional royalties on any additional units sold. When a title reaches this point, it is said to have "earned out." Any money received from that point onward is called "back end" money.

When negotiating a payment schedule, publishers usually prefer that the developer accept smaller advances and higher royalty percentages. In this way the developer shares in the risk and is inspired to create a better game. However, this can be problematic. The advances must be large enough to keep the developer in business. If the developer goes bankrupt, the publisher will lose as well.

Smart developers try to build in some sort of profit margin during development because the publisher could decide to cancel the project at any point. Some will even hedge their bets by insisting that a "kill fee" be included in the contract—money the producer will receive even if the project fails in some way.

Royalties. There are no set royalty rates. Essentially, a developer that is willing to assume more risk will be able to negotiate a higher percentage. This is obviously preferable, but if the game does not earn enough to offset the developer's losses, the royalty rate will not matter.

How are the actual royalties calculated?

- *Net receipts:* Ostensibly, net receipts are the actual profit made by the publisher from sales, rentals, and licensing of the title. This figure determines how much the developer will make per unit shipped. Unfortunately, the definition of *net receipts* varies depending on the publisher. Some publishers introduce a long list of "expenses" that will be deducted from the net. Clever bookkeeping techniques can ensure that "on paper" the game will never make a profit. Even a developer with a very high percentage can end up with little or no "back end" payments.

  Ideally, calculating the net receipts consists of taking the gross retail sales of the title and subtracting the COGS (cost of goods sold). This cost will include packaging a manual, other documentation, and CDs. Developers should strongly resist when producers try to subtract marketing, licensing, and distribution overhead costs. After all, developers need to use their advance payments to pay their own overhead while developing the game. Marketing and distributing the game is the publisher's job and should be its financial responsibility.

- *Reserve against returns:* Actual net sales are not final until a game has truly sold through. At any point, a retailer can return unsold units to the publisher for a full refund. Because it is difficult, if not impossible, for a publisher to get back royalty money paid to a developer, it is a common practice to hold back a percentage when a royalty is due; the name of this process is "reserve against return" (RAR). The RAR is usually anywhere from 15 to 30 percent, paid out over a period of 12–18 months.

Ancillary Revenues. As games become more popular, ancillary revenues are an increasingly important issue for developers. Toys, games, action figures, T-shirts, lunch boxes, and other types of items can generate a significant amount of additional income for any game title. However, game developers rarely participate in these profits. The publisher generally owns all rights to toys, T-shirts, and other products. Eidos Interactive made a lot of money on Lara Croft toys and products, but Core Design probably did not.

The license of intellectual property (IP) is another important source of ancillary revenue. For years the game industry has been licensing popular movies and television shows to create games, but recently the reverse has begun to happen. Hollywood has begun looking to the game industry as a source of ideas for big-budget feature films and television shows. More developers and publishers are negotiating for control of these rights, and for good reason; The right intellectual property can generate millions of dollars in profit. The developer should consider these important IP rights:

- The game's title.

- The storyline.

- The game characters.

- Logos and trademarks.

- Art assets.

- Source code.

- Music.

Proprietary Technology. In addition to the creative elements of a game, many developers will create entirely new game engines and other technologies during development. Game engines, in particular, have an enormous potential for creating future revenues. Originally created for games that are no longer popular sellers, Id's Quake Engine, Epic's Unreal Engine, and Monolith's Lithtech Engine continue to generate income for their developers.

Confidentiality. Nondisclosure agreements (NDA) are common in the game industry. Essentially they prevent the developer or the publisher from releasing confidential information to third parties. These agreements state that each party will protect the trade secrets of the other party as it would its own confidential information. The publishing of specific information usually voids the restrictions placed on it. Game developing companies usually ask individuals seeking positions with them to sign an NDA before any interviews or discussions that might reveal confidential information about the company and its projects.

Completion Bonding. An alternative to royalty advances based on milestones involves the use of "completion bonds." This practice, which comes from the world of filmmaking, involves funding development via a bank loan. A separate bond company issues the completion band to the bank and the publisher. This bond guarantees the timely delivery of the project within the specified budget. With the delivery of the game, the publisher pays off the loan.

Because the publisher is not putting money up front, this type of deal can allow the developer to negotiate a better royalty percentage. The publisher benefits by not having to invest money in the project until it is completed. The publisher also gets a much higher return on its investment. The cost of completion bonding is the only disadvantage: It ranges from 12 to 16 percent of the development budget. Delivery of the product usually means the publisher will pay bond fees, banking charges, and interest.

Current Gaming Trends

"History is more or less bunk. It is tradition. We do not want tradition. We want to live in the present and the only history that is worth a tinker's damn is the history we make today."[2]

Game development has come a long way since the days of Henry Higinbotham and his primordial Pong precursor. As history has proven repeatedly, the seeds of future breakthroughs are propagating today.

Before we look at where game development might take us, let's examine several popular trends that are having a tremendous impact on the game industry right now.

Player-Created Content

Player-created content has become an integral part of the game industry. More and more developers are supporting and actively encouraging this growing trend, which can extend the life of individual titles and even bring about major innovations in gaming technology. Let's briefly look at the history of player-created content, also known as "mods."

Players create game mods. The first true game mod was a fan-modified version of the Atari 2600 game Castle Wolfenstein. The 1983 mod Castle Smurfenstein was a tongue-in-cheek conversion featuring characters from the Saturday morning cartoon show *The Smurfs*. The first professional-looking mods began appearing around 1990. Fans of Apogee's original Duke Nukem began creating mods and editing tools for the game and distributing them via the Internet. This took the developers by surprise but was not actively discouraged.

---

[2] Ford, H. (1916). Retrieved on September 26, 2005, from http://www.21stcenturytrust.org/history.html.

Id Software's DOOM (1993) really signaled the start of the modding craze. Doom had an open architecture that allowed fans to easily access the game's code. The game was a hit due to its unique shareware distribution, so Id understood the value and power of the Internet community. Rather than risk alienating the fans, Id supported the modified versions of the game. Id's only request was that modders use registered versions of Doom to create mods, not shareware versions.

The mod community was happy to comply, and many modders even coded their games so they could not run on shareware versions of Doom. Id quickly formed a bond with the mod community and in 1996 released Final Doom, a collection of mods created by fans, as a retail product. Id even gave the mod creators a share of the profits the release earned. Soon other companies began to recognize the value of the phenomenon, and many began looking to the fan community for new employees.

When Id released Quake in 1996, the modding community was newly inspired. Here was a game engine that allowed them to create true 3D levels. When Quake's level editor finally became available, most home computers were not powerful enough to run it.

Nineteen-year-old Ben Morris was a modder from British Columbia. A few years earlier Ben had created a freeware level editor for Doom, and he decided to create a similar editor for Quake. The result was an editor called Worldcraft, and it would prove more successful than he could have imagined. It took the modding world by storm.

Two years later, when Valve Software used the Quake engine to create Half-Life, Valve chose not to use Id's level editor. Rather, Valve hired Morris to create a new version of Worldcraft specifically tailored to its needs. Half-life became a huge hit, and the user-friendly Worldcraft editor was included on every game disk that shipped.

The inclusion of the Worldcraft editor, and the ability to download user-created mods from the Internet, became huge selling points for Half-Life. Valve even went so far as to create the Half-Life Mod Expo to highlight the best mods. In 2000 one of these mods, a multiplayer game, Counter-Strike (2000), was actually purchased by Valve and released as a full-featured retail product. The game sold over a million copies despite the fact that it was also available free as a legal Internet download.

When Id released Quake 2 in 1997, the company supported fan-created mods from the start by releasing a version of the QuakeEd level editor for Windows. One modder, a computer programmer from Texas named Robert Duffy, decided to create a mod with his brother and set out to learn to use the windows version of QuakeEd. He was disappointed to find that the editor was frustratingly complex and did not run well on his home computer. So he created his own version of the utility with a friendlier user interface. Though he and his brother never created their mod, he released his editor on the Internet.

A few months later Id's John Carmack contacted Duffy and offered him a job. His editor, now called QERadiant, was instrumental in developing Quake 3. Later Id began licensing the software and the Quake engine to other companies, which used the editor to create hits like Medal of Honor, Allied Assault, and Return to Castle Wolfenstein. Western Quake 3, an ambitious full-conversion mod for Quake 3, was created by a team of modders, in Denmark.

The year 1998 also saw the release of another popular game engine for the modding community: Epic's Unreal engine, which integrated Unreal's level editor into the engine. It also featured UnrealScript, a coding system that allowed modders to recode different elements of the game easily.

Although first-person shooters seem to be the most popular genre for mods, amateur developers embraced other types of games as well. Fans have created new content for titles as diverse as The Sims and the RTS game Warcraft 3. The role-playing titles Dungeon Siege and Morrowind: The Elder Scrolls both shipped with their own level editors.

In 2002 Canadian developer Bioware sent shockwaves through the modding community with the release of its Dungeons & Dragons RPG Neverwinter Nights. Although the game shipped with a 60-hour single-player campaign, its most publicized feature was its Aurora Toolset. This 3D tile-based level editor was so user friendly that almost anyone could create an adventure to play online with friends. A special Dungeon Master interface allowed one player to act as an invisible referee, effectively bringing the pencil-and-dice D&D experience to the computer with stunning 3D graphics. Over 2,500 fans, using the Aurora Toolset (Figure 9.1), have created Neverwinter Nights modules.

Bill Blakesley, Kaotic Foolz, Entertainment Arts Research

Figure 9.1 City Image.

However, the toolset also contained advanced tools for creating custom content, scripted events, and NPC dialogue trees. This allowed more technically adept gamers to create autonomous, stand-alone adventure modules with complex stories and characters. Many of the modules created by the Neverwinter Nights community have become more popular than the original campaign that shipped with the game. Developers continue to look to the mod community to extend the life of their games and as a source of innovations and talent. With the incredible popularity of next-generation consoles like PlayStation 2, Xbox, and GameCube, dire predictions about the future of PC games continue to circulate. But so long as there continues to be a thriving community of modders, the steady flow of new, high-quality content might prove to be PC gaming's salvation.

Virtual Online Worlds

Although it was not the first online multiplayer game, the success of Ultima Online in 1997 attracted international attention and was the start of a popular new gaming trend. Today massively multiplayer online games like UO, Everquest, Dark Age of Camelot, and Asheron's Call are all established successes. This has inspired developers to move MMOGs out of the "sword and sorcery" niche in an attempt to capture a wider mainstream audience.

As of this writing, these online PSWs (persistent state worlds) have not been as successful as some industry experts predicted. One reason might be that for many people gaming is a solitary experience and not a social form of entertainment. Regardless of how good online games might be, some gamers just do not want to play with other people. Because online gaming grants a certain kind of anonymity, it has a tendency to bring out the worst in people. The "griefer" phenomenon that we discussed in Chapter 1 is evidence of this.

Gamers who enjoy a narrative will always prefer the single-player experience because this is the only way to tell a great story. Once other players begin dictating how the story will go, artistic integrity can be lost.

The industry continues to search for a breakthrough online title that will attract casual gamers and bring the phenomenon to the masses. The discovery of this magic formula could be incredibly lucrative. The selling of most MMOGs in stores alongside regular game titles is one source of profit, but these games also continue to generate income for their developers by charging monthly subscription fees.

The Sims Online seemed like a sure thing for developer Maxis. The original offline version of the game sold more copies than any other computer game in history. Its appeal with nongamers, and particularly with women, seemed to assure the online game's success. Nevertheless, the release of the game brought only luke-warm sales.

As number of other high-profile MMOG titles approach release, a pall has fallen over the market; the lack of an audience caused Electronic Arts' Motor City Online, a game designed for "muscle car" and racing enthusiasts, to fail. That same company's Earth and Beyond Online, a science fiction game developed by Westwood Studios, is still struggling to stay afloat. The cause of the delay of LucasArts' eagerly awaited MMOG Star Wars Galaxies (based on the blockbuster movies and developed by the creators of Sony's Everquest) was perhaps fear that a rushed release might spell doom for the expensive project. After all, historical precedents exist. Who would have predicted that Atari's home versions of Pac-Man and E.T. would help to destroy the home video game market in the 1980s?

Still, the development of a number of ambitious MMOG titles, among them Vivendi Universal's Lord of the Rings Online, Sony's Everquest 2, and Blizzard's World of Warcraft, is occurring. These games are mainly for the established fantasy role-playing MMOG market. Other developers and publishers continue to search for that elusive golden goose project that will be a mainstream hit.

One hopeful note is Disney's Toontown, the first MMOG marketed specifically for young children. Two other contenders, Linden Lab's Second Life and There, Inc.'s There, are online worlds targeting the same audience that turned up their noses at The Sims Online.

However, There and Second Life are unique in that they are not actually games, per se. Both of these titles are virtual environments designed for social interaction and offer various activities and "minigames"; but players can simply wander about, take in the virtual sights, and socialize with other players.

The developers of There have already acquired corporate sponsors for in-game product placement. The player's avatar can actually go shopping in the game and buy virtual Nike footwear or Levi's jeans. (In addition, of course, the purchase of the same real-life product will be just a mouse click away.) In the future, There hopes to use broadband connections to add real-time streaming audio and video to the game. This means that players could potentially enter a virtual sports bar and watch a live sporting event or turn on an in-game radio to hear the latest hit from a major pop star.

Second Life promises to include in-game tools that will actually allow players to create their own virtual homes and other objects. They will be able to import pictures from the real world and place them on walls as virtual "posters" and "paintings." The goal is to provide players with a "sandbox" that will allow them to interact and express themselves creatively and socially.

Will these virtual worlds be successful? Only time will tell. Nevertheless, if one of these new titles finds the magic formula, online games could enter a whole new era of creativity and invention.

Controversy and Censorship in Games

From the *60 Minutes* exposé of Exidy's Death Race 2000 during the early days of arcade games to the current uproar over the ultraviolent and politically incorrect Postal 2 (from Running with Scissors), controversy has always surrounded video and computer games. Let's look at some of the major controversies involving games and discuss their effect on the industry.

Video and Computer Game "Addiction". Controversy regarding the addictive quality of games is nothing new. Back in the early days of arcade games, Space Invaders was among the first titles to appeal to a mainstream audience. As the games began to appear outside arcades in pizza parlors and department stores, a conservative group in Texas attempted to ban the game in its Bible belt community. They watched in horror as children pumped quarters into the machines and believed that the games were corrupting the children because of the addictive properties of the game.

Today the game at the forefront of the addiction controversy is Sony's online sword & sorcery game Everquest. There are online support groups with names like "Spouses against Everquest" and "Everquest Widows." Many people have even taken to calling the game "EverCrack" because of its addictive qualities.

A woman in Wisconsin publicly blamed Everquest for the suicide of her son, a 21-year-old with a history of mental health problems. Obsession with the game was the reason given for a Florida man's fatal neglect of his infant son. Some have even suggested that the game should display some sort of label warning about its addictive properties. But the game has over 400,000 subscribers; these unfortunate events are far from the norm. A large part of the allure of online games is their social interaction. Most MMOGs allow players to chat and interact. This can be especially appealing for introverted or lonely people; having a sense of belonging, even in a virtual world, can become important.

Another captivating feature of MMOGs is their open-ended "leveling treadmill" style of play. There is always another level to reach for or a better item or weapon to obtain. This "dangling carrot" reward system can foster obsessive behavior.

Is Everquest addictive? Virtually any behavior that is pleasurable and feels rewarding can become addictive. The problem is the public's perception that Everquest is something akin to an addictive drug. This places the game developer in the public eye as something of a drug dealer, preying on the weaknesses of others. The truth is that today's online games charge a flat monthly fee. "Addicted" players who stay online constantly use up expensive bandwidth but do not pay any more than the average player. Developers actually lose money with these types of players in the long run.

In a recent editorial on the Gamasutra Web site, game designer Ernest Adams suggested that game developers stop using the word *addictive* to describe their own games. Instead, he suggests substituting the word *compelling*. A simple change in the way developers describe gameplay could help dispel comparison with drugs and exploitation.

Violence and Adult Content. The controversy regarding violence in video and computer games has also plagued the industry from its infancy. Many people are critical of violent games, suggesting that they promote aggressive behavior. Others claim that the experience is cathartic and releases aggression, thereby lessening aggressive tendencies.

There is no question that most games contain violence. Even early arcade games such as Space Invaders saw the player shooting and destroying as many "aliens" as possible. However, the technological advances in recent years have made games far more realistic. Instead of shooting cartoon blobs, modern games feature realistic human beings and buckets of blood and gore.

This violent, gory aspect of modern games seems to increase their popularity. In 1992 Nintendo and Sega both released versions of the game Mortal Kombat. Sega's version was unedited and featured plenty of blood and violent animations. Nintendo altered its version, changing the blood to white sweat and toning down the death animations. The Sega version sold so many more copies than the Nintendo version that two years later both companies released the far more violent Mortal Kombat 2 in unedited form.

In 1994 the increasingly violent games came under attack by conservative groups nationwide. Two different rating systems were introduced in response to these attacks. The first was created by a nonprofit company called the RSAC (Recreational Software Advisory Council). Its ratings, presented in Table 9.1, act as a "thermometer" with four levels of content.

Later that year a congressional hearing on violence in the media prompted the Interactive Digital Software Association (IDSA) to create the Entertainment Software Ratings Board (ESRB). This self-policing group rates interactive games and enforces advertising guidelines (Table 9.2). Of the games released and rated by the ESRB, on the average,

- 75 percent of games are rated "E."

- 19 percent are "T."

TABLE 9.1   The RSAC Rating System.

Level	Violence Rating Descriptor	Nudity Rating Descriptor	Sex Rating Descriptor	Language Rating Descriptor
4	Rape or wanton, gratuitous violence	Frontal nudity (qualifying as provocative display)	Explicit sexual acts or sex crimes	Crude, vulgar language or extreme hate speech
3	Aggressive violence or death to humans	Frontal nudity	Nonexplicit sexual acts	Strong language or hate speech
2	Destruction of realistic objects	Partial nudity	Clothed sexual touching	Moderate expletives or profanity
1	Injury to human beings	Revealing attire	Passionate kissing	Mild expletives
0	None of the above or sports related	None of the above	None of the above or innocent kissing; romance	None of the above

TABLE 9.2   The ESRB Rating System.

	Early Childhood Content may be suitable for ages 3 and older. Contains no material that parents would find inappropriate.
	Everyone Content may be suitable for ages 6 and older. May contain more cartoon, fantasy or mild violence, mild language, and/or minimal suggestive themes.
	Teen Content may be suitable for ages 13 and older. May contain violent content, mild or strong language, and/or suggestive themes.
	Mature Content may be suitable for ages 17 and older. May contain mature sexual themes or more intense violence or language.
	Adults Only Content suitable only for adults. May include graphic depictions of sex and/or violence. Not intended for people under the age of 18.
	Rating Pending Product has been submitted to the ESRB and is awaiting final rating.

- 7 percent are "M."

- Fewer than 1 percent are "A."

A separate division of the ESRB, the Advertising Review Council (ARC), concerns itself with game industry advertising. The following ARC guidelines come directly from the ESRB's Web site at http://www.esrb.org/:

> An advertisement should accurately reflect the nature and content of the product it represents and the rating issued (i.e., an advertisement should not mislead the consumer as to the product's true character).

> An advertisement should not glamorize or exploit the ESRB rating of a product (e.g., an advertisement with a tag line that states "banned by the ESRB" or "a 'T' rating has never been pushed this far"). A sense of responsibility toward the public should drive the creation of all advertisements. No advertisement should contain any content that is likely to cause serious or widespread offense to the average consumer. Companies must not specifically target advertising for entertainment software products rated "Teen," "Mature," or "Adults Only" to consumers for whom the product's rating is inappropriate.

Many lauded the formation of the ESRB, but it did not end the controversy. The revelation that the two students who went on a violent and fatal shooting spree at Columbine High School in Littleton, Colorado, were avid players of Doom and Quake caused the controversy to erupt anew. In June of that year Congressmen John McCain and Joseph Lieberman introduced the Media Violence Labeling Act.

This proposed law called for "the establishment, use, and enforcement of a consistent and comprehensive system in plain English for labeling violent content in audio, visual media products, and services." The Federal Trade Commission (FTC) would demand that media industries voluntarily create a universal labeling system that would be subject to FTC approval. If they did not establish such a system, Congress would give the FTC the power to issue such regulations. To date, this act is still awaiting congressional approval.

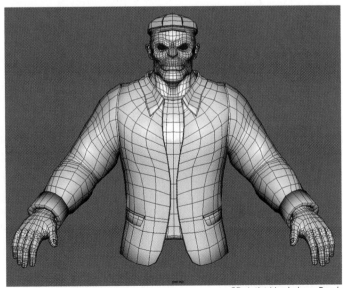

3D Artist Harshdeep Borah

Figure 9.2 Skullhead in wireframe.

The Future of Game Development

"The future, according to some scientists, will be exactly like the past, only far more expensive."[3]

As we examine the current state of computer technology and its effect on game development, remember that the information that we discuss, which is state-of-the-art at the time of this writing, will almost certainly be somewhat out of date by the time you read this book. Such is the nature of technological growth. However, we must begin somewhere. First let's look at some of the ways that advances in computer technology are influencing the world of game development and where these advances might lead.

Technological Advances

In 1965 Gordon Moore, founder of Intel Corporation, made an observation known as "Moore's law." Moore said that the growth of computing power is exponential and doubles every 18 months. That law has held true over the years, and this incredible rate of growth continues to give game developers more options than ever. The lightning-fast speeds of the Pentium 4–2.80 GHz and the Athlon XP 2600 will probably double within 18 months according to Moore's law. Nowhere is the impact of these technological advances more obvious than in the graphics of today's games. The introduction of new and powerful computers affects other facets of game design as well, including

- Environmental graphics.

- Realistic lighting.

- Real-world physics and interactivity.

- Artificial intelligence.

Environmental Graphics. As computing power increased, many 3D game developers sought greater detail for graphics by increasing the number of polygons that make up the objects in a game world. It seemed intuitively obvious that using more polygons would create more realistic, detailed graphics.

When displaying game graphics, the computer makes a number of rendering "passes"; with each pass more detail is added to the game objects. In the past the

---

[3] Sladek, J. (n.d.). Retrieved on September 26, 2005, from the Quotation page Web site: http://www.quotationspage.com/quote/460.html.

standard for 3D games was two passes. The first was for base textures and the second was for lighting effects. If developers wanted more detail, they would add more polygons or increase the detail of the texture maps themselves.

The newest generation of game engines is taking a different approach. Developers have discovered that by increasing the number of rendering passes instead of increasing the polygon count, they can produce highly detailed objects faster and more efficiently. These passes allow them to add lighting effects, shadows, and bump-mapped textures that are rapidly approaching photorealistic quality.

Realistic Lighting. As we discussed in Chapter 4, the game Quake was the first to use lightmaps to create realistic lighting effects. Lightmaps are a type of gray-shaded texture map that overlays the other textures in a game to simulate shadows from light sources.

However, lightmaps are static. Later games introduced dynamic lighting. Shadows would change and react to moving light sources, illuminating objects in the game environment as the moving light encountered them. This introduced another level of realism.

In real life, however, light interacts with an environment in many different ways. Dust or moisture in the air can change its look dramatically. This can be used to great dramatic effect to lend atmosphere to a scene. Ubi Soft's Splinter Cell featured effects like these. Light filtered through horizontal blinds would produce shadows in the air. Swirling fans would cause dramatic movement in a "dust-filled" environment. These effects were faked, however, by using projected texture maps to simulate shadows.

As technology increases the amount of available computing power, developers are rapidly approaching the point where these kinds of "cheats" will not be necessary. Eventually there will be a lighting model that successfully simulates the way real light behaves in an environment.

Real-World Physics and Interactivity. Increased computer power is also affecting the game-world physics of recent titles. As 3D graphics and textures become more photorealistic, the primitive physics models of earlier games simply are not acceptable.

Epic's latest version of its Unreal engine (used for Unreal Tournament 2003 and Unreal 2) was the first to integrate "rag doll" physics. Instead of using simplistic and repetitive death animations, the engine simulates more realistic deaths by turning the enemy's body into an articulated model that falls in accordance with real-world physics. In the original Unreal, a slain enemy would simply fall wherever he was when the action occurred. This meant that a fallen enemy could wind up balanced on a railing or with three-quarters of his body hanging in space off a ledge. The new engine would cause the same enemy to die realistically, falling over a railing or down a flight of stairs and landing with his limbs splayed out at unnatural angles.

Another innovation in game physics is real-time modifications. Historically, game worlds have been indestructible. Certain features like windows or the occasional ventilation grate might be destructible, but most of the game world was static. The player could fire a missile launcher at a rock wall and only leave a slight scorch mark.

This too is beginning to change. Volition Software's Red Faction featured a game engine that allowed players to modify the environment directly. They could use their weapons and explosives to blow holes through walls and reform entire levels of the game.

Volition's Red Faction was the first game with deformable environments, allowing players to blow holes through walls and alter the layout of the game levels. Real-world physics also allow game environments to be more interactive than ever. With many state-of-the-art games, players do not just move through levels searching for specific power-ups or new weapons; they can actually interact with and use many different game world objects in any number of ways. They can move around and stack or climb on furniture; bottles can be broken and used as edged weapons or thrown to distract a guard.

Interactive city environments have also become increasingly popular. Rockstar Games' Grand Theft Auto 3 was the first game to feature a fully rendered 3D city where players had full freedom of movement. They could steal any car and drive anywhere, or board an elevated train and ride it to another part of the city. Illusion Software's Mafia allowed players to use automobiles, trains, and streetcars.

Designers are even designing city games based on real locations. Sony's The Getaway features an accurate, fully rendered 3D model of London. True Crime: Streets of LA from developer Luxoflux features a rendered model of Los Angeles that is purportedly so accurate that players can use an LA street map to find their way around the game. Incorporating more real-world physics and interactivity into games means there seems to be no limit for game development.

Artificial Intelligence. In the past, AI in games has been used primarily for enemy combat behaviors. Most often these would simply be noninteractive scripted events, but occasionally other scripted behaviors were added. As computing power increases, AI is becoming more realistic and responsive. A wounded enemy might try to escape and find a way to heal his or her damage. If the player shatters a glass window, the noise might attract the attention of nearby guards. If an NPC stumbles

3D Artist Harshdeep Borah

Figure 9.3 Final image of Skullhead.

upon the body of another NPC, she or he might become suspicious or even call for backup.

Nevertheless, smarter AI does not necessarily mean that games will be more difficult for the player—just that they will be more realistic. Well-programmed AI will make the same sort of mistakes a person might make. People might get distracted, they might be poor shots, or they might stumble and fall. They might be cowardly or far too brazen. All of these things contribute to realistic and believable gameplay. Ritual Entertainment's Sin was one of the first games to feature reactive AI, but this is becoming more common in recent releases.

Where will the development of AI eventually take us? In the late 1940s British mathematician and computer pioneer Alan Turing proposed an experiment known as the Turing test. The test involved placing a person in front of two keyboards and two computer monitors and having them initiate conversations on both computers. The responses on one computer would be from a real person typing in another room. An AI program in the second computer would generate a second set of responses. Turing suggested that achieving true artificial intelligence would occur when the person initiating the conversations could not identify which conversation was a real person and which was computer generated.

AI that could convincingly pass the Turing test might still be a long way off, but imagine the implications for such technology in game development. This type of AI would truly be the "holy grail" of AI development. One day, possibly sooner than any of us imagine, it might become a reality.

SUMMARY

This chapter briefly examined elements of the gaming business that impact game designers and developers as well as some of the trends affecting the gaming industry both now and in the future. The game designer and developer must negotiate a contract (preferably with the assistance of a good lawyer). The contract will have a great impact on the development of the game because it affects everything from the tools and technologies used to create the game to the production schedule. The contract also determines the delivery of payments as well as the types of payments received. For example, does the developer receive royalties based on game sales? Does the developer receive a share of the money generated by the sale of ancillary products (e.g., T-shirts, action figures)?

A current trend in video games that is likely to continue in the future is the ability of players to create their own content. User modifications, or mods, are available for a number of video games. Some mods (e.g., Counter-Strike) have become so popular that they have been sold commercially. Although mods were initially difficult to produce, current games often ship with editors and scripting languages that encourage the development of additional game content. This helps the user community by keeping the game interesting and also helps the developer and publisher by increasing the lifespan of the games.

Another trend in video games is the development of virtual online worlds. Games such as Everquest, World of Warcraft, and Star Wars Galaxies, among others, let players interact with others in a simulated world. Although many games, including most first-person shooters, provide a multiplayer option, the online virtual worlds go further. Players gain skills, accumulate treasure, and participate in ongoing quests that can range for weeks or months, not just a few hours. Some virtual worlds have become so popular that the "wealth" accumulated within the game can be sold to other players in the real world for real money.

Controversy continues to be a factor in the video game marketplace. Many aspects of video games are topics of discussions ranging from video game "addiction" to the potential impact of video game violence. The Interactive Digital Software Association (IDSA) created the Entertainment Software Ratings Board (ESRB) to help address some of these issues. By providing a rating system for games, it strives to ensure that games are available only to an "age appropriate" audience. While this has helped, controversy over video game content continues.

A number of technology trends will influence the future of video game development. These include advances in graphics (environment graphics, realistic lighting), real-world physics, and interactivity and artificial intelligence. These trends have one thing in common: They all help increase the realism of the

Courtesy of *Into the Pixel*: Chinatown Level Study

Artist:
Rich Mahon, Jon Gwyn, Chandana Ekanayake

games that incorporate them. The graphics and physics help the game world appear and behave in a realistic manner; improvements in interactivity help place the user in the realistic environment; and artificial intelligence makes the behavior of characters generated by the game more "human."

The Business of Game Development

Charne, J. (2002). *Toward an alternative to the advances, recoupment, & royalty model for developers.* Retrieved on September 26, 2005, from the International Game Developers Association Web site: http://www.igda.org/articles/jcharne_royalties.php.

Davies, D. (2001, September). *Exploring the business side of making games.* Retrieved on September 26, 2005, from the Gamasutra Web site: http://www.gamasutra.com/features/20010907/davies_01.htm.

Glosert, D. (1999, November). *Negotiating a great advance and royalty deal.* Retrieved on September 26, 2005, from the Gamasutra Web site: http://www.gamasutra.com/features/19991116/Gloster_01.htm.

Kramer, C. (July, 1997). *On the edge: How current legal issues affect game development and marketing.* Retrieved on September 26, 2005, from the Gamasutra Web site: http://www.gamasutra.com/features/19970707/kramer_01.htm.

Intellectual Property

Rubin, S. (2002, March). *Intellectual property: The game of swords and shields.* Retrieved on September 26, 2005, from the Gamasutra Web site: http://www.gamasutra.com/gdc2002/features/rubin/rubin_01.htm.

Proprietary Technology

Powell, J. (2002, January). *Negotiating contracts that protect your title and team.* Retrieved on September 26, 2005, from the Gamasutra Web site: http://www.gamasutra.com/features/20020123/powell_01.htm.

Completion Bonding

Poitevin, B. (1998, June). *Completion bonding for interactive title development.* Retrieved on September 26, 2005, from the Gamasutra Web site: http://www.gamasutra.com/features/19980619/poitevin_01.htm.

Player-Created Content

Au, W.J. (2002, April). *Triumph of the mod.* Retrieved on September 26, 2005, from the Salon Web site: http://www.salon.com/tech/feature/2002/04/16/modding/.

Chick, T. (2002, December). *The shape of mods to come.* Retrieved on September 26, 2005, from the GameSpy Web site: http://archive.gamespy.com/futureofgaming/mods.

Current top 15 game mods. (2005). Retrieved on September 26, 2005, from the Voodoo files Web site: http://www.voodoofiles.com/top15.asp?cat_id=9.

Hall of fame for modules. (2005). Retrieved on September 26, 2005, from the NeverWinter Nights Vault Web site: http://nwvault.ign.com/Files/modules/HallOfFame.shtml.

Harris, T. (2001, October). *Mod world.* retrieved on September 26, 2005, from the GameSpy Web site: http://www.gamespy.com/articles/october01/gamemods1/.

Virtual Online Worlds

Boutin, P. (2003, May). *Escape from SimCity: At last, an online game without sword fights or pizza-making.* Retrieved on September 26, 2005, from the Slate Web site: http://slate.msn.com/id/2083018.

Eng, P. (2003, January). *Dawn of the avatars? Virtual world evolves online as companies offer new graphical tools.* Retrieved on September 26, 2005, from the There Web site: http://www.there.com/pressABCNews_010903.html.

Johnson, S. (2002, November). *The no-magic kingdom: The Sims Online.* Retrieved on September 26, 2005, from the Slate Web site: http://slate.msn.com/id/2073786/.

Online worlds roundtable. (2003, January). Retrieved on September 26, 2005, from the IGN Web site: http://rpgvault.ign.com/articles/383/383926p1.htm.

Rivera, E. (2003, January). *There is a virtual world.* Retrieved on September 26, 2005, from the G4 Web site: http://www.techtv.com/news/culture/story/0,24195,3414771,00.html.

Controversy and Censorship in Games

Adam, E. (2002, July). *Stop calling games "addictive"!* Retrieved on September 26, 2005, from the Gamasutra Web site: http://www.gamasutra.com/features/20020727/adams_01.htm.

Becker, D. (2002, April). *When games stop being fun.* Retrieved on September 26, 2005, from the CNET Web site: http://news.com.com/2100-1040-881673.html.

Brown, J. (2004, April). *Doom, Quake, and mass murder.* Retrieved on September 26, 2005, from the Salon Web site: http://www.salon.com/tech/feature/1999/04/23/gamers/.

Burman, J. (2000, September). Marketing media violence: An interview with FTC attorney Linda Stock. *The Motion Picture Editors Guild Magazine, 21(5).* Available at http://www.editorsguild.com/newsletter/SepOct00/ftc.html.

Entertainment Software Ratings Board (2005). Retrieved on September 26, 2005 from http://www.esrb.org/.

Janushewski, D., & Truong, M. (n.d.). *Video games and violence*. Retrieved on September 26, 2005, from http://socserv2.mcmaster.ca/soc/courses/stpp4C03/ClassEssay/videogames.htm.

Media Awareness Network (2005). *Media violence*. Retrieved on September 26, 2005, from http://www.media-awareness.ca/english/issues/violence/index.cfm.

Scheeres, J. (2001, December). *The quest to end game addiction*. Retrieved on September 26, 2005, from the Wired Web site: http://www.wired.com/news/holidays/0,1882,48479,00.html.

Future of Game Development

Doat, D. (2002, April). *Designer diary: Tom Clancy's Splinter Cell*. Retrieved on September 26, 2005, from the GameSpot Web site: http://www.gamespot.com/ps2/action/splintercell/preview_6024597.html.

Hodorowicz, L. (2001, March). *Advanced lightmapping*. Retrieved on September 26, 2005, from the Flipcode Web site: http://www.flipcode.com/articles/article_advlightmapping.shtml.

Miller, K. (1999, August). *Lightmaps (static shadowmaps)*. Retrieved on September 26, 2005, from the Flipcode Web site: http://www.flipcode.com/articles/article_lightmaps.shtml.

Real-World Physics and Interactivity

Kent, S. L. (2002, October). *Engines and engineering: What to expect in the future of PC games*. Retrieved on September 26, 2005, from the GameSpy Web site: http://archive.gamespy.com/futureofgaming/engines/.

Kosak, D. & Keefer, J. (2002, December). *Warren Spector on the future of PC gaming*. Retrieved on September 26, 2005, from the GameSpy Web site: http://archive.gamespy.com/futureofgaming/spector/.

Saygin, A.P. (1998, April). *The Turing test page*. Retrieved on September 26, 2005, from http://cogsci.ucsd.edu/~asaygin/tt/ttest.html.

Practice Questions

1. What are the four major types of development deals?
2. What is the difference between an advance and a royalty?
3. What is the purpose of a nondisclosure agreement?
4. What was unique about the level editor used to create the game Half-Life?

Lab Exercise

Pick one of the following important components for the game you pitched last week and create a preliminary design on paper. (Have your partner pick a different component or a separate level.) Your completed designs will be presented orally.

Artistic ability is not as important as attention to detail and concept viability, but you should try to play to your strengths when you choose from the following:

- **Game level:** Sketch a game level on graph paper. Include all gameplay elements (NPCs, mobs, doors, elevators, levers, traps, vehicles, etc.). Describe the objective of the level and the progression of gameplay within it.

- **User interface:** Sketch the game's UI. Include all methods of input and output and describe their functions.

- **Cut scene storyboard:** Sketch a simple storyboard for the game's opening cinematic.

- **Character design:** Sketch simple model sheets for the game's main characters.

- **Environmental design:** Sketch several concepts for key environments in the game.

- **Weapon design:** Sketch several different designs for the key weapons that will be used in the game.

- **Vehicle design:** Sketch several different designs for important vehicles that will be used in the game.

Oral Presentation

Using an overhead projector and any materials you created as part of the homework assignment, present your design components to the class. Describe how the components fit your vision of the game. How will they contribute to the game's look? How will they contribute to gameplay? What are their strongest features? What might still need work?

Courtesy of *Into the Pixel*: Ryu Hayabusa

Artist: Tomonobu Itagaki, Hiroaki Matsui

MANUSCRIPT REFERENCES

Adam, E. (2002, July). *Stop calling games "addictive"!* Retrieved on September 26, 2005, from the Gamasutra Web site: http://www.gamasutra.com/features/20020727/adams_01.htm.

Au, W.J. (2002, April). *Triumph of the mod.* Retrieved on September 26, 2005, from the Salon Web site: http://www.salon.com/tech/feature/2002/04/16/modding/.

Becker, D. (2002, April). *When games stop being fun.* Retrieved on September 26, 2005, from the CNET Web site: http://news.com.com/2100-1040-881673.html.

Boutin, P. (2003, May). *Escape from SimCity: At last, an online game without sword fights or pizza-making*. Retrieved on September 26, 2005, from the Slate Web site: http://slate.msn.com/id/2083018.

Brown, J. (2004, April). *Doom, Quake, and mass murder*. Retrieved on September 26, 2005, from the Salon Web site: http://www.salon.com/tech/feature/1999/04/23/gamers/.

Burman, J. (2000, September). Marketing media violence: An interview with FTC attorney Linda Stock. *The Motion Picture Editors Guild Magazine, 21(5)*. Available at http://www.editorsguild.com/newsletter/SepOct00/ftc.html.

Charne, J. (2002). *Toward an alternative to the advances, recoupment, & royalty model for developers*. Retrieved on September 26, 2005, from the International Game Developers Association Web site: http://www.igda.org/articles/jcharne_royalties.php.

Chick, T. (2002, December). *The shape of mods to come*. Retrieved on September 26, 2005, from the GameSpy Web site: http://archive.gamespy.com/futureofgaming/mods.

Current top 15 game mods. (2005). Retrieved on September 26, 2005, from the Voodoo files Web site: http://www.voodoofiles.com/top15.asp?cat_id=9.

Davies, D. (2001, September). *Exploring the business side of making games*. Retrieved on September 26, 2005, from the Gamasutra Web site: http://www.gamasutra.com/features/20010907/davies_01.htm.

Doat, D. (2002, April). *Designer diary: Tom Clancy's Splinter Cell*. Retrieved on September 26, 2005, from the GameSpot Web site: http://www.gamespot.com/ps2/action/splintercell/preview_6024597.html.

Eng, P. (2003, January). *Dawn of the avatars? Virtual world evolves online as companies offer new graphical tools*. Retrieved on September 26, 2005, from the There Web site: http://www.there.com/pressABCNews_010903.html.

Entertainment Software Ratings Board (2005). Retrieved on September 26, 2005, from http://www.esrb.org/.

Ford, H. (1916). Retrieved on September 26, 2005, from: http://www.21stcenturytrust.org/history.html.

Franklin, B. (n.d.). *Poor Richard's Almanac*. Retrieved on September 26, 2005, from http://www.answers.com/topic/poor-richard-s-almanac.

Glosert, D. (1999, November). *Negotiating a great advance and royalty deal*. Retrieved on September 26, 2005, from the Gamasutra Web site: http://www.gamasutra.com/features/19991116/Gloster_01.htm.

Hall of fame for modules. (2005). Retrieved on September 26, 2005, from the NeverWinter Nights Vault Web site: http://nwvault.ign.com/Files/modules/HallOfFame.shtml

Courtesy of *Into the Pixel*: Enzo in Florence

Artists: Ben O'Sullivan, Gren Atherton, Mark Sharratt, Matt Watts

Harris, T. (2001, October). *Mod world.* Retrieved on September 26, 2005, from the GameSpy Web site: http://www.gamespy.com/articles/october01/gamemods1/.

Hodorowicz, L. (2001, March). *Advanced lightmapping.* Retrieved on September 26, 2005, from the Flipcode Web site: http://www.flipcode.com/articles/article_advlightmapping.shtml.

Janushewski, D., & Truong, M. (n.d.). *Video games and violence.* Retrieved on September 26, 2005, from http://socserv2.mcmaster.ca/soc/courses/stpp4C03/ClassEssay/videogames.htm.

Johnson, S. (2002, November). *The no-magic kingdom: The Sims Online.* Retrieved on September 26, 2005, from the Slate Web site: http://slate.msn.com/id/2073786/.

Kent, S. L. (2002, October). *Engines and engineering: What to expect in the future of PC games.* Retrieved on September 26, 2005, from the GameSpy Web site: http://archive.gamespy.com/futureofgaming/engines/.

Kosak, D., & Keefer, J. (2002, December). *Warren Spector on the future of PC gaming.* Retrieved on September 26, 2005, from the GameSpy Web site: http://archive.gamespy.com/futureofgaming/spector/.

Kramer, C. (1997, July). *On the edge: How current legal issues affect game development and marketing.* Retrieved on September 26, 2005, from the Gamasutra Web site: http://www.gamasutra.com/features/19970707/kramer_01.htm.

Media Awareness Network (2005). *Media violence.* Retrieved on September 26, 2005 from http://www.media-awareness.ca/english/issues/violence/index.cfm.

Miller, K. (1999, August). *Lightmaps (static shadowmaps).* Retrieved on September 26, 2005, from the Flipcode Web site: http://www.flipcode.com/articles/article_lightmaps.shtml.

Online worlds roundtable. (2003, January). Retrieved on September 26, 2005, from the IGN Web site: http://rpgvault.ign.com/articles/383/383926p1.htm.

Poitevin, B. (1998, June). *Completion bonding for interactive title development.* Retrieved on September 26, 2005, from the Gamasutra Web site: http://www.gamasutra.com/features/19980619/poitevin_01.htm.

Powell, J. (2002, January). *Negotiating contracts that protect your title and team.* Retrieved on September 26, 2005, from the Gamasutra Web site: http://www.gamasutra.com/features/20020123/powell_01.htm.

Rubin, S. (2002, March). *Intellectual property: The game of swords and shields.* Retrieved on September 26, 2005, from the Gamasutra Web site: http://www.gamasutra.com/gdc2002/features/rubin/rubin_01.htm.

Rivera, E. (2003, January). *There is a virtual world.* Retrieved on September 26, 2005, from the G4 Web site: http://www.techtv.com/news/culture/story/0,24195,3414771,00.html.

Saygin, A. P. (1998, April). *The Turing test page*. Retrieved on September 26, 2005, from http://cogsci.ucsd.edu/~asaygin/tt/ttest.html.

Scheeres, J. (2001, December). *The quest to end game addiction*. Retrieved on September 26, 2005, from the Wired Web site: http://www.wired.com/news/holidays/0,1882,48479,00.html.

Sladek, J. (n.d.). Retrieved on September 26, 2005, from the Quotation page Web site: http://www.quotationspage.com/quote/460.html.

Glossary

3DO Panasonic's expensive foray into the 32-bit market.

3D Studio Max 3D modeling package used by animators, lead artists, modelers, and texture artists.

A

Act One The first part of classic three-act structure that establishes the setting and main characters, introduces the conflict that will drive the story, and contains an inciting incident and a hook.

Act Three The third and final part of classic three-act structure, which has the hero resolving the primary conflict of the story.

Act Two The second part of classic three-act structure and the longest of the three acts, which contains many obstacles, twists, and reversals and usually a dark moment for the hero.

actors and voice-over talent Professional actors used to perform recorded dialog and voice-overs.

advances Unrecoupable royalties paid to the developer before the release of a game, usually tied to milestones.

Adventure Vision A tabletop LED game with interchangeable game cartridges, released by Entex in 1982.

alpha testing A testing phase that begins when an alpha version of the game has been completed. This version is usually playable from beginning to end, though it may have gaps or incomplete features.

ambient lighting A general flood of light that illuminates objects evenly and does not indicate the source of light.

ancillary revenues Additional profits made by a game property, including merchandising and licensing to other media.

animation cycles Animated character movements that repeat to create the illusion of continuous action. Types of animation cycles include running, walking, sneaking, attack, and so on.

animator An artist who adds life and movement to the characters and creatures that populate the game world.

antagonist The primary villain of a game.

art assets All of the various models, textures, and components created by the art department for inclusion in the game.

art bible A style guide that includes concept art, character sketches, equipment design, and the like. The art team will refer to it throughout the development process as they create new art assets for the game.

art lead The head of the art department and the person responsible for a game's look. He works with the lead designer to develop a consistent visual style for the game world and the objects and creatures that inhabit it.

Asheron's Call This MMORPG from Microsoft and Turbine Entertainment has a loyal following

and releases new and original content every month.

associate producer A position that varies from company to company but that generally involves assisting the producer by managing various aspects of production and taking on administrative and support duties.

Asteroids A hit vector graphics game released by Atari in 1979. This was the first game to allow players to enter their initials in a list of high scores.

Atari Jaguar Atari's failed 64-bit home system.

Atari VCS (2600) Atari's first programmable home system (1977).

audio output A method of feedback using audio sound effects, music, or spoken dialogue.

audio settings A menu reached via the user interface that allows the player to select audio options like dialogue volume, music volume, and sound effects volume.

augmented reality Games where the player interacts with a virtual world through actions in the real world. Augmented reality games require a heads-up display so the player can see objects in both worlds.

B

background modeling The use of simple geometric shapes known as *primitives* to create the walls, floors, vegetation, and so forth for a game environment.

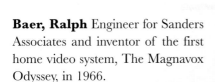

Baer, Ralph Engineer for Sanders Associates and inventor of the first home video system, The Magnavox Odyssey, in 1966.

Berserker, the A player archetype that prefers fast-paced gameplay and usually attempts to solve most problems through combat and/or destruction.

beta testing A testing phase that begins when a beta version of the game is complete. This version is usually "feature" complete and very close to the final version of the game.

blending An animation technique that allows animation cycles to transition to different cycles via shorter bridging motions.

Blizzard Software Developers of the RTS franchises Warcraft and Starcraft.

branching events A method of creating nonlinear gameplay by giving players multiple choices at key points in the game and allow them to pursue several different courses of action.

Breakout The first simulated color video game (1972).

bump mapping A process that uses light reflection calculations to create the appearance of small bumps, thereby adding detail to an image map without increasing the polygon count.

Bushnell, Nolan Founder of Atari and considered by many to be the father of modern video games.

C

Carmack, John A game developer with Id Software who developed Wolfenstein 3D, Doom, and Quake.

Castle, Louis Founder (along with Brett Sperry) of Westwood Studios; developer of the first RTS game Dune II and the Command & Conquer franchise.

Castle Wolfenstein An Atari 2600 8-bit title from 1982 that served as the basis for Id's Wolfenstein 3D.

casual gamer: A broad category of gamer characterized by a casual gaming style and a desire for simple and intuitive gameplay. The casual gamer might play a game for just 20 or 30 minutes at a sitting and wants to have some feeling of accomplishment in that short time.

Cavedog Games Developer of the groundbreaking 1997 RTS title Total Annihilation.

Channel F The first programmable home system, released by Fairchild in 1976.

character descriptions Descriptions included in the design document covering the PC, friendly NPCs, enemy NPCs (or mobs), and boss NPCs.

character modeling The creation of characters and creatures that will populate the game world. These character models are fitted with skeletal frameworks that determine their kinetic movements.

Civilization The most popular god game of all time, created by Sid Meier and released in 1991.

COGS (cost of goods sold) The total cost of a game, which includes packaging, the manual and other documentation, CDs, and the like but usually does not include the publisher's costs (like marketing, licensing, and distribution overhead).

collision detection Programming that makes objects in the game world solid and causes them to perform a predetermined action when they collide with other objects.

color depth The number of distinct colors displayed by each pixel at one time.

Colossal Cave Adventure A hugely popular text adventure game created by Willie Crowther in 1976 and later refined by Don Woods.

Comp IV The first handheld electronic game, released by Milton Bradley in 1977.

completion bonding The process of funding development via a bank loan and using a bond to guarantee the timely delivery of the project within the specified budget.

completion funding deal A development deal wherein a developer begins financing and creating a game and later has a publisher provide the financing to complete it.

composers An outside contractor hired to create original theme and/or atmospheric music for a game.

concept art An important component of a game's proposal document, design document, and art bible.

concept document A two- or three-page document that describes a game in brief and simple terms, used as a sales pitch to get financing.

conceptual artist An artist who creates the initial sketches and artwork that will make up the art bible and define the visual look of the game.

control configuration Allows players to customize and remap the keyboard controls of a game.

Conway, John H. British mathematician that created the Game of Life, a cellular simulation game that opened up a new field of mathematical research, the field of cellular automata.

core gamer A broad category of gamers characterized by a serious and dedicated devotion to games. Completing (or beating) a game is paramount, and they tolerate complex rules and long hours of gameplay. The more difficult and complex a game is, the more satisfied they are for having completed it.

cross-media games Games that incorporate multiple types of media, including but not limited to e-mail, Web sites, phone calls, classified ads, and instant messaging.

cut scenes Short movies triggered during a game, usually at the end of a level or at a key moment in the story line, that move the plot forward and reveal important information to the player.

D

Death Race The first controversial video game, based on the B movie *Death Race 2000* (1976).

depth cueing An effect that causes objects farther away to appear hazier and darker, used to create the illusion of depth, fog effects, and underwater effects.

depth of field Refers to the distance between the nearest and farthest objects in view that are in sharp focus. In photography, depth of field is determined by the camera's aperture setting. In games it can add depth to an environment or be a cinematic device in cut scenes.

Descent The first game that rendered true 3D virtual space, released in 1994 by Parallax Entertainment.

design document An important document that contains all the technical specifications for the game and covers every design aspect including story, gameplay, interface, and structure. It serves as a road map for the team during production.

Detective, the A player archetype that prefers more deliberately paced gameplay, logical puzzles, and problem-solving exercises. They derive pleasure from finding clever ways to solve problems and often seek to avoid combat.

Deus Ex Hybrid action/stealth/role-playing game developed by Ion Storm and released in 2000.

diffuse lighting Lighting that comes from a specific direction, casts shadows, and doesn't change when viewed from different positions.

Doom An incredibly successful FPS game by Id Software in 1993, distributed as shareware.

Dragon's Lair The first laser disk game (1981).

Dune II The first real-time strategy computer game, created by Westwood Studios in 1992.

Dungeons & Dragons A pencil-and-dice role-playing game that had a huge influence on game development.

E

emergent gameplay Gameplay that arises spontaneously from the artificial intelligence programming that controls NPCs, enemies, and monsters in a game. Depending on a player's location, choices, and actions, NPCs can respond in surprisingly different ways.

ESRB, the (Entertainment Software Ratings Board) A self-policing body created by the IDSA (Interactive Digital Software Association) in 1994 to rate the content of interactive games and enforce advertising guidelines.

Everquest This Sony/Verant game is the most popular MMORPG to date.

Everyman, the A popular type of game protagonist that is easy to identify with: a normal man or woman caught up in extraordinary circumstances.

external producer A producer who works for a game publisher and serves as the publisher's liaison to the developer.

F

Famicom (short for family computer) Nintendo's home gaming unit released in Japan in 1983. Later the unit was redesigned and released in the United States as the NES.

final release The completed game fully tested and ready to ship.

first-person perspective The most immersive player perspective, where the player sees through the eyes of the character he or she is playing.

Foley artist An outside contractor who uses props to create specific custom sound effects in the recording studio.

force feedback An output device, sometimes built into custom control devices like joysticks, steering wheels, and game pads, that uses vibrations to simulate rumbling engines, explosions, and the like.

free play A mode of play where players can go anywhere and do anything they like. Grand Theft Auto 3, Mafia, Morrowind, and Freelancer all feature this optional type of gameplay.

Freeware Software and games released for free download in the hopes that consumers will purchase the complete version. (Also called *shareware*.)

G

Galaxian The first true color video game (1979).

Game and Watch A series of handheld LCD games released by Nintendo in the early 1980s.

Game Boy Nintendo's handheld 8-bit black-and-white system with interchangeable cartridges, released in 1989.

Game Boy Advance Nintendo's next generation color handheld, released in 2000.

Game Boy Color Nintendo's 1998 color handheld unit, which was backward compatible with existing Game Boy titles.

Game of Life, the A cellular simulation computer game created by British mathematician John H. Conway that opened up a new field of mathematical research, the field of cellular automata.

game overview A section of the design document that describes the target audience, target platform, key features, story summary, environments, competitive genre titles, and risk assessment.

game pad controllers Input devices used for most console games.

gamma correction An adjustment to the brightness of a game's graphics.

Garriot, Richard Creator of the Ultima series and founder of Origin Systems.

global positioning system (GPS) A satellite-based system for determining a user's location.

"god" games Simulation games that give the player control over the simulation as a sort of omnipotent overseer.

Grand Theft Auto 3 Controversial hybrid game (third-person action/driving game), developed by Rockstar Games, that featured a fully rendered interactive city and nonlinear gameplay (2001).

Griefer, the A player archetype whose primary motivation is making others miserable in online games. This practice is counter to the end user agreement of most games and can result in a player being permanently banned.

GUI (graphic user interface) displays The graphics that frame the game world at the edges of the screen, providing feedback and clickable icons for player input.

Gunfight The first game to use a microprocessor (1975).

H

handheld game console A portable device for playing video games.

hand painting For some high-end close-up work, texture artists sometimes use a significant amount of hand painting to add detail to a texture map.

Heath-Smith, Jeremy Founder of Core Design and developer of Tomb Raider.

high concept A one- or two-line description that describes a game in a simple and exciting way.

Higinbotham, William A. A nuclear physicist at the Brookhaven National Laboratories who invented the first electronic game, Tennis For Two, in 1959.

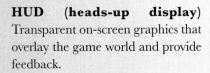

HUD (heads-up display) Transparent on-screen graphics that overlay the game world and provide feedback.

Human Pac-Man An augmented reality version of Pac-Man. The player walks around a real-world playing field "eating" virtual dots.

Hunt the Wumpus The first text adventure game, created by Gregory Yob in 1972.

I

idle animation An animation cycle that makes characters seem like living beings, even when not moving, by giving them simple movements like scratching their heads, shifting their weight, looking around, and the like.

Id Software Developer of the classic FPS titles Wolfenstein 3D, Doom, and Quake.

inciting incident In classic three-act structure, an event in Act One that kicks off the events of the story.

in-game tutorials Tutorials that are incorporated into the first level or mission of a game to educate the player about the game's controls.

input Actions taken by players via the user interface that allows them to interact with the game environment.

Internet and LAN multiplayer modes An important section of the design document detailing the various types of multiplay (such as team-based, head-to-head, or capture the flag).

IP (intellectual property) rights The rights and control of a game's title, characters, story, assets, source code, and so on with regard to sequel games, spin-offs, ancillary revenues, and licensing to other media.

isometric perspective A player perspective with tilted, three-quarter views from above, popular for many RPG and RTS games.

J

Jones, Dave Founder of Rockstar Games, creators of the Grand Theft Auto series.

joystick An input device sometimes used for flight simulation, air combat, and space combat games.

K

keyboard An input device that features the most control options and allows familiar game conventions to be used.

Kingdom The first city simulation game, released in 1970 (also known as Hammurabi).

King's Quest A classic graphical adventure game created by Roberta and Ken Williams of Sierra Online.

L

lead designer A key position on a development team and the person with the vision of what the game will be like. Responsibilities include maintaining the design document and managing the design team.

Legends of Kesmai The first graphical online game, created in 1983 by Kelten Flinn and John Taylor.

level designers Designers who take all of the assets created by the modelers and programmers and create an area of the game world through which the player can move and interact with the environment.

level editor A software program that lays out game levels and previews 3D objects imported from modeling programs; it places triggers that run special scripts when the player enters a certain area or performs a certain action.

licensed properties A common source of game concepts involving a licensed property like a film, television show, or celebrity sports figure.

Lucas, George Hollywood director and founder of the LucasArts game development company.

M

Maniac Mansion LucasArts game that introduced the point-and-click adventure game interface called SCUMM (Script Creation Utility for Maniac Mansion).

market analysis A section of the proposal document that analyzes the game's target market and other similar titles in that market, comparing the selling features of those games.

massive multiplayer online role-playing game (MMORPG) Games such as World of WarCraft, where thousands of players interact in the virtual game world.

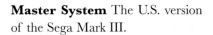

Master System The U.S. version of the Sega Mark III.

Meier, Sid Creator of the most popular god game of all time: Civilization, released in 1991.

Meridian 59 An early online graphical game that boasted 30,000 paying players at its peak (1995–2000).

Microsoft Xbox Microsoft's next generation console, released in 2000.

Microvision The first programmable handheld game, released by Milton Bradley in 1979.

Miller, Rand and Robyn Brothers who created Myst and formed Cyan Games.

mixed reality See **augmented reality**.

modeler An artist who uses 3D modeling packages like Maya and 3D Studio Max to create the models that will represent objects, characters, and scenery in the game environment.

modeling The creation of virtual objects using 3D wire meshes that define their size, shape, and properties.

mods Modified versions of published games or game content created by players, usually with the support and encouragement of the original developers.

Moore's Law An observation made by Intel founder Gordon Moore in 1965 that states that the growth of computing power doubles every 18 months.

motion blur In photography, a blurred effect that is the result of a slow shutter speed and has come to represent dynamic motion. When used in games it can add realism to movement.

motion capture A technique for creating realistic character animation that involves the placement and tracking of motion sensors on an actor's body, allowing the computer to recreate captured moves with a rendered character.

mouse An input device familiar to all computer users (even nongamers) that is simple to use and non-threatening.

MUDs (multi-user dungeon or multi-user dimension) Online text-only role-playing environments where multiple users can log on and interact.

music supervisor An outside contractor responsible for all of the music in a game.

Myst CD puzzle-solving adventure game created by Rand and Robyn Miller.

Mystery House The first graphic adventure game, created by Roberta and Ken Williams in 1980.

N

NEC Turbographix-16 NEC's 16-bit home unit released in 1989.

NES (Nintendo Entertainment System) The revamped version of the Famicon, released in the United States.

net receipts The actual profit made by the publisher that determines how much the developer will make per unit shipped, calculated by taking the gross retail sales of the title and subtracting the COGS (cost of good sold).

Nintendo 64 Nintendo's 64-bit system, the first to support 3D graphics, released in 1995.

Nintendo GameCube Nintendo's next generation console, released in 2001.

Nintendo Seal of Quality After the crash of 1982, in an attempt to gain the confidence of retailers, Nintendo created this new software licensing program whereby third-party game developers would have to meet a stringent set of standards.

Nintendo Super NES Nintendo's 16-bit system, released in 1991.

nondisclosure agreements A common legal document that prevents a developer or publisher from releasing confidential information to third parties.

O

Odyssey The first home video game system invented by Ralph Baer in 1966 and released by Magnavox in 1972.

output Feedback given to the player from, and about, the game world via the user interface.

P

Pac-Man A phenomenally successful maze game designed by Namco's Toru Iwatani (1980). The title

character became the first video game superstar.

Parallax Entertainment Creators of Descent, the first game that rendered true 3D virtual space.

personal digital assistant A small handheld computer with limited functionality.

pervasive games Games that can be played anywhere on a broad range of devices.

photo manipulation A common technique used to create texture maps to photograph real surfaces, scan them, and touch them up with photo manipulation software (like Photoshop) to fit the needs of the situation.

pick-up deal A development deal wherein a developer finances a game with its own money and shops the completed game to various publishers.

pitched deal A development deal wherein a developer pitches a concept to a publisher and seeks financial backing to develop it.

pixel hunt A poor design decision in an adventure or role-playing game that involves placing a small but necessary item in a huge, dimly lit area. The object is virtually invisible to the naked eye. The only way the player can locate it is to slowly move the cursor over every part of the area until the cursor changes shape.

player-created content Modified versions of published games or game content (also called *mods*) created by players, usually with the support and encouragement of the original developers.

polygonal models 3D models that are actually present within the virtual environment and can be viewed from any angle.

Pong The first successful arcade video game, a simple tennis game released by Atari.

Populous The first true god game, created by Peter Molyneux in 1989.

Power-Leveler, the A player archetype that prefers open-ended games and derives pleasure from increasing their character's abilities and wants to obtain the best of everything (weapons, armor, and the like). They are usually willing to endure tedious, repetitive gameplay to achieve their goals.

procedural texturing A process (sometimes also called *algorithmic texturing*) by which texture artists can alter the appearance of an object by using mathematical computer algorithms to change the appearance of a surface.

producer A key position on a development team. Producers are responsible for hiring, scheduling, budgeting, and acting as liaison between departments and with the publisher.

profit and loss statement A statement that estimates the development cost and projected revenue of the title.

proposal document An expanded and more detailed version of the concept document containing more information that the publisher will need before committing to funding a game's development.

proprietary technology Any new technology, tool, or game engine created during the development of a game.

protagonist The main character, or hero, of a game.

prototype A working demo that is the end result of the preproduction process. It affords a glimpse of what the game will be like upon completion and demonstrates to the publisher that the project is viable.

Q

Quake Id's first game in true rendered 3D, released in 1996.

R

real-time strategy A genre of games where gameplay occurs in real time whether the player makes a decision or not, thus adding a constant time pressure and increased stress level.

reserve against returns A portion of royalties held back from the developer to cover retail returns.

resolution The level of detail used when the graphics are drawn on the screen, indicated by figures that represent the number of horizontally and vertically displayed pixels.

Rosen, David An American who founded an art export company called Rosen Enterprises in 1951, which later merged with a jukebox manufacturer in 1965 and changed its name to Sega, a contraction for Service Games.

royalties Payments to a developer based on a game's net receipts once a game has earned out and covered any advances.

S

scripted events Important events that are prescripted in a game and are triggered automatically when the player enters a certain area.

SCUMM Script Creation Utility for Maniac Mansion.

secondary characters Secondary or nonplayer characters that are often the mirror through which the player sees the character he or she is portraying.

Sega A successful game company founded as Rosen Enterprises by an American named David Rosen in 1951, which later merged with a jukebox manufacturer in 1965 and changed its name to Sega, a contraction for Service Games.

Sega 32X Sega's 32-bit Genesis add-on, which was a spectacular flop.

Sega CD A CD-ROM add-on for Sega Genesis, released in 1993.

Sega Dreamcast Sega's 128-bit console that developed a loyal following due to an impressive flood of arcade-quality titles but eventually halted production in 2001.

Sega Genesis Sega's 16-bit home unit, released in 1989.

Sega Mark III A home gaming unit released in Japan in direct competition with the Sega.

Sega Saturn Sega's affordable 32-bit system, which failed because its engineering was too complex for many third-party developers.

serious games Usually a simulation of a real-world process with the purpose of training users in some discipline.

shareware Software and games released for free download in the hopes that consumers will purchase the complete version. (Also called *freeware*.)

side scrolling A third-person player perspective where the player remains in the center of the screen while the environment scrolls from side to side.

Sierra Online Company formed by Roberta and Ken Williams, creators of the first graphical adventure game, Mystery House.

Sim City The first of Will Wright's popular Sim games, released in 1989.

Sims, the The most popular computer game of all time, created by Will Wright and released by Maxis in 2000.

simulation games A genre of games that simulate real-life events or circumstances.

Socializer, the A player archetype in online games that sees games primarily as a social experience and views all other aspects of gameplay as secondary.

SoftImage 3D modeling and animation package owned by Avid, used in films, commercial, and video game production.

software engineer The team members who make the designer's vision a reality by writing the code that affects every aspect of the game.

Sonic the Hedgehog An ultra high-speed, graphics-intensive game released by Sega to highlight the weaknesses of the SuperNES's slow CPU.

Sony PlayStation Sony's incredibly successful 32-bit unit that began development as a CD-ROM add-on for the Nintendo NES.

Sony PlayStation 2 Sony's next generation console, released in 2000.

Sony PlayStation Portable (PSP). A handheld version of the PlayStation 2

sound designer An outside contractor responsible for assembling all of the sounds that will be heard in a game.

sound engineer An outside contractor that handles the technical aspects of recording and voice processing.

source lighting Lighting that comes from a specific source in the environment and will change if the source is moved.

Space Invaders A phenomenally successful game developed by Taito Corporation engineer Toshiro Nishikado in 1978.

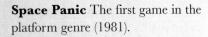

Space Panic The first game in the platform genre (1981).

Space Wars The first game to utilize vector beam graphics (1977).

Spacewar! The first computer game, created by a group of students at MIT in 1961 using the PDP-1, a refrigerator-sized mainframe computer with a CRT display.

specularity The amount of light reflected from an object's surface, which depends on the light hitting the object and the location of the viewer.

stand-alone tutorials Tutorials that exist outside the game world and are optional training exercises that the player can choose to take.

Starcraft Blizzard Software's sci-fi RTS game, released in 1998.

steering wheels Input devices sometimes used for driving games.

Strategist, the A player archetype that prefers games with complex rules and high attention to detail and statistical issues. They usually derive pleasure from tactical decision making.

Stratovox The first game with synthesized speech (1980).

Super Game Boy Nintendo's 1994 add-on unit that allowed gamers to play Game Boy cartridges on the SuperNES home console.

superhero, the A popular type of game protagonist that is fun and exciting to play: a larger-than-life character with abilities far beyond those of the average person who will take chances and perform heroic deeds almost as a matter of course.

T

Taylor, Chris Designer for Cavedog games who developed the 1997 RTS Total Annihilation.

tech lead The lead programmer, responsible for the technical design document, the game architecture, and managing the programming team.

technical design document (1) This document lists all the required programming tasks for the game, which programmers they have been assigned to, and target dates for their completion. (2) A document that lays out the technical design strategy for the game.

test lead A key member of the development team responsible for overseeing the QA team and making sure that when the game ships it will be as bug-free and polished as possible.

test plan A document that mirrors the schedule of the design document and details the team's bug-reporting system and tracking process.

texture artist An artist who creates detailed 2D surface textures for the environments, structures, creatures, and objects in a game.

texture detail Usually low, medium, or high settings that are dependent on the system specifications and the desired frame rate.

texture mapping The process of wrapping a texture skin around a model.

texture skins Skins used to cover and wrap around 3D wire mesh models, giving them a more detailed appearance.

Thespian, the A player archetype that primarily enjoys the role-playing aspects of a game. They want to immerse themselves in an alternative reality and see their character as an alter ego.

Thief: The Dark Project Hybrid first-person action/stealth game developed by Looking Glass Studios and released by Eidos in 1998.

third-person perspective A more detached player perspective where the player can actually see the character he or she is controlling.

three-act structure A dramatic structure first identified by Aristotle that divides a narrative (story) into three distinct sections or acts.

Tomb Raider A hybrid puzzle-solving adventure/third-person action game that featured the industry's first female protagonist. Developed by Core Design in 1996.

top-down perspective A player perspective using two-dimensional graphics, viewed from directly above.

Total Annihilation A groundbreaking RTS title released by Cavedog in 1997.

turn-based strategy A genre of strategy games where games are divided into turns; A player makes a move or series of moves, and then the next player has the opportunity to do the same.

tutorial A method for teaching a new player how to play a game via stand-alone or in-game lessons.

U

Ultima Online The first popular massively multiplayer online role-playing game (1997).

Ultima Underworld This 1990 RPG created by Blue Sky Productions is considered by many to be the ancestor of all modern first-person 3D games.

underdog, the A popular type of game protagonist for whom players root: a down on his or her luck but inherently likable person who begins the game at a disadvantage.

Unreal A 3D game from developers Epic Games and Digital Extreme that introduced the new and popular Unreal Engine in 1998.

Unreal Script A powerful programming language created for the Unreal Engine that was embraced by amateur mod makers.

user interface The controls and feedback devices that determine how the player will interact with the game environment and what feedback will be given back to the player by the environment.

V

variable perspective A player perspective that allows the player to zoom in and out or rotate the view in any direction.

vector beam graphics A black and white CRT display invented by Larry Rosenthal in 1977 that could render only straight lines between points but had crisper and brighter graphics than the heavily pixelated games of the time.

video display settings A menu reached via the user interface that allows the player to select graphical options like resolution, color depth, texture detail, and gamma correction.

Virtual Savannah Wireless educational game research project where students play a pride of lions on an African savannah.

visual representation A method of feedback using visual graphics rather than written text or audio cues.

voice director An outside contractor hired to cast the various roles required and direct the audio recording sessions.

voice processing A process where recorded lines are cleaned up and edited for quality, then processed to sound right in a 3D game environment.

W

Warcraft Blizzard Software's fantasy RTS game, released in 1994.

WASD keys Four keys on the left side of the computer keyboard that are often used as directional keys, freeing up the player's right hand to fire or perform actions using the mouse.

wearable computer A small portable computer. It is designed to be worn on the body, integrated into clothing, or attached to the body.

Williams, Roberta The creator of the first graphical adventure game, Mystery House.

wireless games Games that incorporate wireless technology.

Wizardry Groundbreaking series of games created by Andrew Greenberg and Robert Woodhead in the early 1980s.

Wolfenstein 3D The original FPS title developed by Id Software in 1992.

work for hire deal A development deal wherein a publisher hires a developer to create a game based on a specific property that the publisher owns or has licensed.

Wright, Will Designer that founded Maxis and created the incredibly popular Sims series of games.

writers Writers work with the lead designer to develop a detailed bible for the game world containing history, backstory, background information, and major characters. They also write scripts for cut scenes, game dialogue, on-screen text, and so on.

X

Xbox, Xbox 360. Game consoles produced by Microsoft.

Z

Zork A popular text-based adventure game—the first to become a true commercial hit, created by M.I.T. students Marc Blank, Joel Berez, Tim Anderson, and Bruce Daniels.

Photo Credits

A Special Thanks...

Figure 1.13: The Thespian

Artist: John Walker

Company: Entertainment Arts Research

Figure 1.14: The Griefer

Artist: Craig Brasco

Company: Entertainment Arts Research

End of Chapter margin: Chinatown Level Study (2005)

Artists: Rich Mahon, Jon Gwyn, Chandana Ekanayake

Company: Shiny Entertainment

Game Title: The Matrix: Path of Neo

End of Chapter margin: Yellow Room (2005)

Artist: Stephan Martiniere

Company: Cyan Worlds

Game Title: Uru, the Path of the Shell

End of Chapter margin: Ryu Hayabusa (2004)

Artist: Tomonobu Itagaki, Hiroaki Matsui

Company: TECMO

Game Title: Ninja Gaiden

End of Chapter margin: Enzo in Florence (2004)

Artists: Ben O'Sullivan, Gren Atherton, Mark Sharratt, Matt Watts

Company: Microsoft Game Studios

Game Title: PGR – 2

Chapter 2 Opener:

Artist: Bill Blakesley

Company: Entertainment Arts Research

Chapter 3 Opener:

Artist: Harshdeep Borah

Figure 3.1: Sugmas Toning

Company: Liquid Moon Studio

Figure 3.2: Jupiter

Company: Liquid Moon Studio

Figure 3.3: Kalsus

Company: Liquid Moon Studio

Figure 3.4: Intry

Company: Liquid Moon Studio

Figure 3.5: Earth 3D

Company: Liquid Moon Studio

Figure 3.6: D_Koei

Company: Liquid Moon Studio

Chapter 4 Opener:

Artist: Bill Blakesley

Company: Entertainment Arts Research

Figure 4.1: Various Textures of Light

Artist: Bill Blakesley

Company: Entertainment Arts Research

Figure 4.2: Ambient Lighting

Artist: Bill Blakesley

Company: Entertainment Arts Research

Figure 4.3: Diffuse Lighting

Artist: Bill Blakesley

Company: Entertainment Arts Research

Figure 4.4: Source Lighting

Artist: Reggie Boon

Figure 4.5: Specularity

Artist: Bill Blakesley

Company: Entertainment Arts Research

Figure 4.6: 3D Model Character

Artist: Ola Gardener

Figure 4.7: 3D Character

Artist: Joe Gardener

Figure 4.8: Animation Choices

Artist: Joe Gardener

Figure 4.9: Animation Choices at Work

Artist: Joe Gardener

Figure 4.10: Modeling

Artist: Joe Gardener

Figure 4.11: Reminiscence

Artist: Harshdeep Borah

Figure 4.12: Mai – The Spider Killer

Artist: Harshdeep Borah

Chapter 5 Opener: Navy Shipyard (2005)

Artist: Tyler West

Company: EA

Game Title: Godfather

Chapter 6 Opener:

Artist: Bill Blakesley

Company: Entertainment Arts Research

Figure 6.4: The King

Artist: John Walker

Company: Entertainment Arts Research

Figure 6.6: Kaos Character Model

Artist: Bill Blakesley

Company: Entertainment Arts Research

Chapter 7 Opener:

Artist: Bill Blakesley

Company: Entertainment Arts Research

Figure 7.2: Kaotic Foolz

Artist: John Walker

Company: Entertainment Arts Research

Figure 7.3: Storyboard

Artist: Haji Abdullah

Company: Entertainment Arts Research

Figure 7.4: Boss NPC

Artist: Bill Blakesley

Company: Entertainment Arts Research

Figure 7.5: Soldier

Artist: Harshdeep Borah

Chapter 8 Opener:

Artist: Bill Blakesley

Company: Entertainment Arts Research

Figure 8.2: Screenshot

Artist: Kenneth Karr

Company: Entertainment Arts Research

Chapter 9 Opener: Design & Construction (2005)

Artists: John Kendrew, John Machin, Darren Douglas, Lee Carus

Company: Production Design Lead - Sony Computer Entertainment Europe - Studio Liverpool

Game Title: Wipeout PSP

Figure 9.1: Kaotic Foolz

Artist: Bill Blakesley

Company: Entertainment Arts Research

Figure 9.2: Skullhead in Wireframe

Artist: Harshdeep Borah

Figure 9.3: Skullhead

Artist: Harshdeep Borah

Index

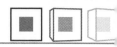